DYNAMICS OF YOGA

Published by
Prakash Books India Pvt. Ltd.
113/A, Darya Ganj,
New Delhi-110 002
Tel: (011) 2324 7062 – 65, Fax: (011) 2324 6975
Email: info@prakashbooks.com/sales@prakashbooks.com

ISBN: 978 81 7234 390 3

Processed & printed in India

DYNAMICS OF YOGA

R.R. VARMA

PRAKASH BOOKS

Dedicated to Sri Sri Daya Mata

ACKNOWLEDGEMENT

Teachings of the great spiritual Masters of Kriya Yoga dispensation — Sri Sri Lahiri Mahashya, Sri Sri Yukteshwara Giri, Sri Sri Paramahansa Yogananda and Sri Daya Mata are treasures beyond time. They are based on reason, advanced intuition and direct God contact. To guide the destiny of mankind through the balanced use of spirituality and science, these teachings offer a rare opportunity not to be missed.

Thirty years back, I was lucky to have become a member of the Yogda Satsang Society of India. Practising Kriya teachings and reading various works of these great masters have helped me physically, psychologically and spiritually as it has helped many others, both in the west and in the east. Therefore, I must acknowledge with reverence that the works of these masters have been a constant source of inspiration for me. Widely acknowledged and famous works of these great masters, which have greatly benefited me, are *Autobiography of a Yogi*, *God Talks with Arjuna* (a unique commentary on *The Bhagwad Gita*), *Man's Eternal Quest*, *Journey to Self Realization* and *Spiritual Diary* by Paramahansa Yogananda; *Holy Science* by

Yuketshwara Giri, Sri Lahiri Mahashya's *Adhyatmik Dipika* with Shri Upendranath Sanyal's commentary in its Hindi version spanning three volumes and also *Finding the Joy Within You* and *Only Love* by Sri Sri Daya Mata (President of SRF Los-Angeles). Guruji said that if one reads for an hour, he should write for two hours and meditate for four hours. Since my retirement from the IPS, following broadly this advice has helped me among other things, to present this fourth book to the readers.

I must also acknowledge that studying many works published by the *The Bhagawad Gita* Press, Gorakhpur and Ramakrishna Mission, particularly the creations of Swami Vivekananda have benefited me a great deal in understanding the concepts of Vedanta and Yoga, apart from being a source of great joy.

Various works of western and Indian scientists, philosophers and historians have helped me to give direction to the ideas mentioned in this book. Important among these are 'Cosmos' by Carl Sagan, 'A Brief History of Time' and 'Universe in a Nutshell' by Stephen Hawking, writings of Jagdish Chandra Bose, and Mani Bhaumik; various books by Bertrand Russell, H.G. Wells, Dr. Radhakrishanan and 'A Study of History' by Professor Toynbee.

I am very happy to express my gratitude to the publishers, Prakash Books India Pvt. Ltd. and particularly to Shri Ashwani Sabharwal, who has published this fourth book of mine.

I must express my thanks to Ms. Sonalini Chaudhry for editing the book and also Ms. Meena and Mr. Pawan Chandel for their great help in typing the manuscript.

I am always grateful to the monks of Y.S.S. Ranchi for their sincere and dedicated endeavour to train and teach us special

Kriya Yoga techniques to imbibe the wondrous truth of Yoga science.

Above all, I am grateful to my wife Mrs. Rama Varma, a devoted housewife, for her services to keep me unencumbered from various household responsibilities during my preoccupation with this work, as also for being a constant source of encouragement and inspiration to me.

CONTENTS

INTRODUCTION

Broadly speaking, the purpose of education, apart from acquiring skills, is to build character and develop the mind to understand the mysteries of life and the universe to enable creatively inspired people to work for prosperity, peace and enlightenment of humankind. It is, therefore, through the pursuit of education that humanity, struggling through ages has reached the present era of affluence marked by a surfeit of goods and services along with the explosion of knowledge. However, the long history of humanity for many people is a tale of grim struggle and penury that they had to brave through centuries. In this background, this present phase of abundance seems a sheer interlude, because our future stands threatened by grave dangers, which are the consequences of our own making unleashed by greed and ignorance. It seems that the instinct of violence has affected our genes. Even if we talk of history since the Christian era, it is a record of violence and wars motivated by the fear of hunger and greed forever more. It becomes even more agonising to know that those wars and carnages were perpetrated not for need and want but for greed, vengeance and aggrandisement. It is this aberration, which continuing through centuries, ultimately exploded in the 20th century in the conflagration of two World Wars. As if this was not enough for the world to learn its lessons, the 21st century inaugurated its advent with worse carnages of 9/11/2001 and 26/11/ 2008. Stark realities tell us that the prime movers of these tragedies are the human instincts of fear, greed and vengeance.

The dangers of man-made challenges that are confronting the world now are nuclear arsenals, terrorism and global warming. The crisis of sub-prime episode had pushed the world economy to the brink. Corruption, tax havens, drug trafficking and mafias are blooming because it is greed which is calling the shots. Business conglomerates, corporates, governments, academia, media et al are players in this game of minting money, in which some are proactive and some helpless.

It is not that men and women who are at the helm of affairs in various fields all over the world are not capable and responsible people. Most of them are outstanding and honourable people, and it is in spite of the capable and experienced world leaders that the dangers of destruction are looming ever large and solutions seem to be slipping through their fingers.

At this juncture, we must sit up and ponder whether everything is really correct with the main system of education that we have been following across the world; because it is education which is the real source of knowledge, which breeds wisdom to guide and bail us out in dire situations.

It is an understood fact that the system of education that we have been pursuing is incomplete. No doubt on the material plane, knowledge derived from education has served humanity beyond expectation but it has not been able to cater to the spiritual dimension of human life, which is the very essence, and substance of life. We should never forget the principal teachings of scriptures which proclaim that the real man is soul because man is essentially the soul and has a body. The prevailing system of education caters to intellectual pursuits and cannot access the soul within. This is the root cause of imbalance in the development of human personality. Since the existing system of education develops the mind and cannot relate to soul, which is the core and essence of every human being, therefore existing education is an incomplete source and medium of knowledge to develop the holistic and balanced human personality. No doubt, books for ages and computers of late are the source of knowledge which has showered, among other blessings, awakening and prosperity, but lack of basic values and scourge of greed have unleashed the monster in people which has robbed peace and threatened our existence. Therefore, now there is need to recognize that beyond human mind there is a higher, nay the highest knowledge; the human soul which is the source of love and peace and the supreme knowledge, which the present system of education cannot access.

In support of this view it may be said that the Yoga system of education is a time honoured and trusted system of ancient and yet ever new knowledge to discipline and use the mind creatively and access the soul slowly but certainly. Yoga is not against the present system of education but rather applauds its contribution to improve the basic material dimension of life so important for human growth and development. In fact, the role of modern education and Yoga are supplementary to each other. The essential role of Yoga-based education begins where the role of mundane education ends; but the importance of the latter is necessary to provide for the basic needs of physical life. Science and technology are the main forces, which have catered to material well being by alleviating the suffering of people, yet modern man stands bereft of individual peace and social harmony. Consequently, now greed, insecurity and violence have become nightmares of humanity. The Yoga system of education is a dependable methodology of education to culture and transmute the human mind and ultimately lift the consciousness to the spiritual dimension of higher life.

Like natural sciences, Yoga also is a science but it is a higher and finer science. Compared to the science of Yoga, other natural sciences lack advanced intuitive subtleties. Natural sciences deal with energy, matter and mind but the science of Yoga begins from where the physical sciences give up. Yoga deals with the astral and causal and spiritual dimensions of life and matter. Yogis know for certain that behind the phenomenon Universe and the body of man, exist their astral and causal counterparts, from where evolves energy and macrocosm of the cosmos including man's mind and body. Yoga education teaches that the source of mind, energy and physical forces and forms, which make the universe, are soul and spirit. All bodies and physical objects are operated in their actions and motions by their astral counterparts, which enliven, motivate and operate the manifest world of senses. Yogis have developed special techniques and scientific methods based on experiments and trials to culture and control the mind and senses to specialise in the art of interiorization so essential to establish soul contact. The lab of Yoga is the human body and mind is its tool to use it to realize spiritual ends, and finally the mind itself is transcended to reach the spiritual pinnacle. Yoga is an occult science, which uses different methods to unravel the inner astral mysteries of higher and finer life. It works through intuition, acquired through intensive concentration and long meditation, as taught by a guru.

The main objective of the Yoga system of education is to transform the mind and transcend it to ultimately attain the highest level of consciousness called the soul or spiritual consciousness. This spiritual consciousness is the source of love, higher knowledge and peace. Now medical science knows that the left hemisphere and the *Sahasrara* (the thousand petalled center in the brain) controls our body-mind functioning but yogis knew from ancient times that the right hemisphere and the *Sahasrara* (the thousand petalled centre) in the brain are the source of higher knowledge, pure love and deep peace. This theme has been touched to some extent by Dr. J.B. Taylor in her book 'My Stroke of Insight'. Yoga teaches us how higher consciousness is attained by mastering systematically the discipline of Raj Yoga or Kriya Yoga, following the rigorous practice of special techniques, exercises and deep meditation. Medical science yet does not appear to be aware of the existence of astral and causal bodies nor does it have any clue aboutthe seven astral centres in the spine and brain. But for Yoga education, these are the basics unless the astral body is manifested through techniques of Yoga, and seven chakras (centres) in the spine and brain are targeted, which are the sources of life and consciousness; it is not possible to change the mindset and attain ascendance to the higher level of consciousness, which is the source of pure knowledge, universal love, deep peace and harmony.

The education of Yoga does not depend on script or language to impart yogic instructions but discovers and develops its distinct symphony of astral sounds, lights and colours generated with the ecstatic effect of Pranayama. It is through this methodology that Yoga system of education changes the conventional mindset of its students. The approach of Yoga is to culture and train the mind to inculcate positive and creative thinking and feelings. To achieve this end special emphasis are laid on training the mind to develop qualities of service, sacrifice and love. These ideas are dinned in through repeated esoteric practices to ensure that results are perceptible.

After long practice through concentration and meditation, ardent followers succeed in transcending the mind and rise to the spiritual level of consciousness where a person feels love for others and derives happiness from helping and serving them. They develop a habit to serve others unconditionally and even sacrifice their comforts and necessities for the sake of others. The basic approach and ultimate purpose of Yoga-based education is to develop and train the mind to generate a fount of love in the human heart from which peace, love and harmony will flow.

The purpose of this humble study is to create awareness of the great potentials of Yoga as a source and medium of complete education, to transform human attitude and mindset to serve and love others. To transform human mind and uplift human consciousness is the speciality of Yoga, which the existing system of education is unable to achieve. Perhaps I owe it to my karma that for the last over thirty years, I have been able to maintain regularity in practice of Kriya Yoga meditation twice daily. Therefore, the views expressed in this book are inspired by the works of Gurudeva Paramahansa Yogananda, Sri Daya Mata and other great masters of Kriya Yoga dispensation, and are also based on my own experiences.

Yoga teachers are of unanimous view that there is a pressing need to reorient human thinking to prioritize ethical and spiritual values in the present system of education. Since Yoga system of education recognises and prescribes adoption of ethical and spiritual value system in its educational curriculum, it is necessary that scientific Yoga methodology should be introduced as a subject in schools. It is the teachings and practices of Yoga that leads a person to spirituality. Spirituality essentially means to believe, feel, experience and realize the spirit within, which is the highest source of knowledge, peace, love and harmony. The best means to realize spirituality is through the scientific techniques and methods of meditation and selfless service. It is now a well-recognised fact by Yoga practitioners that the unmanifest spirit can only be known through the practice of deep meditation, as this is the only science, which can unravel the unknown dimension of the infinite and omniscient spirit.

The world knows that there is no substitute to science and technology to promote material progress of the planet. Now it must be realized by the world leaders that there is no substitute to Yoga-based methodology of education to generate a new atmosphere of peace and harmony that the world cannot delay. It is good that now thinking people at various places in the world have realized that parallel progress of both spirituality and science, in this world overloaded with nuclear weapons and threatened by global warming, is necessary for global security, progress and peace. Creative people know that the union of spirituality and science will provide a strong and lasting base for the accelerated advent of new global order, which may make inter-state rivalries and consequent wars a subject matter of History books. Since attainment of a balanced development through science and spirituality needs more effort, therefore, there is need to update the system of education. Endeavours of human annals are there to indicate that great attainments call for bold initiatives and consistent struggle to attain the desired results. The attempt to introduce scientific Yoga in the education curriculum, sensitivities of various individuals and groups, being as they are, could be an onerous task but its power to creatively reorient human thinking, is a potent inspiration to work sincerely for its success. The credentials of Yoga to serve, reform and unite people of all origins and classes being flawless can therefore serve as a strong base to accelerate the advent of a better world order. To achieve this noble end, Yoga based education can provide a strong input because Yoga science believes in and preaches the fatherhood of God and brotherhood of mankind. I hope the readers will bear with me for the repetition of various Yoga themes and terms in the following chapters, which is unavoidable as Yoga and spirituality are not elaborate theories but are a scientific reality, which is to be dinned in, through repetition and re-emphasis for the improvement of practical behaviour in daily life.

GOD AS THE COSMIC SPIRIT

Since the prime concern of yogis is discovery of the self within which is the presence of God in all who is the source of all knowledge, power and love, therefore, it is just and right that this humble workstarts with a prayer to the almighty to evoke His blessings. Therefore, this chapter is not a discourse but an oblation of devotional petals at His holy feet.

We all have often heard scriptures and yogis preach that God is omnipresent but many people say that if He is omnipresent then why can't He be seen? But scriptures and yogis declare that God not only exists everywhere but it is His omnipresence which vibrates all hearts and permeates all atoms of creation. Yet in some quarters, a question arises — Could God be a Paradox, an Enigma or both? Now it must be said that scriptures and yogis are the unique sources of knowledge and wisdom and they enjoy time-tested credibility because scriptures are the statements of God and yogis are the spiritual masters who are in communion with God. However, an inquisitive and rational person wonders as to why the omnipresent and omnipotent God who needs nothing and has everything should hide Himself even from people who pray to Him? To some people this Divine elusiveness is a mystery which deepens to see when even ardent seekers pass on unrewarded in their quest to see God. In this wake some people ask, 'Is God there at all, or is He so indifferent?' Therefore, the standing questions in the minds of doubting individuals' are- What is God? Where is God? Why does He live in Hiding and how can God and so much of injustice exist simultaneously? So many people suffer so much for none of their faults and so many people enjoy for none of their efforts? All these questions have answers but before such answers are spelled out, it must be properly realised that such questions emanate from the mind and are based on reason. However, reason can only understand and explain the facts related to the world of senses. God, the infinite cosmic spirit cannot be cognised and understood by the finite mind and reason. The higher realm of spirit can only be cognised by a high level of intuition which can be acquired through advanced techniques of Yoga after purification of the heart. Divine syntax is an unlettered science which can be learnt by the pure at heart. There are two ways to know the divine mystery; the art of Nididhyasana and the science of Pranayama. The subtle truths of Divine designs are inscribed on the diaphragm of our heart, which are decoded by the eye of intuition, promoted by meditation based on deep concentration. Secondly, these answers can be known from the lessons of life learnt from the book of nature, authored by God to guide everybody to become like Him through the endeavour of pure action. There is no short cut to learn these secrets but sincere students do master the art of knowing the unknown without asking questions. They know that the art of spiritual pursuit is a saga of Divine romance. It is an unlettered epic and its quest thrives on faith and devotion which with persistent effort culminates in the highest knowledge of intuition. This intuition cannot be acquired with mind and senses and is beyond these instruments which nature has provided to man to know the outer world of senses. To know the Divine mystery, man must change from within.

Now we may attempt to answer the first part of the question, as revealed by the knower of truth that — What is God? Frankly, no human mind has an answer to this question, because mind is finite and God is infinite, the finite cannot know the infinite. Therefore, God and this cosmos, being His own creation, are a mystery unresolved since times immemorial. Rig-Veda, the oldest spiritual monument in the annals of humanity, so precisely explains this mystery of God and the universe, "That whole is full (God), this whole is full (cosmos), from the whole comes the whole, but the whole ever remains!" Through countless cycles of evolution and involution, as Hindu scriptures reveal, man has learnt many arts and secrets, some of which are documented and some lost. However, the art of God contact is a matter of personal experience, which cannot be taught through intelligence and mind. These instruments and their creations of mundane arts and sciences can only guide a student but divine contact is to be pursued through the odyssey of Divine love and devotion, which are taught by the promptings of heart from within.

Now let us look at what scriptures say and what yogis tell us about God and nature. Scriptures say that God is *Anadi* (birth-less and eternal) and is the sole fundamental cause of birth, continuity, end, creation and recreation of the universe.

Therefore the universe never ends; it changes from gross to astral and vice versa. This explains how the prakriti (invisible and visible worlds) is also called *Anadi* (*The Bhagawad Gita* 13/19). In this world which is based on cause-effect relationship, nobody else is *Anadi*. Everybody is subject to birth and death including devas and rishis. The entire creation — this expanding universe, is the product of God's divine will. In this *Jagat* (creation) all people live on the mind level of consciousness but human mind and intelligence cannot know the infinite God (cosmic consciousness). God can only be known through spiritual consciousness because knowing God is not an imaginative or a theoretical concept. It is a matter of unmistakable reality based on direct personal experience of the soul within (*The Bhagawad Gita* 2.16). Therefore, it does not mean that nobody has had the privilege of knowing God in this world. The way to know God has Himself been indicated by God in *The Bhagawad Gita,* verse 7/3 and 10/3, where God says, "One in thousands endeavours to know Me and of them the rarest of the rare succeeds to know My reality." God contact is possible only after conquering *prakriti* — God's powerful Maya. To simplify matters for an individual Maya means one's mind, conquering the mind means conquest of Maya. In fact, it is a major challenge as Maya or mind can only be controlled through the mastery of Yoga and this important aspect is separately explained in this book. Nevertheless, those who have realized God say that it is a unique experience. Human mind can never imagine the etherealizing effect of this spiritual contact because it is so much above the physical mind, which is why God says in *The Bhagawad Gita* and Upanishads, that even devas and rishis do not know Him. The fact is that no physical being who lives on body-mind consciousness be it an angel, deva, or rishi can know God. God is the unmanifest cosmic spirit, which can only be seen or realized by the soul. The spiritual law is that for attaining divine consciousness, body and mind consciousness must be dissolved into spiritual consciousness. Therefore, a God seeker must transcend the mind consciousness and attain spiritual consciousness, which is the highest state of human evolution. Angels and devas who have not attained this pinnacle of evolution cannot know God. It is true that angels and devas do not have physical bodies but they have astral bodies because all angels in heaven have astral bodies, but astral bodies are only finer forms of physical bodies which bind them to return to the world after enjoying and exhausting the rewards of their good actions performed earlier in this world. Those great divine seekers who have succeeded to glimpse the spirit here in this life, through Yoga and allied spiritual endeavours, shed the bondage of three forms of their bodies; gross, astral, causal, and as pure souls, they know God and ascend to Him bypassing all heavens, even the Brahamaloka.

Now we may attempt to discuss what is God and how can God be known. Cursorily we may say that God is infinity and eternity, the source of all and everything, therefore beyond human kin to fathom Him but super human beings have endeavoured to discover the ways to know God and have also experienced Him. It is such masters who provide the key to know the ways to contact God. It is said that there are four ways to know God. The first is through revelations made by God Himself about Himself. The second source is the Holy Scriptures; the third source is the vision of prophets and views and experiences of God realized spiritual masters and the fourth source is realization of the soul from within as realized in *Samadhi*. Let us first deal with the divine revelations made by God Himself. These are wonderful disclosures having immensely inspiring effect. There is nothing in the world, which can be a greater source of truth than such divine pronouncements. To begin with, we may mention *The Bhagawad Gita* as a book full of divine revelations about God; in this regard, it is a unique record. In fact, the whole of *The Bhagawad Gita* is the speech of Lord Krishna Himself. In its eighteen chapters, Lord Krishna repeatedly declares that He is the supreme God of Gods. He is the cosmic spirit, the cosmic consciousness, the creator, the preserver and the destroyer of all. Cosmic evolution and involution start from Him and end in Him, to evolve again as per His divine laws. He is the source of matter, energy, life, love, beauty, consciousness and the super conscious. Everything good, great and divine emanates from Him. He is bliss and eternity. He is beyond time, birth and death. The cosmos of a trillion worlds is on His finger tips and nothing happens and moves without His divine will. God's own pronouncement in *The Bhagawad Gita* 10/42 signifies the saga of His wondrous powers, "O Arjuna, wonder not about details — I support the universe with a single fragment of Myself." Chapter eleven of *The Bhagawad Gita* in which God reveals His cosmic form is the wonder of wonders which, human mind cannot understand correctly. The spiritual theme is that the duality of good and bad exists in the relative worlds of cause and effect phenomenon but not in the infinite realm of His divinity, where only one science of love and truth prevails. Among various revelations, Lord Krishna reveals that *para* and *apara* (life and matter) are

His creations (*The Bhagawad Gita* 7/-4-5). God says that *para* is the life element and *apara* is eight fold: intelligence, mind, ego, space, air, fire, water and earth; it is lifeless matter. It is God's higher prakriti (para) from which life flows to the eight fold lower (apara) prakriti. The Infinite divine is the birth-less, deathless, omnipresent, omnipotent and omniscient, blissful eternal power, which permeates and transcends the universe or multi-verses. He is above both *para* and *apara prakritis (The Bhagawad Gita* 7/6-7, 14/3).

Divine revelations about the origin, nature of the universe and powers of God and the ways to realize Him are contained in various Shrutis. Four cardinal sayings of four Vedas: (1) "Consciousness is *Brahmn*" (Aitereya Upanishad of Rig-Veda), (2) "I am *Brahmn*" (Brahadaranayaka Upanishad of Yajur-Veda), (3) "Thou art That" (Chandogya Upanishad of Sam-Veda) and (4) "This Atman is *Brahmn*" (Mandukya Upanishad of Atharwa-Veda), are Shrutis — the divine sayings heard in Samadhi. Important Yoga texts i.e. Udhava Gita, *The Bhagawad Gita*, Yoga Vashistha, Karma Yoga, Jnana Yoga, Bhakti Yoga also contain divine revelations. These revelations are heard by yogis in the state of *Samadhi*, which is why yogis declare that the magnetic pull of a seeker's pure love, (bhakti), is irresistible to God. God is always looking forward to the devotees drunk with love for Him and He always hastens to embrace them.

If we talk of Upanishads, they are the unique source of revelations of the divine experiences of rishis (enlightened ones) who describe God (the self within) as the source of everything and as the only reality called the Absolute truth. Discovery of the self as the presence of God inside is the great achievement of Upanishads. It is said to be a unique experience of indescribable bliss rendering the Rebecca effect a drab comparison. This blissful experience of soul contact is based on the personal experiences of these spiritual pioneers.

Most of the eighteen Puranas are full of stories describing God's appearance in miraculous ways to protect, bless and divinize His devotees – and destroy the demons. The stories of Dhruva, Prahalada, Bali Raja are only a few to illustrate such events. In these Puranas, God lays down various spiritual laws to be followed by common people for worldly success and spiritual salvation.

The great epics, *The Ramayana* and *The Mahabharata* are inspiring examples and revelations, indicating how God incarnates to protect the pious, to restore the majesty of righteousness (dharma), and to ensure continuity of the world along the path of virtue. Examples of incarnations of God at various epochs during the course of evolution are foolproof facts revealing the unique power of God to become and perform what He wants for the good of the creation.

Talking of these and other scriptures as a source to define God, it is the belief of common people and experiences of the enlightened ones that they are the best source to describe the existence, nature and powers of God. The holy *Bhagawad Gita*, *Bible*, *Koran*, Buddhist texts and other great scriptures like Yoga texts abound in such inspiring examples and stories. But there is one thing about the great scriptures of the world that they are highly symbolic, and full of metaphors. They can be correctly interpreted only by spiritually advanced people. All scriptures define God as the source of all powers, knowledge, love, mercy and the spirit of sacrifice. All scriptures reveal the secret ways to know God, such as unconditional surrender, faith, love, devotion, sense of service and sacrifice. These commitments when performed sincerely with deep faith and devotion generate the power of intuition in such people. Intuition, as mentioned in various pages of this work is a great knowledge of the highest kind. It is direct knowledge, independent of the senses and mind power, which reveals the hidden truth and secrets of life and divinity. However, it takes time to develop intuition to attain higher levels. In Yoga, precise methods are listed to develop this unique source of knowledge. It is the highest knowledge of intuition and spiritual revelations, which is the basis of great scriptures of the world. No wonder these scriptures are treasures against time. The truth stated therein is relevant for all times and ages and is the best means to be adopted for spiritual benefits and inner evolution. All scriptures directly or indirectly reveal with conviction that there is the highest power which creates and controls the universe and creates life and beings in their diverse forms.

The third source to describe what is God is the personal experience of God realized by spiritual masters and prophets. These spiritual masters are unique personalities in many ways. They are gifted with super perceptions acquired by them through the divine art of intuition. This high level of intuition is a flash of flawless direct knowledge. Due to this knowledge of intuition, spiritual masters and yogis see through and read the thoughts of people and not their faces. Yogis through esoteric and intuitive means of meditation acquire this supreme knowledge of intuition and it takes a long time to master this great art. Based on their personal experience and direct face-to-face contact with God, Indian yogis and spiritual masters define God as *sat-chit-ananda* (existence–consciousness-bliss). This means that God as *sat* is above time and space and therefore, as cosmic spirit, is present always and everywhere. He permeates the whole universe as all beings are in Him and He is in all. As consciousness, God is the cosmic consciousness who knows everything in this expanding universe and all knowledge flows from Him. God is the material and sentient cause of this universe, the universe is made of divine content just as gas, steam, vapour, clouds, ice and snow are all made of the water source. Everything and every being emanate and evolve from God–the cosmic spirit. As various things grow from the earth, similarly everything and being evolves from the un-manifest spirit. Cosmic nature works under the supreme will of God (*The Bhagawad Gita* 9-10 to 9-19). Spiritual masters and yogis know through intuitive experience that the divine and cosmic powers of God described in chapters 7, 9, 10, 11, 13, 15 and 18 of *The Bhagawad Gita* and proclaimed by God Himself and by prophets are eternal truths which can be known through superb knowledge of intuition, acquired through Yoga.

In this context, I may quote only two of the many verses from *The Bhagawad Gita*, which describe the liberated state of a yogi attained through meditation at the time of death; and the state of another yogi who has qualified to know God by fulfilling five conditions through pure action.

The Bhagawad Gita 5/27–28: "Shutting out external objects, fixing the gaze between the eyebrows, equalizing the outward and inward breaths moving in the nostrils, the sage who has controlled the senses, mind and the intellect, who is solely yearning for Liberation, who has caste away desires, fear and anger, he verily is liberated."

Verse 11/55 :"He who works for Me, who looks at Me as the

supreme, who is devoted to Me, who is free from attachment and who is without hatred for any being, he comes to Me, O Partha." For excellent commentary on these verses, one may study Sri Sri Paramahansa Yogananda's – 'God talks with Arjuna', a translation and commentary on *The Bhagawad Gita*.

For the benefit of readers interested in meditation, I am quoting a few sayings of Gurudeva Paramahansa Yogananda from his book "Spiritual Diary". Reading this book and to practice its contents will greatly help serious students in their spiritual progress.

"But the best gifts cannot be purchased and given. The gifts and graces of the soul must be acquired by patient daily practice. All will surely be yours in time, for if you do not obtain them in the position to which God has called you, where, in the entire world, are they to be found." "If others fool away their time, you be lost in God. You will go ahead. Let your example change other's lives. Reform yourself you will reform thousands."

"I will be calmly active, actively calm. I will not become lazy and mentally ossified. Nor will I be overactive, able to earn money but unable to enjoy life. I will meditate regularly to maintain true balance."

"All souls are equal. The only difference between you and me is that I made the effort. I showed God, I love Him, and He came to me. Love is the magnet from which God cannot escape."

"Why should God surrender Himself easily to you? You who work so hard for money and so little for divine realization! The Hindu saints tell us that if we would give so short a time as 24 hours to continuous, uninterrupted prayer, the Lord would appear before us or make Him known to us in some way. If we devote even one hour daily to deep meditation on Him, in time He will come to us."

"You are punishing the soul by keeping it buried, slumbering in matter life after life, frightened by nightmares of suffering and death. Realize that you are the soul. Remember that the Feeling behind your feeling, the Will behind your will, the Power behind your power, the Wisdom behind your wisdom is the Infinite Lord. Unite the heart's feeling and the mind's reason in a perfect balance. In the castle of calmness, again and again cast off identification with earthly titles, and plunge into deep meditation to realize your divine kingship."

"Do not think that you can comprehend the infinite Lord by reason. Reason can grasp only the cause-effect principle that pertains to the phenomenal worlds. Reason is powerless to understand transcendental truth and the nature of the Causeless Absolute."

"Man's highest faculty is not reason but intuition: apprehension of knowledge derived immediately and spontaneously from the soul, not from the fallible medium of the senses or reason." – by Sri Sri Paramahansa Yogananda.

The soul within everybody is the fourth source to know God and the ways that lead to Him. This soul is the omnipresent Guru within everybody, always keen to guide a true seeker to turn in to see God and taste the ambrosia of His indescribable presence. Five sheaths called koshas cover the presence of God as soul in every heart: Anandmaye Kosha is the chitta (the power of feeling) which experiences ananda (bliss). It is the first sheath which covers the soul. The second sheath covering the soul is the Jnanamaye Kosha. It is the buddhi (discriminating power). The third sheath is the Manomaye Kosha; the mind element, which is based on, senses i.e. the five knowledge senses. The fourth Kosha is Pranaamaye Kosha, which is made of *Pranaa* energy-and activates our senses. The fifth covering is called Annmaye Kosha it is the outer body-gross cover, which is caused by various gross elements including food. These sheaths have been discussed in the famous book, 'The Holy Science" by Param Guru Swami Sri Yuketshwara Giri. To experience the soul after uncovering these five sheaths is a matter of determination and a trial of patience. In his epoch making book Yoga-Sutra, Patanjali says that the soul experience is not possible without overcoming the four obstructing forces of kelesh, karma, vivak and ashya. These four terms have been explained in the chapter on 'What is Yoga'.

It is the spiritual quest which can lead a person to attain Samadhi (the state of God contact) and then to Nirvikalpa Samadhi, which the yogi enters after dissolving the five sheaths screening the soul. In this supreme state of consciousness, the yogi realizes what is God but words cannot describe this Divine experience. The best possible description to define God is Sat-Chit-Ananda (Existence-Consciousness-Bliss.)

To attain this supreme state the best path is scientific meditation. To realize the wonders which lie beyond the mind and are the source of love and bliss can only be attained through intuitive and scientific meditation.

WHAT IS YOGA?

Yoga is a science, which teaches that man is not flesh and blood, but the eternal spirit, which has become this body. Yogis practically experience this reality and teach this to their sincere students, who can realize it themselves. Yoga practitioners know, that if practised sincerely, its learning and practices are enjoyable and the effects are highly rewarding. No doubt this needs patience. In the wake of this basic reality of Yoga teachings, an attempt has been made in the following pages to explain what Yoga is and how its wondrous truths should be realized. Truths that have the potential to reinvent the human thinking not only to generate the spontaneity to serve and love the humankind, but also to bestow the power to realize God.

Therefore, Yoga is the art of Divine union, and yogis call it a spiritual science, which lifts tha Kundalini Shakti from mooldhara (coccyx) to sahasrara (the brain), to establish its union with the cosmic spirit. Soul is the Self within and spirit is the supreme God, therefore Yoga is the union of the soul and God. This spiritual union is necessary because without this rare feat, perfection in life and salvation (*moksha* — the final liberation) are not possible. Yoga liberates us from the cycle of rebirths by connecting us to God, the cosmic spirit and may bestow on us eternity and bliss. To achieve this miracle, Yoga is the sole avenue. Simply stated, Yoga is a Science to culture the brain and spine to discover the self within by mastering the techniques to control the modifications of the mind through special concentration exercises and intuitive methods of meditation. The key point to be noted is that in this great adventure of self realization, breath is the most important factor. Being the only important link between life and death, breath occupies a key position in mastering the science of Yoga. Nobody can survive without breath beyond a couple of minutes, yet Yoga is a science which enables a person to live without breath, because it is a state of breathless life. Without resolving the mystery of breath, nobody can become a *Yogi*. It is by culturing and controlling breath by special *pranayama* system that a Yogi secures freedom from body bondage and even from death. The spiritual adventure of *pranayama* system is clearly mentioned by Lord Krishna in verses 4/29 and 5/27–28 of *The Bhagawad Gita* and is the main theme of Patanjali Yogasutra. The beauty of *pranayama* practise is that if performed properly, it gives long and lasting joy. Ancient rishis who discovered this great science must have been geniuses par excellence. The world will slowly, but surely, awaken to appreciate the uniqueness of this great science and commend Indian spiritual culture for gifting the world with this great knowledge called the sovereign knowledge — Brahma Vidya in the *Gita* and *Upanishads*.

This aspect has been discussed at length in separate chapters on Kriya Yoga and Patanjali Yoga. However, it may be pointed out at the outset that the brain and spine to be cultured by Yoga are the astral counterparts of the physical brain and spine, which have to be contacted after diligent practice of Yoga at the physical level. Surely, no sensible person is expected to imagine that the wonderful knowledge of Yoga which enables a person to become perfect, to know the Self and God can be an easy or a simple pursuit. Therefore, let us begin with a brief genesis of Yoga.

Yoga is an ancient science and predates the invention of scripts and evolution of languages; therefore, its base is not script or a language and it predates even Vedas. Vedas or mundane sciences mainly teach about energy, matter and mind, but Yoga teaches all this apart from God- the cosmic spirit, which is why Yoga is called *Brahmn vidya,* a knowledge that leads to God. This is the theme of Upanishads, essence of *The Bhagawad Gita* and conclusion of Braham sutra. Upanishads are the thesis revealing the spiritual experiences of the great rishis who proclaimed and taught to their ardent students that Yoga is the path to discover the Self within. *The Bhagawad Gita* of course is the spiritual spring spurting from the divine mouth to quench peoples' spiritual thirst by drinking from the fount of Yoga. Braham sutra is the final word to proclaim that Parambrahman (supreme God) is the source of everything because the universe emanates from Him. No doubt, Yoga is a difficult study but is a sure path to lead to the self within and the cosmic Infinite called the *Brahmn*. Besides these sources, Patanjali Yogasutra reveals that right practice of eight-fold path of Yoga empowers a person with superhuman powers (Vibhuti Yoga). Besides, Yoga also trains a person in the art of humility by dissolving the ego and teaches a person the virtues to serve and love all. Such indeed is the spiritual marvel of Yoga. Mastering Yoga lifts a person above the constraints of time-space and causation. Mind and intelligence become redundant for a yogi and moving beyond these mundane faculties yogi acquires the divine art of intuition knowing which he knows all he wants to know. Another passion which Yoga rouses in a yogi is to love God and serve others unconditionally. "Yogi seeks to do brave and lovely things left undone by most people. He gives gifts of love and peace to those whom others pass by" – Paramahansa Yogananda in his spiritual diary. Yogis know that happiness comes by making others happy and the highest happiness oozes out of the honeycomb of meditation. Meditation is the medium and method, which makes a person yogi.

A gist of the methodology of meditation containing the basics to guide a beginner in Yoga is carefully mentioned by Lord Krishna Himself in *The Bhagawad Gita* in the 6th Chapter – "The Yoga of Meditation". The relevant verses to learn how meditation should be done are 10th to 28th. Due to their usefulness I am reproducing these verses but for proper and precise understanding it will be very beneficial if a student interested in Yoga studies the commentary on these verses in the book "God talks with Arjuna", *The Bhagawad Gita*, written by Paramahansa Yoganandaji. These Verses are:

(10) Away from crowd sitting alone in a quiet place free from desires and craving for possessions, disciplining the body and mind the yogi should concentrate his mind on God.

(11) The yogi's seat in a pious place should be firm, neither toohigh nor too low covered

with kusha grass, a deer's skin and cloth in a respective order and on it the yogi should sit still.

(12) Concentrating the mind, controlling the senses and chitta (the feeling power) on one point, sitting still on asana the yogi should practice Yoga for purification of the self. (It is important to note that the main purpose of Yoga is to purify the body and mind with prescribed energising exercises and Pranayama).

(13) Keeping the body (spine) and neck erect and the head firm the yogi should fix his gaze on the tip of the nose ensuring that he does not squander his attention. (According to Paramahansa Yoganandaji tip of the nose means the base of the nose in between the eyebrows –Nasikagram).

(14) Peaceful, fearless and firm in Brahmacharya, observing austerity, mind and thought under control and surrendering himself to Me, the yogi should meditate on Me.

(15) The yogi in communion with soul – due to deep meditation on the self and having fully controlled the mind, saturated in peace attains moksha – the final liberation.

(16) Final liberation or samadhi cannot be attained by a person who eats too much or too little. Also not by him who sleeps too much or too little.

(17) For him who is moderate and awake and austere, travelling, recreation, sleeping and working pains do not afflict him.

(18) When the desires of a man for the sense objects have been overcome and the serene chitta (feeling) is deeply settled in the self, such a yogi is called yukta (united to God).

(19) As a lamp does not flicker in a windless place so is the mind of a yogi, firm and steady, unhindered and undistracted by the vagaries of the world.

The following four verses describe the state of a spiritually enlightened yogi.

(20) It is a state in which the soul (ego) having attained the self by the self through meditation is tranquil and all bliss.

(21) It is a state in which the mind transcends; yogi experiences the infinite bliss and finds himself irrevocably settled in the supreme state.

(22) Attaining this blissful state the yogi imagines no joy or gain greater than this and entrenched in this state where no pain can ever touch him.

(23) This highest state of disconnection from pain is called Yoga – the pain free state. This Yoga is to be pursued with determination and performed with devotion.

To become a yogi it is necessary to have a guru — who is God realized. No scholar of Yoga texts or scriptures be it *The Bhagawad Gita*, Upanishads or brahmansutra can bestow enlightenment on a person. Only a God realized master knows the spiritual art and its skills to pull up a person from the cosmic delusion of Maya (body-mind consciousness) and uplift to the infinite realm of the spirit. It is true that such great Gurus are very few but a person having the spiritual quest is sure to meet his Guru. Time and space are no barriers for such a guru; he can identify the genuine learner at the first glance. Only a Guru or his authorized spiritual monk can help a person to learn the correct methods of meditation. Most important step in meditation is to learn how to disconnect the mind and senses from the outward sensory phenomenon. The mind through senses is always tied up with the outer world. It can be disconnected only by using the scientific methods of meditation which yogis master after long practice as is explained in the chapter on Kriya Yoga. No doubt controlling and disconnecting the mind and senses from the outer world is a very difficult task therefore common people do not find it easy even to believe let alone doing it. Yogis therefore explain this wonderful science to disconnect the mind and senses from the outer world in a simple but scientific way. Yogis explain the obvious fact that at night in sleep every person becomes a yogi because in deep sleep when the body is resting, the Pranaa Shakti (the life current), which operates and externalizes the consciousness, withdraws itself from the motor and sensory nerves. Resultantly the mind being disconnected from the senses stops feeling the body consciousness and relaxes enjoying the subconscious state of deep sleep. Since in sleep mind is in subconscious state, on waking up it does not remember where it was and what it saw during the sleep but only feels the good effect of the deep sleep. Yogis in deep meditation and samadhi state perform consciously this feat to withdraw the consciousness (mind) from motor nerves and sensory nerves and concentrate it at the Kutastha centre in between the two eyebrows. This centre unlike other five lower centres of the spine which control and regulate the body and mind functioning is the centre of spiritual consciousness. In this super-conscious state the mind becomes ecstatic experiencing glory of the soul. Great yogis demonstrate this ecstatic and blissful state by consciously attaing the state of breathlessness through yoga techniques of the super-consciousness to their good Yoga aspirants. In this state the yogi's heart becomes still and his breath, nerves and heart stop. At will the yogi resumes the state of mind body consciousness remembering his ecstatic and blissful experiences of the super-conscious state. But this art of withdrawing consciously and at will the mind and life current from the motor and sensory nerves which disconnect the senses from the outer world and interiorize the mind can be done by using scientific Yoga techniques which a guru can teach and it takes time, deep devotion and deep concentration to achieve this feat. But even if one does not succeed to become a yogi for some good reason he/she never loses the good effects of Yoga which become a part of yogi's life and benefit him in the next birth. This theme is well described by God in *The Bhagawad Gita* verses 39 to 47 of the Sixth Chapter. Even in worldly life yoga helps a person to develop balance outlook which distinctly helps him to perform better.

The main concern of Yoga is to purify the system, body, heart and mind. Human psyche for countless incarnations in the past is deeply submerged under the piles of desires related to worldly attachments. These desires not only corrupt human body and mind but also percolate to affect the astral and causal counterparts of the human system. Therefore purification in Yoga context is an intensive and elaborate endeavour because only a pure heart and balanced mind can enable a person to do good in life. To attain higher spiritual consciousness chita is to be dissolved through Yoga sadhna into its causal form from where it cannot re-emerge because then the seeds of its vritis (modifications) are burnt.

The most effective and widely accepted system of Yoga to purity chita is the path of Raj Yoga. Raj Yoga means the Royal or the highest Yoga among various Yoga systems such as Laya Yoga, Mantra Yoga, Hath Yoga etc. No Yoga is complete without using some of the basic tenets of Raj Yoga in one or the other form – Raj Yoga as a system to attain spiritual realization is prevalent in India for the last many thousand years. In fact Yoga being God's own creation and gift to mankind for spiritual evolution is eternal (changefully eternal) like nature and man. According to the level of the evolution of human mind, spiritual masters or divine incarnations modify this ancient science of Yoga to suit the spiritual needs of people in the prevailing scenario. Therefore in each epochal cycle *(yuga)* this Yoga is used in different forms and names in different societies by different people. In the present age Maha Avatar Babaji (the deathless divine incarnation who lives in Himalayas and appears before sincere devotees in many parts of the country) through Shri Shri Lahiri Mahashya has introduced the spiritual science of

Kriya Yoga for the spiritual salvation of mankind. Kriya Yoga is only an advanced form of Raj Yoga which through the use of special techniques liberates a person from the prison of body bondage and makes him a spiritually enlightened person.

Raj Yoga is also called the Ashthanga Yoga – the eight-fold path of *Yoga*. By performing sadhna on the eight parts of *Raj Yoga,* the yogi becomes aware that the human system of 24 evolutes is different –mere matter, from the soul who is the real master and the only conscious power of human being. Following are the eight parts of *Raj Yoga*:

Yama, niyama, asana, Pranayama, pratyahara, dharna, dhyana and *samadhi.*

1. **Yama:** Non-violence, truth, non-stealing, Brahmacharya and continence, these five are called Yama.
   (i) *Ahinsa* or non–violence is the first step of the eight-fold path of Raj Yoga and therefore marks its importance in the series of don'ts to be strictly observed in his conduct by a yogi. Non-violence is to be observed and practiced in thought, speech and action. This means violent thoughts are to be banished from mind and also the violence inciting or provocative speech. At no cost should a yogi perform an act of violence except to save life and uphold the truth. But justification for such exceptions must meet objective standards. Use of an alibi will have adverse effect on the Yoga progress. For peace to prevail and love to flourish *ahinsa* as described in Yoga is the secret. No wonder Mahabharata the great Hindu epic says – ahinsa parmo dharma. *Ahinsa* is the prime *dharma.*

(ii) Truth – Truth in Yoga means right statement and right behaviour. Right statement means to speak correctly what has been seen, heard or known without adding or concealing anything and without fear or favour. Truth is God and therefore speaking the truth means half the Yoga is accomplished.

(iii) Non-stealing: It means non-appearance of a feeling or thought in mind to cause wrongful loss to others or wrongful gain to oneself by depriving another person of his/her property. Only such a state purifies the mind from greed and stealing instinct. Non-stealing also means to banish from mind the thoughts and feelings of tax evasion, bribery or acts of corruption.

(iv) *Brahmacharya*: It means to protect the purity and vital energy of the body and mind by banishing from mind all feelings and thoughts about any form of sexual behaviour. Yoga prohibits amorous contact with the opposite sex and also contact with people of doubtful character. Yoga also recommends keeping distance from such audio-visual contacts which incite sex feeling and also non-eating of aphrodisiac and exciting foods and drinks.

(v) Continence (*aprigraha*): It means the absence of feeling and desire to amass wealth and properties with greed for selfish ends and gain. It means the absence of such feelings in the mind.

The good effects of these practices will benefit a

yogi when he/she attains this state of perfection at all times, places and in all situations. It is also suggested in scriptures that a beginner yogi should counter his negative feelings by promptly feeling and visualizing opposite and positive feelings to nip the evil feelings in the bud.

2. The following are five **niyama** (dos): *Shauch* (cleanliness), santosh (contentment) tapa (austerity), swadhyaya (study of the self and scriptures) and Ishwar Pranaidhana (surrender to God).
   (i) Shauch: It means cleanliness of the body, clothes, dwelling houses, and other households to avoid infection and diseases. This is called outer cleanliness and it also includes using clean ways and dealings to arrange supply of food articles and fair dealings with all. Internal cleanliness means to ensure purity of mind and feelings towards others by eradicating from mind the pro and anti feelings and the feelings of attraction and repulsion from the antaha-karna (the mind stuff). This condition promotes equanimity.
   (ii) Santosh: Contentment. It means to remain contented and even minded by performing duty to the hilt irrespective of the results that may follow.
   (iii) Tap: Austerity. It means to bear all pressures and pains patiently involved in performing the charter of duty in life.
   (iv) Swadhyaya: It means to analyse the mind dispassionately and study scriptures with

devotion and to adopt their advice and content in life.

(v) Ishwara Pranaidhana: It means faith in God and unconditional surrender with devotion to God. In fact it is only unconditional surrender to God which ignites love for God in human heart. It is only God love which showers grace on a yogi to bless him/her with spiritual enlightenment.

3. **Asana:** Asana means to sit still comfortably for meditation. Asan also means on which a person sits for meditation and that should be firm and comfortable, this helps in concentration. Perfection in asana makes a yogi impervious to the effects of the pairs of opposite i.e. hot-cold, pain-pleasure etc.

4. **Pranayama:** It means to control the life force (Prana Shakti). Its main objective is to stop breathing at will or rather to attain a stage through the performance of Pranayama where breathing stops automatically and the state of breathlessness is attained which is a state of deep joy. Some people think that Pranayama supplies additional amount of oxygen to purify the blood and strengthen lungs, nerves, cells etc. In fact Pranayama does much more. Good Pranayama through special technique distils the life force (Prana Shakti) from the extra inhaled oxygen and deposits it in the brain to rejuvenate the brain cells and all other weak and fatigued cells, nerves and muscles. Using more advanced Pranayama in intuitive meditation lead to spiritual enlightenment. To attain cessation of the breathing process, which is the real essence and prime

purpose of yoga, is a delicate operation and requires use of special Yoga techniques. Without Pranayama there is no success in Yoga, therefore Pranayama is the very soul of Yoga. There are many forms of Pranayama but the best system of Pranayama is that which, besides successful and honourable life, leads a person to attain spiritual realization. Pranayama is a science of regulating and controlling breathing, cessation of breathing (kumbak) (stopping inhalation and exhalation) is an automatic effect of the proper performance of Pranayama. An important system of Pranayama used in Kriya Yoga for spiritual realization is described, to the admissible extent, in the chapter on Kriya Yoga.

As a person progresses in Pranayama his delusion (the effect of Maya) diminishes even his sanchit karma (cumulative effect of all past actions) improves and his spiritual ignorance declines. His interest in sense objects drops, mind becomes steady and man moves towards the spiritual centre.

5. **Pratyahara:** It is the state when after long practice of Pranayamasenses lose interest in all sense objects and revert to chita (inside) and get absorbed there. Mind becomes interiorized and becomes fixed on one inner or outer object, such as the lotus of heart or the forehead. After attaining success in pratyahara all senses are under the control of a yogi.
6. **Dharna:** *Dharna* is a state of concentration which means fixing the mind with deep concentration on any internal or external part of the body as indicated

in pratyahara but dharna is longer and deeper concentration than pratyahara which precedes it. The difference is not only quantitative but also qualitative because without purity dharna does not succeed.

7. **Dhyana:** Dhyana is meditation. Its importance is indicated by the fact that in the pure and arduous successive steps of Yoga practice its turn in the hierarchy is at sixth position. This means that dhyana can only be performed after successfully performing the five preceding steps of Raj Yoga. Concentration in dhyana on God should be deep and long. It is to be performed so intensively that a person is only aware of himself and of the object meditated upon. Meditation lasts for hours and a person gets lost in its joy and wondrous spiritual experiences emitted by the intensity of meditation. Deep and long meditation is a state of divine romance. Meditation is the bridge that connects to God.

8. **Samadhi**: When there exists only one consciousness of the object meditated upon (God) and even self consciousness is non-existent; that consciousness is samadhi, in fact it is the state of super-consciousness or the state of being with God. There are degrees of samadhi which are discussed in the chapter on Patanjali Yoga and Kriya Yoga). Samadhi is the highest state of Yoga in which a yogi is united to God by merging his soul in the cosmic spirit through the ecstatic medium of mediation. Talking of Kriya Yoga technique of meditation, it is mentioned in *The Bhagawad Gita* of Swami Parmananda (6/46) that sitting on asana

> performance of 12 Pranayama (each Pranayama being of ½ minute duration) make one pratyahara, multiplying by 12 (144) make one dharna, multiplying dharna by 12 times make one dhyana (1728 Pranayama) and multiplying dharna by 12 times (20736 Pranayama) make the samadhi.

The secret of Yoga meditation is the art of concentration which is based on special techniques which are taught by the guru. It is the skill to master the art of meditation which when mastered lifts a person above the mind consciousness and lands him on the plane of spiritual consciousness. These two levels are said to be poles apart. Mind through ten senses knows the matter (the phenomenon world – Jagat) and spiritual consciousness acquired through intuitive meditation knows both spirit and energy (matter). Matter or the phenomenon universe is very big but the spirit is infinite and cannot be known by mind. This theme is discussed in the following pages. Here it may be briefly mentioned that the self (soul) is the reality the only absolute reality. Body is unreal because it is subject to six fold modifications and dies. Our human body-mind machine like the world that we live in is a polarity. It is motivated by two fundamental forces and both these powers are always at work. They are variously named in scriptures; Nivriti - Pravriti, divine – demonical, Nar-Narayana, and Sat-asat i.e. Ishwara and Maya. They are variations on the same basic theme of Purusha and prakriti which enjoys consensus among the three important schools; Sankhya, Vedanta and Yoga. These two forces represent the divine and the mundane. Nivriti force attracts a person towards the Divine and through inner conscience guides a person to take to moral and spiritual pursuits by working for others and God.Pravriti force pulls a person to the material lures of the world which offers varieties to attract the mind and senses, making a person outwardly oriented. Nivriti can take a person, moving on the path of Yoga, to God and pravriti can take even the best performers to a spell in heaven and then a person must revert to restart in the drudgery of this world. Basically Yoga preaches that the cosmic design is essentially of the spiritual essence and the purpose of Yoga is to unfold this design. The essence of this divine design is that God – the cosmic spirit at the universal level and human soul at the individual level is the source of the visible cosmos and the human body respectively. This is the ever ongoing process of cosmic evolution and involution. Spirit is the source – through a long drawn-out process, matter evolves from the spirit and following the reverse order matter, reverts to the original spirit and this state is called *Pralaya*. Sankhya and Yoga schools, despite some differences which are discussed in separate chapters, explain this course of cosmic ascendance and descendance as follows.

According to Sankhya, Prakriti is an independent basic creative power and according to Yoga, prakriti is the creative power of God and works under Him but unwittingly believes itself to be the cause and creator of the universe. From Prakriti begins the evolution. Prakriti is made of three gunas (basic qualities): Sattava (positive), Rajas (dynamic) and tamas (negative). From their interaction begins the evolution of nature, this theme has been discussed separately. (1) The first of the 24 evolutes is mahatatva – chitta. (2) From chitta evolves budhi (discriminative power), (3) third evolutes is ego, (4) fourth is mind. Ten senses, five tanmatras and five mahabhutas; these are the 24 basic evolutes which evolve from Prakriti in accordance with the divine design. The 25th is the purusha. Even according to Sankhya, without the presence of purusha (the soul) prakrikti cannot function.

It is the spirit which is the source of the evolution of our bodies and the cosmos. As Chandogya Upanishad reveals that God's will to become many from 'One' is the cause of what we are and what exists around us.

Just as without water its other variations like vapour, clouds, rain and ice are unthinkable similarly without soul, intelligence, mind, body and societies would be non-existent. But this soul is inconceivable and unimaginable and therefore incommunicable, yet the only reality and the only source of everything else. As indicated above there are two realities in the world called Ishwara and Maya or sat and asat, absolute and relative respectively. Atman (soul) is the absolute reality and everything else; mind, senses and their objects, abstract or tangible, are asat – unreal. *The Bhagawad Gita* also subscribes to the same theme. The soul pulls a person towards the divine for salvation and nara (energy element) pulls a person to the material world where prakriti rules. This Maya is a powerful deluding force projects the real as unreal and the unreal as real. Maya cannot be understood by mind and intelligence because they are its instruments. No power on earth or in heaven can outwit or defeat Maya. Yoga is the only power which can liberate a person from the delusion of Maya. The method used by yogis to defeat Maya is the master art of breath control, a technique in which two Prana forces (life currents), Prana and Apana, are used to neutralize maya. Prana abides in Kutastha center and apan abides in coccyx centre. Prana and Apana both exist in astral spine and are continuously busy pulling each other up and down. Parana current pulls up Apana from coccyx centre and Apana current pulls down Prana from ktastha (spiritual point between eyebrows). According to Yoga, it is this continuous Prana and Apana combat which causes the breathing process. When Prana pulls up the Apana, inhalation takes place and when Apana pulls down Prana, exhalation occurs. It is a continuous process. It is this breathing which causes modifications and restlessness of the mind as is explained at length in a separate chapter on Kriya Yoga. Yogis have developed special breathing techniques called advanced Pranayama system which involves time and patience but when mastered, it stops breathing and stills the heart, thus enabling a person to experience his soul. This technique is separately discussed in Kriya Yoga chapter.

In the treasure house of Hindu spirituality four Vedas stand out as the unique source of spiritual knowledge. Antiquity and intuitive base of Vedic knowledge occupy the position of pride in the spiritual annals of mankind. There are four Vedas: the Rig Veda, the Yajur Veda, the Sama Veda and the Atharva Veda. Each Veda contains two parts: Samhita and Brahmana. Samhitas contain hymns and prayers to invoke deities by offering oblations in fire and performing rites whereas the Brahamnas are spiritual treatises and are also called the Aranyaka. The best part of Brahamnas is the Upanishads. Upanishads teach the supreme art to realize the self. The discovery of the self within is the unique achievement of the rishis of the yore. They were the spiritual pioneers who discovered and realized the self, the only source of "bliss and eternity". It is this spiritual art which led the ardent seekers to the higher knowledge of *Brahmn* – the Supreme Being – the absolute reality. World should be indebted to these spiritual masters who discovered through self-realization this unique spiritual source described in scriptures as sat-chit-anand (existence–consciousness-bliss). Upanishads teach the absolute truth about the individual soul, the universe and the Param Brahamn. Upanishads are called Shruti (the knowledge based on what is heard in samadhi or heard by spiritual masters in communion with God). Shruti is a spiritual and not a mundane sound and is also called Divine revelation. Shruti or the knowledge taught in the Upanishad, if learnt as per guru's instructions can reveal to an ardent seeker, pure unchanging absolute truth. Vedanta (Upanishad) defines *Brahmn* as the pure consciousness and All-Bliss. This pure consciousness is the source of animate and the inanimate universe, as against the views of many philosophers and scientists that matter is the source of life and the phenomenon nature.

The crux of Vedanta is that the individual self and the supreme self are identical. The four cardinal sayings (mahavakya) of the four Vedas clearly declare this truth:

1. "Consciousness is *Brahmn*", Aiterya Upanishad of Rig Veda.
2. "I am *Brahmn*" (Brhadranayaka Upanishad of Yajur Veda).
3. "Thou art that" (Chandogya Upanishad of Sama Veda).
4. "This atman is *Brahmn*" (Mandukya Upanishad of the Atharva-Veda).

One of the great modern yogis Paramahansa Yoganandaji, is also firm in his views that spirit is the source of animate and inanimate evolution. Life, thought, energy and matter all evolve from the spirit and on death and destruction dissolve back into the spirit.

In chapter nine of *The Bhagawad Gita,* God declares Yoga as the supreme, sovereign and secret knowledge. In verse 9/2, Yoga is described as the king of all sciences, the highest secret, great purifier, fully righteous, the truth itself, and the supreme enlightenment and easy to perform. These terms are significant, therefore their import must be properly explained.

It is the supreme knowledge and sovereign science, the king of all sciences because Yoga qualifies a person to know both the Spirit and Matter, in fact it can teach everything worth knowing in this world and fully satisfies seeker's quest for knowledge. Consequently seeker's doubts vanish and calmness soothes his mind. Yoga is the highest secret because it cannot be known by reading, writing and discussion, it can be realized only by accessing the Kutastha (point in between the two eye brows where spiritual experience is felt) where yogi sees the inner spiritual light, manifesting the spiritual eye by ardently practising Yoga techniques given by the Guru. Yoga is a great purifier because esoteric Yoga exercises, performed correctly as demonstrated by Guru for a long time, purifies the heart fully. Purified heart feels no ill will and no negative feelings and thoughts enter the mind. To attain this level of attainment, performance of basic Yoga steps such as yama, niyama, asana, Pranayama and pratihara practices are important. Yoga is called 'dharma' – righteousness which shows the path leading to God. It also develops equanimity of the mind which breeds absence of discordance and presence of cordiality, which is a fertile background to promote love, devotion and peace in life.

For worldly people, Yoga lays down the four fold path of duty. The four pillars of this socio-spiritual enterprise are dharma (righteousness), artha, (material needs) Kama (family desires) and Moksha (salvation). The purpose of spiritual realization to those who seek God, is integral to this pursuit because these four fold duties are to be performed with detached mind by unconditional surrender to God. Yoga is the direct and perfect perception of truth which needs no evidence or external testimony to discern the absolute reality because this direct knowledge is realized unaided by mind and senses. Yoga is the supreme realization due to which a yogi sees the self within and the unmanifest spirit everywhere. *The Bhagawad Gita*'s view that Yoga is easy to perform does not mean that it is easy even to realize. It is easy to perform because it involves no academic excellence and financial or any other extraneous obligations but only seekers' loyalty and dedication are the prerequisites.

The question, that Yoga is easy to perform and difficult to realize, needs proper elaboration. Therefore, let us recapitulate what Yoga is and what are the methods to master this sovereign since called the king of sciences. As already explained Yoga is a unique spiritual knowledge to know God through esoteric techniques and practices. In this context Yoga is essentially science of the management of the mind, because mind is both help and hurdle on the path to spiritual realization. In the beginning the theory of Yoga can only be understood with mind and senses. This may be important but it is not Yoga.

Yoga education begins with esoteric exercises and practice of techniques to introduce psychological and physiological changes in the spine and brain. It takes long time to effect these changes. To initiate this course God realized guru is needed. The teachings of such a guru can remove mind's hurdles. It can be done by means of correct use of esoteric methods of concentration and meditation. Beside these, important prescribed exercises (asana) and Pranayama techniques are to be followed. Important techniques of shrawan, manan, darshan and nididhyasan are to be used to interiorize the mind. These steps are necessary to manifest the astral body because without manifesting the astral body, (body of light, sound and energy) which exists inside the physical body, higher progress in Yoga is not possible. Gradually by performing other important intuitive meditation techniques yogi succeeds to still the mind. But it is a very difficult thing to do, in fact the most difficult of all the attempts that man may undertake, as Arjuna also complained in *The Bhagawad Gita* 6/34-35. It is imperative to note that mind and heart cannot be stilled unless cardio-vascular system is fully purified. Mind, heart and lungs are intimately interlinked. To purify and still the heart special Yoga techniques are to be used and this practice takes a long time. We know that mind and senses are closely interconnected. It is paramount for a yogi to snap this connection so that mind is interiorized. Senses are permanently externalized because their function is to know the phenomenon world therefore mind too is externally disposed but unless mind is internalized its modifications cannot be stopped. Yogis have found effective scientific methods to interiorize the mind by disconnecting senses from their objects and stilling the mind by slowing and then stopping the working of cardio-vascular system. This extremely sensitive process is mastered by mastering the twin art of Yoga practices and renunciation. The main purpose of this process is to disconnect the connection between the senses and their object i.e. sound, touch, sight, taste and smell and the external objects. Without adopting proper scientific Yoga techniques, no renunciation and Yoga are possible. (These issues are discussed separately in the following pages).

Yoga view is that mind, senses and their objects are parts of Prakriti i.e. represent the world at large. This world for every person exists within the five spine centres viz. cervical, dorsal, lumbar, sacral and coccyx. Infact coccyx to lumbar plexus is related to the mundane life and from dorsal upwards is the sphere of higher life. Above these five spinal centres is the Kutastha (seat of spiritual awareness) and from Kutastha to sahasrara (brain) is the realm of the Divine. Five lower spine plexuses; coccyx to cervical and five knowledge senses are the realm of the mind. Mind, in waking and dream states, is always engrossed in this terrestrial world of senses which is the vast and infinite universe of three gunas and 24 evolutes. Birth after birth and age after age mind (read man) must live this worldly life of bondage to Prakriti (read matter). If man is to move upwards to savour the higher spiritual life he must take recourse to Yoga. With full determination, following the Guru's Teachings and techniques, man must lift the mind to Kutastha (the point in between the eye brows) where spirit and space (prakriti) meet and separate this being. An arduous endeavour requires no hold-barred perseverance to interiorize the ever externalized senses and mind. Mind is externalized because it is dependent on externalized nature of senses which are externalized by the power of Prana Shakti. Prana is the powerful life force called the cosmic energy.

Everything in the world, animate or inanimate, is operated and propelled by the Prana energy. Prana emanates from God (Aum power) and permeates the whole world. The origin and nature of Prana energy, due to its importance, is also separately discussed in the following pages at various places but it may be mentioned here that Prana energy emanating from God (Aum power-Pranava principles) enters the human brain which stores and regulates the use of cosmic energy in the body. From brain, it moves down through the spine nerves and operates and directs the flow of senses and mind outward to know and understand the outer world of senses. Therefore mind and senses are always disposed externally. They know little of what happens within the complex inside of every being. The knowledge of external world, gained through mind and senses, educates man to promote material development. The consequence is lack of balanced growth in the individual's life. Therefore man develops material mindset and aspirations, and finer ethical, social and spiritual values get ignored which result in imbalanced individual personality. The process being contagious produces imbalanced societies. Therefore, man has exploited and mastered for material gains, the phenomenon world, but has deprived himself of the internal knowledge which is the means to know the self and the infinite spirit. When senses are internalized and mind managed through concentration and meditation, then only man begins to know the inner world of higher life. It is with this regular and continuous progressive Yoga endeavour that man acquires the power to realize the self. This supreme knowledge is called 'jnana' – knowledge of the self acquired by interiorizing and controlling the senses and mind through Yoga practices and other spiritual pursuits. After acquiring this 'jnana' a person attains equanimity of the mind and loses interest in the material world of senses. A yogi is then immersed in peace and bliss. But this does not mean that a yogi abandons his worldly interests and responsibilities. On the contrary, a yogi performs his worldly responsibilities as already said in other chapters, more vigorously and joyfully, with deep sense of service and sacrifice. Simultaneously yogis develop a sense of commitment to inspire others to serve people and God.

How yogi attains this supreme state needs brief explanation. Patanjali in Yoga Sutra says that this highest state of complete liberation called Kaivalya is attained by the cessation of the modifications of mind. This is done by adopting the process of purification which is a package of important practices and observances; Brahamacharya, renunciation, non-violence, control of five forms of vritis (Yoga darshan 1/6), control of five basic distractions (Yoga darshan 2/3) and practice of Ashtang Yoga. These issues are properly examined in the separate chapter on Patanjali Yoga SutraHowever, it appears necessary to mention here that Patanjali describes four elements, which are major obstructions on the path to attain Kaivalya, Kalesh, Karam, Vipak, and ashya and unless these four are uprooted from the system, purity is not possible. There are five forms of kalesh; Avidya, Asmita, Rag, Davesh and Abhinivesh. Briefly, it may be said that Avidya is the worst form of obstructions and it means ignorance. Due to Avidya, man knows only gross matter and body as the reality and is unmindful of the subtle forces like the soul.

Asmita, it may briefly be said, is the near impossibility to distinguish between (budhi) intelligence and the soul. This confusion is not possible to resolve till samadhi is attained.

Raga and Dvesh (attachment and repulsion) feelings are a challenge to eradicate them from the human psyche.

Abhinivesh is the deep feeling of fear due to repeated death experiences during various births and deaths; therefore it is only in samadhi that this deep feeling of fear can be eradicated.

Klesh, Karam, Vipak and *Aashya* are interrelated and form a chain of forceful obstruction series to be overcome by a person in this world. Karma here means worldly or material actions, vipak means the results of actions and ashya means sanskar-The effects of action results which impact the mind and bind a person to perform similar actions during the successive births. The only permanent remedy to eradicate kalesh, karma, vipak and ashya from the mind is attainment of samadhi.

Infact, in this world, discovery of the self is a priceless gift of Upanishads to mankind. Different Upanishads show the way to master the science of the self. A study and practice of the contents even of three Upanishads; Brihadaranyaka, Katha-upanishad and Chandogya Upanishad will reveal the secret and teach the essence of life and death. Katha Upanishad unfolds the secrets to know the life after death and reveals the mystery of death. *The Bhagawad Gita* in its 18 chapters for understanding the world and God through spiritual realization reveals the inevitability of various Yoga means such as performance of duty with devotion, to surrender and love God, the art of renunciation and above all reveals the methods to perform Yoga and yagya. The three main Yogas discussed in *The Bhagawad Gita*; Karma Yoga, Bhakti Yoga and Gyan Yoga, provide the most useful material to control senses and to transcend and spiritualize the mind.

The basic issue is that yogi is a seeker of the self within. Attainment of 'Brahimisthiti' - spiritual realization, through self purification, is his prime concern. The reason being that yogi knows that the self within and the cosmic spirit as already said, are the basic source of the origin and evolution of a being and of the universe. Spirit is the source of all forms of forces be it consciousness, life, gravity, energy, nuclear, electrical, mechanical or chemical. This supreme power; the self, cannot be accessed unless the mind is dissolved and transcended. Till then, permanent happiness and absolute knowledge are not possible. Therefore a yogi believes that no sacrifice is big enough for such an abundant spiritual treasure. Due to personal experiences, yogis know that this self is nothing else than the God Himself who pervades the entire universe and is also present inside every person as soul and 'Aum', as His indicator.

To access the power of 'Aum' and then the Self, a yogi adopts the spinal route. There are other methods also such as rational approach and devotional path but yogi adopts the scientific method of Yoga to reach the inner spiritual realm through the sushmana nerve hidden inside the spine. Inside sushmana nerve is the vajra nerve, inside vajra is the chitra nerve and inside chitra is the Brahamnadi. Brahamnadi is said to be infinitesimally thin hollow tube of astral light. This is said to be the route to the supreme self inside the brahamrandra in the Sahasrara (brain). But it is not a direct royal ride through sushmana to brahamrandra. Inside the physical spine there is identical astral spine. In the astral spine there are seven astral centres called the plexes. In ascending order they are called coccyx at the bottom, the second above it is sacral plex, the third is lumber, fourth dorsal, fifth is cervical, the sixth medulla oblongata and the seventh is the sahasrara (brain). The nature and importance of these plexuses has been discussed separately. Here it may suffice to say that these plexes are centres of energy, life and consciousness. Our mind consciousness or physical consciousness of five basic elements is within these centres. Our consciousness of the gross matter and smell sense is due to coccyx plexus, our consciousness of the liquids and taste sense lies in sacral plexus. Our visual consciousness and the sight sense lies in lumber plexus. Our touch sense and consciousness of the gaseous substances lies in dorsal plexus and our space, ether or sound consciousness lies in cervical centre. These five astral centres of our spine control and condition our physical and psychological life. Each of these spine centres is said to have separate astral colours and sounds which a yogi can see and hear in deep meditation. The art of meditation unfolds the charm and attraction of these beautiful sounds and colours which enthral the yogi and reveal to his delightful astonishment, the wonders of the astral world. However a Yogi does not get attached to these attractions and continues his efforts to rise to higher centers. The other two centres, medulla and brain, deal with the higher level of super consciousness. This aspect has been separately discussed in a different chapter. The five lower centres are directly concerned with our five knowledge and action, senses and keep the mind connected always with the outer world of senses. These spinal centres, like the rest of the body's vital organs and parts such as, heart, lungs, excretory system, central nervous system etc, are operated by the Prana energy. The Prana energy continuously flows from brain through the spine centres to coccyx centre which uses the cosmic energy (Prana power) to operate the physical body outwards and keeps all the five senses and the mind tied down and connected ceaselessly to the outer world of senses as mentioned earlier. It is important to note that the physical nature like physical human body has its counterpart; the astral universe, which is also operated by the finer Prana power. Our senses and mind work due to the cosmic Prana power. Unless the flow of Prana power is reversed and turned inward, man cannot disengage his mind from the external world. The concentrated and inward turned attention is an important step in meditation which can reveal the real inner astral life to a person. This is called manifesting the astral body, without which,achieving higher progress in Yoga is not possible. It is only Yoga education which can teach the techniques to acquire this great knowledge.

Now it can be said that Prana power occupies important position in Yoga system of education. Management of energy (Prana) and consciousness is the prime task of the knowledge of Yoga system, therefore it is said that Yoga teaches superb skills to manage the interplay of consciousness, energy, will, cells, nerves and tissues. It is an esoteric saga of intuitive knowledge and victory in this adventure is possible with guru's guidance and divine grace.

It has already been said that the science of Yoga teaches that the cosmic spirit is the source and cause of the universe. In human body its abode.It is said to be inside the Brahamrandra (brain centre) and this cosmic intelligence manifests itself as

Aum. Therefore, in Yoga pursuit the priority is to contact Aum through meditation. Aum contact means to transcend and spiritualize the restless mind. Subsequently more intuitive meditation can lead a yogi to God contact. It is said to be the state of bliss and eternity. For this experience the restless mind must be purified which can be done by mastering the time honoured spiritual art of Raj Yoga or any other perfect Yoga system but the tried scientific method is based on Kriya Yoga techniques preached by the great modern yogi Paramahansa Yogananda. It is an advanced form of Raj Yoga, spiritually designed to suit the conditions of the modern world. This Kriya Yoga technique scientifically channelizes consciousness and energy (Prana power) to activate and energize the spinal centres to extract quickest and maximum spiritual benefits. This Yoga system is discussed in a separate chapter on Kriya Yoga.

As already said the basis of Yoga to establish God contact is the route of the spine to reach the brain. The inside of the spine is said to be hollow. Through this hollow space passes the hollow sushmana nerve from coccyx centre at the bottom of the spine to the brain. The mouth of hollow sushmana nerve at coccyx is based on four petals. As already mentioned inside the spine there are six spiritual centres one above the other.

The first centre; coccyx at the base of the sushmana has four petals, the second centre sacral has six petals, the third lumber centre has ten petals, the fourth dorsal centre has twelve petals, the fifth cervical centre has sixteen petals and the sixth Agya centre has two petals. These fifty petals and their six centres along with the Aum sound are said to be the source of 50 alphabets of the Sanskrit script Devanagri (the home of gods), because the sounds of these alphabets (phonetics) emanate from the Aum sound. The origin of these fifty petals and 50 alphabets is in sahasrara (brain). These fifty petals of the six spine centers are dormant and largely inactive and their petals are closed. When through correct Pranayama practice they are opened and turned upward; these petals generate more energy and higher consciousness. Sushmana nerve passes through these six centres. At a point below medulla and above cervical plexus (centre) sushmana divides itself into two parts and both parts of sushmana enter brahamnrandhra at two different points in lower part and upper part as mentioned in Pranaava Gita. The part of sushmana entering brahamrandra at the lower end carries Prana power and the upper part of sushmana's mouth is closed.It opens only when a spiritual person dies, this is called bursting of the brahamrandra and the spiritual person's astral body escapes through this exit. In the spine Ida and Pingla are two other very important nerves which operate and control our breathing or the cardio-vascular system to decarbonize and oxygenize the blood. These nerves start from the coccyx, the same point from where sushmana starts. They flank sushmana nerve, Ida on the left and Pingla on the right, and cutting criss-cross sushmana at each one of the four successive centres join sushmana at the agya centre in between the two eyebrows. Through Pranayama techniques (as per the guru's brief) Pranaa power is distilled from inhaled and exhaled oxygen through special technique and is to be coursed and lifted upward through sushmana nerve. This esoteric Pranayama practice turns the petals of spine upwards and step by step lifts the mind's consciousness from each spinal centre to the Kutastha, where after long persistent Yoga practice, the mind becomes spiritualized. Unless the mind is spiritualized it cannot be controlled and uncontrolled mind is the antithesis of spirituality. Restless mind is the world and spiritualized mind is the spirit. Human mind is a store house of restlessness and its modifications are countless. In a minute its infinite pace can cover nearly the whole world. However, yogis due to their experience have divided the stages of mind into five forms:

1. *Kshipt* – It is the unstable and restless state of the mind. In this state mind remains full of changes and modifications.
2. *Murh* – It is a state of lack of knowledge i.e. ignorance. In this state the mind is full of desires, anger, laziness etc.
3. *Vikship*t – It is a state of short-lived stability when mind likes an object or experience. This state lasts for a short time. Mind vacillates between alternates of stability and restlessness.
4. *Ekagrta* – In this state, mind remains concentrated and attached to a good object or experience for a long time and enjoy it.
5. *Nirudh* – It is a state of complete absorption and deep concentration in which mind forgets itself and becomes one with an object or experience, and gets lost in objects' causal state losing even its own identity. It is a sort of Samadhi state.

There are different methods of different Yogas to attain samadhi but Kriya Yoga techniques have been introduced and scientifically devised by Paramahansa Yogananda to ensure quicker spiritual results. It is an inclusive method covering activity, knowledge and devotion, devised after realizing the fact that Yoga is both spiritual action (vigyan) and spiritual knowledge (gyan). Both are interdependent because without Yoga there is no spiritual gain and without spiritual gain Yoga (God contract) does not last. God realization being the only real knowledge can be attained through Yoga and its perpetuity is ensured through the ideal combination of pure action and pure knowledge. Yoga never means to disconnect with the world; it is inclusive of mundane and spiritual because both exist in God and Yoga eliminates only greed and selfishness from the bounty and beauty of the world. In fact pure life, led through spiritual discipline (*yama-niyama*), is the key to spiritual consciousness. It is the observance of spiritual discipline which orients a yogi to the inner astral sounds and sights which is called *Shruti*. *Shruti* means the ecstatic and spiritual sounds heard in transcendental state of meditation or in *samadhi*. It is the silent speech of the soul which cannot be cognized by the power and imagination of mind..

In this concluding para now, I am attempting to recapitulate in a few lines the discussion narrated in the above pages. The main object of Yoga is to bestow on man's physical, mental and spiritual perfection to enable him to establish God contact. During his practice the main hurdle that a yogi experiences in this endeavour is the restless mind. Mind is always restless due to continuous modifications and is always attached to the outer world through the senses. Unless the mind is detached from the senses and senses from their objects, no progress is possible in Yoga. The means to do this is meditation. Precisely meditation means to manage the mind and experience the

Self. Mind being the part of invincible Maya is not easy to control. Therefore in meditation proper techniques are used to control the mind, both by ignoring it and by concentrating the attention on God who is the master of maya. Mind is also controlled by being a silent spectator, a neutral witness of the thought modifications, without attempting to interfere. Use of right techniques of concentration by remaining detached, a witness patiently waits for the thoughts to dissolve. Watching the mind with deep concentration is the key to a good meditation. *The Bhagawad Gita* also preaches that powerful prakriti (maya) can be controlled by ruthlessly ignoring it and by concentrating on God (*The Bhagawad Gita* 15/3-4). The secret of meditation is to look within, concentrate within, watch the inside and ignore the mind and manage it by detaching senses from their objects. Gurudeva Paramahansa Yogananda has taught effective techniques in Kriya Yoga to transcend the mind by concentrating on the Self. This is done through special Pranayama and other esoteric techniques which are scientific and therefore very useful for success in meditation. Quality meditation bestows intuition upon a person and with intuition; a yogi may contact the self and earn final liberation by being one with God. But Upanishads reveal that God realization, despite best efforts, cannot be attained without divine grace. This secret is explained even by Swami Paramahansa Yogananda in his spiritual diary. "The soul is bound to the body by a chain of desires, temptations, troubles and worries and it tries to free itself. If you keep tugging at that chain which is holding you to mortal consciousness, someday an invisible Divine Hand will intervene and snap it apart, and you will be free." Guruji in the same spiritual diary adds, "The

Infinite source is an infinite dynamo, continually pouring strength, happiness and power into the soul. That is why it is so important to rely as much as you can upon the Infinite source." The bottom line is that unconditional surrender to God is the key to success in the supreme art of Yoga. Only unconditional surrender to God earns a person, the gift to love God and be loved. Loving God is said to be bliss par excellence because God loves His own lover the most; therefore, the effect of this response is indescribable. In fact the best and the only means to understand the world and realize the spirit is the art of meditation. Without meditation, there is no Yoga, no wisdom, and no bliss. No wonder Gurudeva Paramahansa Yogananda cautions us "Don't say tomorrow I will meditate longer. You will suddenly find that a year has passed without fulfilment of your good intentions. The most destructive shaft of Maya delusion is unwillingness to meditate. First things must come first; when you awake in the morning, meditate. When you seek God, make even a short meditation so intense, that it will seem you have spent hours with Him. The more you meditate the more helpful you can be to others and the more deeply you will be in tune with God. Selfish people remain spiritually hide-bound, but the unselfish ones expand their consciousness. When you find your omnipresence in meditation you will find God. If He is pleased with you, all nature will work in harmony with you. Learn to talk to Him with all your soul. No matter what happens to your body, meditate. Never go to sleep at night until you have communed with God. Your body will remind you that you have worked hard and need rest, but the more you ignore its demands and concentrate on the Lord the more you will burn with joyous life, like a globe afire. Then you will know that you are not the body." "What joy awaits discovery in the silence behind the portals of your mind no human tongue can tell. But you must convince yourself; you must meditate and create that environment." These are a few lines I have quoted from Guruji's spiritual Diary and other great works like God Talks with Arjuna. Any person interested in Yoga and meditation must read, apart from Patanjali Yoga Sutra, Swami Yogananda's books – Autobiography of a yogi, *The Bhagawad Gita* - God talks with Arjuna and Spiritual Diary. These treasures against time offer wonderful material to uplift and internally transform an individual to rise above selfishness and commit oneself to the cause of common good. It is this orientation which will enable a person to envision the Infinite Essence, from which flows the grace to build a new socio-psychological field to liberate the creative forces of Yoga and spirituality, which moving hand in hand with science, will generate the right values and unleash fresh élan to found a new world order for the new global society. It is to be noted that Yoga is not only meditation, it also means action because spiritual and material are two sides of the currency of life, therefore, this balance must be maintained which is possible by pursuing both science and spirituality. Before concluding I may answer the question, what is Yoga, with these words: Yoga is the highest and the oldest knowledge yet ever new and the ever latest to bestow wisdom and enlightenment on man to love all.

WHY YOGA EDUCATION?

At death when we quit this physical body it is our astral body which survives and moves out of the dead physical body, along with the soul, to enter a new body as per our karma. During our life it is the astral body which enlivens and activates our physical body to perform various physical and psychological functions, and the physical body, despite our belief to the contrary has a little role to play in all our actions of the present life, as has been explained at various places in this book. Astral body is our subtle and finer body inside the visible physical body. It is made up of 17 elements; intellect, mind, five Prana energies and 10 senses. Yogis say that unless we manifest this astral body through the knowledge of the science of Yoga, it is not possible to contact the soul within and to rise spiritually to the higher realm of super consciousness. Therefore, it may be said that Yoga as a system of education, is different and a markedly higher knowledge. The lab and library of Yoga system of knowledge are the human spine, brain and a network of nerves in the body. Through the scientific use of various esoteric exercises, special concentration techniques, and intuitive meditative methods and by controlling breath, yogis disconnect the mind and senses from the external world and fully reverse the consciousness inward. Through Prana energy, will power and consciousness, interiorisation and purification of the mind is achieved. After a long practice when the mind is purified through special Pranayama system, the consciousness rises to the higher realm. Keeping this background in view an attempt has been made to explain that why it is necessary to introduce Yoga system of education in the present academic curriculum.

Why Yoga education, is a question which cannot be answered in words because Yoga is a matter of practical performance and personal experience. However, to satisfy the intellectual curiosity of readers, it can be said that Yoga is the only knowledge which can teach about both God and the world. In fact Yoga is said to be the highest knowledge that the world has yet to know it properly because it intuitively understands and properly explains the ever-conscious spirit and lifeless matter, along with their mutual relationship. It is a flawless and inclusive knowledge covering important aspects of the animate and inanimate parts of the world. Its specialty is the self but life and mind in all aspects; concerning conscious, subconscious, unconscious and the super conscious levels are also well within the scope of Yoga knowledge and simultaneously its study also includes the fields of matter and energy. The course of evolution and involution both at individual and cosmic levels is also explained in Yoga texts. Of course the basis of this study is intuitive knowledge but intuition acquired through Yoga, being the highest flawless knowledge, therefore leaves little scope for error and doubt. Primarily the concern of Yoga is two fold; to acquire knowledge and experience of the individual soul and the cosmic spirit including the relationship between the two and secondly, to obtain knowledge of the principles and process by which the spirit descends, following various steps, to become man (Jiva). Next, Yoga teaches how man ascends back to evolve as the spirit and dissolves himself in it. This is done by following Raj Yoga, Kriya Yoga and Laya Yoga disciplines, strictly following the instructions imparted by the guru. To attain this spiritual level through the science of tested and tried scientific methods of Yoga, precise techniques of concentration and meditation are to be mastered which are spelled out in Yoga texts and great scriptures; *The Bhagawad Gita* and Upanishads, which of course need an expert to guide and interpret. According to Yoga texts and spiritual masters, Yoga knowledge being a matter of practical realization, can be mastered by following a precise Yoga methodology under the guidance of a Guru. Its progressive training programme is to be followed in a successive order and its each step is to be mastered to elevate to the next higher stage. No doubt, it is an arduous pursuit but when accomplished, it exposes the seeker to an ecstatic spiritual marvel. It first turns a person into a good human being and then step by step uplifts him to the wonder of the spiritual pinnacle. To master this process a yogi moves successively upwards inside the spine, as is also explained in *Pranaava Bhagawad Gita*, from coccyx to cervical, dissolving the earth element into liquid element, the liquid into fire element, the fire into air element and the air into ether, then ether into *tanmatra, tanmatra* into mind, mind to be dissolved into intelligence, intelligence into ego, ego into *Mahatatva (chitta), chitta* into *mool prakriti (avyakta or aum)* and *moolprakriti* into *purusha* (acme of spiritual realization). This is the yogic ascending course prescribed to realise the spirit. This outline explains the reverse course of man's evolution which he must adopt to spiritualize himself through the path of Yoga to contact God. This brief description which is an answer to the question, "Why Yoga Education", is the subject matter of discussion in the following pages.

Before spiritual discussion regarding dissension and ascension of human soul through Yoga, meditation is initiated, it is necessary to describe some of the more pragmatic and tangible benefits of Yoga-based education, which may positively help common people, when they begin Yoga practice, to attain the benefits of physical health and mental joy. So far as physical fitness and health are concerned, Yoga, through its various methods, techniques, exercises and asana practices, offers highly useful and easily doable ways to ensure to its regular practitioners, completely disease free health, vigorous body fitness and vibrant mental health. The best thing about Yoga therapy and health guidelines is that they are fully cost free. Every Yoga practitioner can perform them in his/her small room, having proper ventilation and fresh air. Yoga medical therapy and health care packages prescribe regular use of special practices; yama, niyama, asana, Pranayama and pratyahara. It is to be noted that these exercises are not common physical, breathing and concentration methods. They are to be performed scientifically with full care and attention to get the necessary benefits in respect of physical, psychological or spiritual requirements. For physical health and fitness different emphasis are prescribed and for spiritual benefits different nuances and techniques are to be observed, as briefed by the guru. For physical health and ailments, Yoga is a great healer. There are specific asana for different ailments. If the asana provided in Hatha Yoga are performed properly and regularly they not only cure the disease permanently but make the body strong like steel and flexible like rubber. These different asana are performed with special techniques by using Prana Shakti and consciousness, first to cure and then to strengthen the body. Use of Prana Shakti (cosmic energy), consciousness and will power have special role in Yoga methods for cure and treatment. This combine is to be timed with the physical performance of the specific asana for prescribed time duration.

Yogis have intuitively and with personal experience known that Prana Shakti (cosmic energy) is an unlimited and a wonderful source of food, force, power, medicine and relaxation. Accordingly, they have devised and developed methods to harness and use this cosmic abundance for the help and benefit of mankind, all animals and plant life. Yogis claim that some of their health care and cure techniques effectively work as preventive vaccines, curing medicines and source of energy, strength and relaxation.

They say that Pranayama system is one of the very useful and effective methods to prevent and cure many diseases and to make body fit and keep the mind relaxed and balanced. There are various types of Pranayama. With my personal experience, I can say that a few Pranayama that are prescribed and used in Kriya Yoga system are very useful to cure some of the diseases related to cardio vascular system, respiratory system and nervous system. These Pranayama affecting our tissues, cells, nerves and consciousness are of great benefit to feel healthy, energetic, relaxed and happy. Pranayama, as taught in Kriya Yoga, is a very good source for energy intake at will and to counter fatigue and tension. Pranayama system is a wonder therapy to cure and treat diseases which are difficult to cure, like some cancers, Alzheimer etc. It builds the body defence system and can help to ward off diseases like AIDS. I am of the view that if only two of the eight basic steps of Yoga covering important asana and Pranayama are taught to school children to be performed properly and regularly our children will develop good health and sound character. Yama and niyama parts of Yoga, if observed, can yield very good results for character building and spiritual growth. The other three stages of Yoga wiz dharna, dhyana and samadhi are mainly for higher spiritual benefits and are therefore discussed in separate chapters. Yogis who can attain the samadhi (super conscious) become disease proof and also can cure other peoples' incurable diseases.

Since time immemorial master yogis have mastered this unique art through intuitive meditation by using special techniques of concentration. One of the great modern yogis of the 20th century, Paramahansa Yoganandaji, through Kriya Yoga techniques has educated a large number of Yoga students in USA and many other countries of the world. Quite a few of these students have become dedicated monks. They have set up four hundred Kriya Yoga centres in USA and Europe alone and 170 such centres are functioning in India too. These Kriya Yoga centres are overflowing like beehives with devotees. American and Indian monks have dedicated themselves with missionary zeal to educate and train willing people to acquire physical fitness and build character and avail themselves of the golden opportunity of Kriya Yoga science to spiritualize them and inspire others.

Scriptures reveal and yogis say that God gifted this knowledge to mankind at the time of creation. This sovereign knowledge is known by two names -- Yoga and yagya. In essence, both these branches of spiritual knowledge are similar, when earnestly pursued, because both lead to God contact. The path of Yoga is meant for the meditative and the path of yagya (pure action) is meant for the active as is also laid down in *The Bhagawad Gita* 3/3. Essentially the purpose of Yoga and yagya is to purify the heart, for this paramount purpose Yoga and yagya, prescribe important rites and spiritual practices as are also strongly recommended in *The Bhagawad Gita*, Upanishads, Puranas, Vedas and darshans (including Yoga darshan). In *The Bhagawad Gita* the third chapter on Karma Yoga is mainly dedicated to the performance of yagya to attain spiritual liberation. In verse 3/9 *The Bhagawad Gita* lays down that yagya (yagna) means pure action (done for God and others) and must be performed with a sense of sacrifice to attract the gains of spiritual excellence. Verses 3/14-15, of Gita reveal that God is inevitable though unmanifest presence is always there in every act of yagya (yagna) which showers His grace and blessings on the performer. Yagya (yagna), due to its pivotal position in Hindu scriptures, may have several interpretations but in essence yagya is an act of devotional sacrifice done for God, in fact it is the greatest sacrifice in which the performer offers his soul as oblation into the fire of the cosmic spirit. In verses 3/14-15 *The Bhagawad Gita* reveals a grand summary of the existence and evolution of man from spirit through God's creative will in which the instrument of yagya performs a key role. These verses reveal that beings become from food, food is produced by rain, rain is produced by yagya, yagya is born of karma, karma is born of Veda, Veda from the imperishable Brahmn. Therefore the omnipresent God is anchored in yagya (devotional spiritual action) in which lies the seed of man's evolution and destiny. This is simple translation of the verses 3/14-16. The deeper meaning of these verses is that the supreme God causes evolution/ involution through His divine laws. From Him, emanates 'Aum', the creative vibratory power. From Aum, emanates the sound element *(shabad Brahmn),* and then successively emerge ether, air, fire, water and earth. These five terms are mere symbols of various forces of life and energy *(para /apara prakriti).* The essence of these verses is that the performance of Yagya is the secret to spiritual liberation. In fact, verses 14-16 of chapter III of The Gita, intuitively spell out the saga of the descension of man from the spirit and his spiritual ascension back to the spirit, following the path prescribed by Yoga. This is well explained in The Gita bySwami Pranvananda.

Yagya is a spiritual ceremony and is performed for the welfare of all but without the input of sacrifice it loses the effect. Below are mentioned the five forms of yagya (yagna) which Hindus perform for their own and others spiritual benefit:

1. *Pitri yagya* – Is offerings for the benefit of the ancestors who have bequeathed rich and diverse heritage to us. Pitri yagya also means to emulate the devotional and creative deeds of the worthy ancestors.
2. *Nri yagya* – Offering food and other useful things to deserving contemporaries to discharge our social responsibilities. This promotes coexistence, peace and harmony.

3. *Bhuta yagya* – Offering food and nutrition to the non-human kingdom of creation such as animals, plants etc. for their preservation and maintenance. This promotes ecology.
4. *Deva yagya*- Is performed for Devas and angels as a mark of devotion to attract blessings.
5. *Brahmn yagya* – This is the highest spiritual sacrifice performed to God, with deepest devotion and sense of gratitude, for what He has been doing for his creation. This sacrifice is offered by people having spiritual awareness.

God Himself praises the spiritual merit of yagya (yagna) in verse 5 of the 18th (last) chapter of *The Bhagawad Gita,* where God exhorts all to perform the three virtuous acts of sacrifice viz- yagya, dana (alms giving) and tapa (austerity), at all costs. These virtuous acts purify a person and make him fit to perform higher spiritual rites of Yoga. In verses 4.25 to 4.29 and 9/15-22, God Himself explains the merit of various yagyas to be performed by devotees to attract divine grace.

Now we may briefly talk of *The Bhagawad Gita* as the source of Yoga. *The Bhagawad Gita* is the greatest source of various important branches of Yoga. Therefore, this important aspect of relationship between Yoga and *The Bhagawad Gita* has been discussed while dealing with each of the important branches of Yoga. Here I may mention only two links of the vital relationship between the two. The best definition of Yoga is contained in verse 48 of the second chapter of *The Bhagawad Gita,* "O Dhananjaya, being fixed in Yoga, perform actions renouncing attachment (to fruits), remaining even-minded in success and failure is Yoga." The main aim of Yoga is to attain equanimity of the mind which is extremely difficult because mind is always restless and full of vritis (modifications). Equanimity and mind are poles apart. To attain evenness of mind, mind is to be stilled which can be attained by detachment from the desire of rewards of actions. No doubt, to perform action without attachment to rewards and results of actions is also an uphill task. But there is a spiritual law which resolves the complexity of this difficulty. This spiritual law states that the outcome of the results of all actions is laid down by the universal law of cause and effect. It is an unexceptionable law just as when oxygen and hydrogen are properly mixed, water will be the result even without intent. Therefore a person must act whole-heartedly to improve the quality of action rather than dilute the attention on desire for results. The karmic law states that good results are bound to follow quality actions. It is this attitude which makes the mind even. But it is to be noted that pure action in Yoga context also means meditation. If all actions are performed with detached and dedicated mind which is the consequence of quality meditation, equanimity of the mind, which means Yoga, is bound to follow.

The second link between Yoga and *The Bhagawad Gita* is clearly established by the fact that each one of the headings of 18 Chapters of *The Bhagawad Gita* has Yoga as suffix – *Vishada Yoga, Karma Yoga, Gyana Yoga* etc. This not only proves the inseparable link between Yoga and *The Bhagawad Gita* but indicates identity between the two. In fact *The Bhagawad Gita* without its Yoga content ceases to be the spiritual force. Now it can be said that *The Bhagawad Gita,* as a spiritual song, is a unique source revealing the glory of Yoga to attract God. No wonder Guruji proclaims that yogis are God's Achilles' heel.

It is an irony that people should know so little about this ancient and great knowledge. Antiquity of Yoga is proved by its references in oldest scriptures and God's own pronouncement in Bhagwat Purana and in *The Bhagawad Gita* 4/1-3 "I gave this imperishable Yoga to Vivasvat: Vivasvant taught it to his son Manu and Manu gave it to his son Ikshwaku. Through its regular transmission, the royal sages knew it. Due to long lapse of time this Yoga lost its impact in this world. The same ancient Yoga, indeed the supreme secret, has been told you by Me today because you are My devotee and friend."

These three verses of *The Bhagawad Gita* being God's own pronouncements reveal volumes about the antiquity, authenticity and uniqueness of Yoga. These verses are full of symbolism, as is also interpreted by Paramahansa Yoganandaji in his *The Bhagawad Gita* book, God talks with Arjuna. Vivasvat does not refer only to the historical king Vivasvat. Symbolically, Vivasvat personifies God's cosmic light and intelligence, the source of highest knowledge. Manu, the second king to know this spiritual knowledge, personifies intuitive mind and *Ikswaku* means the intelligent mind of man and Royal sages mean the disciplined senses. Human mind and senses being involved with the phenomenon world lost the secret of this supreme science which is why Lord Krishna revealed this supreme science of spiritual realization to His devotee and friend Arjuna so that all deserving souls would benefit from this divine gift. It is due to the mercy and grace of God that this eternal and immutable divinizing science of Yoga, moving through the trackless track of time, reaches the parching hearts of yogis. Various great yogis and spiritual masters of different times and lands have divinized themselves through the master key of this Yoga, which may have been known by different names in different places, but in spiritual essence it is the same truth. Yoga is the only immutable art which internally connects the soul to the spirit. According to the divine scheme human soul descends from God – the cosmic spirit and in this world on taking birth becomes a jiva. This world is the realm of Prakriti – God's powerful maya. This Prakriti has two forms; Para and apara – higher and lower respectively. Apara Prakriti is made of eight parts: intelligence, ego, mind, akash (ether or space) air, fire, water and earth. Para Prakriti is the life element and has consciousness and intellect but the eight fold apara Prakriti is lifeless matter. Here jiva in this world becomes part of Prakriti, unaware of his soul and the divine origin, and gets involved in the intense struggle of bread and butter. Prakriti is an infinite phenomenon. Life and living in the realm of Prakriti is full of mixture of good and bad, pain and pleasure. There is no escape from the rule of powerful Prakriti; its power covers earth, heaven and the nether land. In simple words, Prakriti for an individual means body and mind consciousness and to raise above this body consciousness, the only remedy is to attain spiritual consciousness. This is possible by acquiring gyana (soul experience) and through Yoga. In spiritual context, soul contact is the real Midas touch. It is the only philosopher's stone which turns the iron cage of life into the smiling blossom of the divine bliss.

It must be noted that knowing the soul is a great event. In fact, the biggest achievement that a person can attain in this life because it is the supreme knowledge knowing which man knows everything worth knowing. Therefore, Yoga is the only science which has the precise knowledge about three dimensions of human personality; physical, mental and spiritual. Yoga also offers means and measures to make the body fit and healthy. It can improve and discipline the mind and reveals right methods to build character. Most importantly, Yoga bestows the knowledge to establish contact with the unmanifest soul.

Yoga, through its esoteric methods and techniques, imparts flawless intuitive knowledge about inorganic, organic, plant and animal kingdoms. Therefore, the nature and scope of Yoga study extends to cover in its wide range of knowledge i.e the animate and inanimate regions of the world. Yoga is claimed by its acknowledged masters and famous yogis as the only science which knows and imparts knowledge to its ardent students about which science and secular knowledge knows little. Mundane knowledge does not know about what is *Brahmn* (eternal spirit), what is Adhyatma (soul), what is karma (creative and spiritual actions born of Aum), what is Adhibhuta (all physical beings having body consciousness), what is Adhidaiva (astral beings –angels), what is Adhiyagya (the supreme creative and cognizing intelligence of Ishwara) and about the fate after death of a common man, a good man, a failed yogi and an accomplished yogi. And what is death and how can death be conquered? All great and God-realized yogis know these secrets and have answers to these basic questions. Answers to these questions are also given in *The Bhagawad Gita*, Bhagawad Purana and Upanishad particularly in Kato Upanishad and Brihadaranyaka Upanishad. According to these scriptures, Brahamn is the supreme, eternal cosmic consciousness, Anadi-beyond birth and death and the origin of all.

Adhyatma is the soul knowledge and its realization called *Kuthastha* consciousness, the power of super-consciousness, through which a yogi knows intuitively what happens anywhere in the world.

Karma means detachment from worldly and material things and performance of detached action for God and others. Karma also means the effect of actions which impact our future life. It signifies the quality of conduct a person should perform to lead a balanced life to develop spiritually. *Adhibhuta* means all physical objects and beings that live on body mind level of consciousness. It includes animals, plants and organic substances. It is through Karma that Adhibhuta becomes Adhideva.

Adhideva means higher beings like angels and devas, who due to karma or yoga pursuit. go to heaven but on return from heaven, through Yoga sadhna (spiritual endeavour), can attain salvation.

Adhiyagya means the supreme will and sovereign spiritual power of God to create, protect and love all beings and the whole universe; causal, astral and physical. God is the supreme sacrificer who creates all beings and things for their good. Nobody else is a creator in this world because nobody else can create matter and life.

Yoga texts reveal that a common man who has not made a mark in any creative field in this life goes after death to mrityuloka, the big and diverse region of the dead, as per his/her karma. The average life span in this Mrityuloka is said to be 500 years. The good doers go to vast and diverse heavens, some to lower and others to higher heavens. As per their karma, they enjoy the life of pleasures, joy and beauty for long spans.

After exhausting the rewards of their good karma, they have to return and get reborn in this world. Even in Braham loka, the highest abode of joy and happiness, God-realization is not possible. However at the end of cosmic cycle such great souls who enter the *Brahma-loka* merge with the supreme God.

Yoga showers imperishable benefits. Even bhrasht (unsuccessful) yogis who are of two types; depending on the degree of their advancement in Yoga never lose the rewards of their spiritual endeavour. Less advanced (unsuccessful) yogis, after death go to the highest heavens and after exhausting their long and glorious term return to earth. Here, they are reborn in spiritual families where they find favourable atmosphere for their further spiritual progress. More advanced unsuccessful yogis, after death do not go to heaven but due to their merit in Yoga, get rebirth in the family of yogis and there they quickly progress spiritually and become Yogarurh (fit to attain God realization) and attain salvation. This theme is well explained in Upanishad and in *The Bhagawad Gita* 6/41-42 and 8/25-26.

The Bhagawad Gita, Yoga scriptures and texts categorically reveal that death is wrongly understood and wrongly interpreted in this world. There is no such thing as an end of life. Life never dies and never ends; its end is salvation which in fact is deathlessness and not death because salvation is eternity and bliss. Of course salvation is to be earned through Yoga and spiritual sadhna. Body death is followed by rebirth and new fresh life according to individual karma. This theme is elaborately discussed in *The Bhagawad Gita* 2/17 to 30 and in various commentaries. Yogis through personal experience know that death is a welcome change from physical body to astral body.

Yoga texts reveal and great yogis say that yogis, through spiritual sadhna conquer death because they at will walk out of this physical body when it is no longer of any use to them. Modern famous yogi Paramahansa Yoganandaji had told in advance his disciples of his will to leave the body at a given time. There are many such instances mentioned in a world famous book autobiography of a yogi where yogis quit the body at will. Swami Pranavananda, during his life time, used to move out of his body at will and back into it and simultaneously appear and act at more than one places. In this book, an important example of dying at will and reappearing in the same body the following day at three different places at the same time is of Shri Shri Lahiri Mahashya the great founder of Kriya Yoga. Shri Shri Lahiri Mahashya, by mastering the science of Yoga had humbled death and even revived the dead. These achievements are not uncommon for yogis but it is uncommon to become a yogi. How to become a yogi is explained within permissible limits in separate chapters on Kriya Yoga and Patanjali Yoga. Yoga is an exhaustive and intuitive knowledge which teaches about life, space, energy and matter, revealing an exciting chain of the origin, continuity and evolution of the epochal events from the cosmic spirit to gross matter and their reverse process, from the gross back to the spirit. Therefore, Yoga is an intuitive knowledge of cosmic evolution and involution and also the study of involution and evolution of the life of man.

The 'implicate and explicate' orders of the growth and evolution of the manifest(outer world) and the unmanifest (inner life) are accessed and then explained by yogis through intuitive insight. Such intuitive knowledge and observations are explained by Yoga philosophy and texts for the benefit of Yoga students. But this great intuitive knowledge can be acquired after soul realization through meditation. It is well known in some circles that yogis make predictions about future events and perform miracles. To curious readers I may suggest to read two great books of our time, *autobiography of a yogi* and *man's natural quest* by Paramahansa Yoganandaji. It is a study which answers many questions and explains many mysteries.

The scope and aim of Yoga study is to experience and expand the spiritual dimension of human personality and its core is human soul, which is the source of life, love, compassion, happiness bliss and eternity. In fact the secret of human glory reflected in noble deeds and laudable institutions through the ages is attributable to the fount of soul virtues. Yogis know from personal experiences that the self is the source of the abundance of pure love. With soul contact, spurts the elixir of divine love, which is an inexhaustible source of infinite romance. This divine romance being contagious affects all seeking ardent hearts. Yogis know that divine love is the only force which binds Jiv, Jagat and Ishwara, with its invisible tendrils and Yoga is the path which leads a committed seeker to this unique discovery of the divine bliss. It is the feeling of love and power born of spiritual experience, which commits a yogi to the cause of universal love and universal service. A yogi or a spiritualist finds satisfaction only by loving and serving others. I have personally seen this commitment to selfless service on the part of many monks of Yogda Satsanga Society of India. They dedicate themselves sincerely to serve people and out of love, try to educate and enlighten them.

Due to their intuitive knowledge of inorganic, organic, plant and animal lives, yogis are aware of the interdependence of various forms of living species and inorganic substances, therefore, they endeavour to promote balance in nature. Maintenance of internal and external purity in living beings, on earth and in atmosphere, to ensure a balanced life, is the main concern of yogis because without purity and balanced life spiritual development is not possible. For a yogi life is the school for spiritual training and his centre of consciousness is not the body but the soul, which he must realize and inspire others to follow him, to know the hidden and unmanifest knowledge of the universe.

The need and importance of Yoga can be explained in a simple way. In fact the question that why Yoga, is well answered by another question, that why food? As food feeds and nourishes our bodies similarly Yoga knowledge feeds, purifies, improves and disciplines our mental faculties and reveals to us the self, which is the source of our life, peace and enlightenment. Therefore, Yoga is unique. This uniqueness is clearly illustrated by the fact that there is no other branch of knowledge be it arts, sciences or technology which can bestow on man the power to realize the spirit which transfigures a person into a divine being called the super man. Secondly, the unique power of Yoga is to bless a seeker with the gift to remain permanently happy and blissful. There is no means in conventional or mundane education which can even aspire to attain such powers. In fact this supreme art is unattainable unless consciousness is raised to the level of the super-conscious level and this capability can only be taught by Yoga. Thirdly, Yoga has the power to conquer death, which means that a yogi knows beyond any iota of doubt that there is no such thing as death of life. Life never ends, it only ascends to become the spirit with salvation even after a trillion years, but Yoga can accelerate this process! Due to his mastery of Yoga, a yogi can choose his time and the method to quit this mortal frame at will.

No doubt, to attain the spiritual level in which these high states are attained is very difficult but these statements are not the claims from speculative realm. These views are facts based on the realization and personal experience of several yogis (Gita 2/16). It is true that such Yoga masters though still there, may not be many in the present time, but if they were in sizable number in the past and creatively inspired people whoimpacted their socio-cultural outlook to create harmonious societies, why should not such inspiring people be more in the future. The reason for the lack of their presence in the modern time is explained by obvious reasons. The most important being the radical shift towards material attraction in the modern system of education which has opaqued people to social, moral and spiritual qualities of life. To overhaul the education system through proper planning as envisaged by yogis, is necessary to shape the growth and development of various global societies to meet the needs of the new age. Yogis have clear vision about the future and proclaim that the world will develop into one political organization, a sort of one global order, which can be accelerated by evolving the right system of education which will inform people that mankind has evolved from one common source; we have common needs and aspirations and common stakes concerning security, prosperity and peace. The new education system should teach scientific Yoga which has the capability to creatively transform the outlook and mind-set of students so that real values like love, compassion, fellow feeling and sense of service and harmony are developed. This is possible because the techniques and methods used by Yoga teachers to promote such qualities and to produce such desired results are demonstrable and can therefore convince people that Yoga can produce creative and people friendly socio-spiritual culture. It is the system of education which holds the key to effect necessary changes in peoples' thinking. Let us admit; there is need for fundamental change in our system of education, which must be designed to transform a student from within and Yoga specializes in this spiritual art. The need of the hour is to introduce change in the mindset and thinking of a few intelligent people, once they have been trained they will act as the dynamo of change to inspire and transform others. It is the internal change which can transform people. Yoga specializes in this art to change creatively people from within. Such transformed minority will generate the ripple effect. Being focused and committed they can yield spectacular results. All major changes in human societies since immemorial times have been brought about by a committed intelligent minority. The cardinal teaching of Yoga philosophy is that the course of human evolution can be improved and accelerated by moral and spiritual inputs which Yoga teachings and practices can provide in ample measure. Induction of these values in education system is the prime need of the hour to redeem man from greedy materialism. Yoga, being an inclusive life approach, does not exclude basic material needs of life which are necessary for progress; on the contrary Yoga teaches methods to attain comfort and leisure in life without which spiritual progress cannot accelerate and methods are cost effective and result orientated. Yoga preaches right ways to alleviate poverty because poverty is a curse and balanced life is the ideal which yoga education can produce. Yoga education is different. It is not based on reading, writing, discussion and lectures, infact, these basics of conventional education system form only elementries of the Yoga teachings. Yoga teachings are based on certain esoteric proven techniques, methods, exercises and strict observance of physical, mental and spiritual discipline of which even cyber science and latest information technology are unaware. These techniques are aimed at directing the flow of cosmic energy within the body to charge cells, nerves, muscles and vital body parts, including various involuntary and voluntary systems of the body and brain. Through yogic techniques, dormant, fatigued and ailing neurons can be energized by augmenting the energy which will supply additional power to the brain. Yoga techniques and its strict discipline radically improve the character of a person and purify his capabilities to conceive new ideas and perceive hidden facts. No doubt only a few can achieve such high standards of performance. But there are always a few selected great people who creatively lead the masses, transform societies and form new cultures. Yoga has the power to create a team of leaders across nations who will be filled with the new and distinct élan unleashed by spiritual spark lit inside them. It is such a class of leaders that is needed which Yoga can produce, which will usher in a new phase of life bereft of violence, hatred, jealousy and the revenge instinct. On the positive side it will promote love, fellow-feeling, fairness and deep concern for others.

No doubt, the creative and elite segments of different societies comprising statesmen, scientists, media, academia and creative thinkers have been expressing, for a long time in the past, their views to organize violence and hatred free world order, but in the past the essential basics of infrastructure to implement such noble thoughts did not exist. Now, advances in science and technology have done the ground work to facilitate the advent of a new globalized world society. The Yoga-based spirituality will supply the software of universal love and service to transform people from within. Undoubtedly, the catalyst of Yoga can humanize and mobilize people to usher in a ketter world society in which prosperity and peace for all will have a chance. Yogis say that these socio-spiritual dynamics are programmed in the course of evolution but human effort can do a lot to accelerate the process. The irony is that people are not aware of the wonderful potentials of Yoga. Yoga based education and meditation techniques can transform the world because Yoga transforms a person from within and it changes human mind and thinking. A person becomes different and starts liking, helping and loving others. As a result, a new dimension is added to human personality. Such people develop patience and courage. For the information of those who will find these conclusions doubtful and may term them as speculative, it may be reiterated that basically Yoga is a different system of education. It does not target the mind through reason; it rather ignores this aspect of the mind. Through special Pranayama by manipulating the chemistry of breath and other well tried techniques, Yoga methods target the psycho-physiological system by directing and diverting consciousness, and energy through concentration techniques and will power, to achieve the desired results for peace and progress. These special Yoga techniques work on the untapped subtle centres in the spine and brain by targeting nerves and cells. These techniques concentrate on disconnecting contact between senses and the sense objects by withdrawing the consciousness from senses by turning inwards the flow of Prana Shakti which operates the senses. As a result, the senses become as if dead, loose contact with the outer world and the mind then, automatically turns inward and is further channelized towards inner centres of life and consciousness. These techniques produce great amount of additional energy in the brain. Yogis become more knowledgeable, relaxed and peaceful. Their inner strength increases to counter gainfully the external threats. It can be said that if Yoga based education is earnestly started, it will produce a creative culture to produce balanced people. The major challenges which confront the world today can be neutralized through the pursuit of a new system of education based on Yoga. It will produce a different culture based on brotherhood of humanity because we all come from one source as has been scientifically proved by the decoded human genome. Such a society will be the home for prosperity, peace, freedom and love. In-fact due to its importance a separate chapter has been devoted in this book to explain the concept of a new education system based on teachings of Yoga.

KARMA YOGA

In simple words, Karma Yoga is an earnest spiritual endeavour to know God- the cosmic spirit, through the performance of pure action. Therefore these two words, Karma and Action, need to be properly explained. Karma is a Sanskrit word and its English translation is 'action'. Whatever action we do is karma. However, in Yoga and Vedanta concepts, the word karma has distinct connotation involving the higher spiritual essence. Therefore, karma means actions, which produce immediate and long lasting effects; therefore karma also means the effects of actions. These effects of actions are called Sanskars. Sanskars are the impressions caused in mind by the effects of actions performed, which become the cause for future actions. Therefore, karmas and sanskaras generate a psychological chain of cause- effect series in our mind to follow and affect us life after life till we have been able to neutralize this chain of cause and effect, by the power of karma (pure actions). This is why Karma, our action, is the cause which binds and also liberates us. Therefore, the best action to secure liberation from earthly bondage is to always perform good actions. It is this pursuit which leads a person to the state of akarma, actionlessness, and enables to realize the action-less pure soul. According to scriptures, karma in Hindu philosophy is an immensely important reality. It guides and conditions our activities not only in this life but also in lives hereafter. Therefore, the quality of life lived in this world and how we may begin the life after death depends on the quality of karma we perform in this life. The concept and reality of karma is so central to the Hindu view of life from birth till death and for life after death, that every other mode and philosophy of life is secondary to the fact and philosophy of karma. It is to be borne in mind that karma not only means gross actions but includes speech and thoughts too. All actions of people are caused by the three gunas of Prakriti i.e. Sattvic (creative), Rajasic (dynamic) and Tamsic (negative) which form the basic nature of all human beings. They not only affect the nature of our actions but our actions in turn regularly affect the nature of these gunas for the better or worse, depending on what karma we do. It is a complex and interdependent situation. That is why lord Krishna tells Arjuna in *The Bhagawad Gita* 4/17, "the nature of Karma is hard to fathom." The secret is that karma is to be performed to attain *akarmanta* (state of actionlessness) and after attaining *akarmanta,* actions performed, automatically become akarma (spiritual actions) 4/18. Therefore let us begin from square one and analyse that why and how karmas benefit and harm us. According to scriptures, the reason of our birth in this world is our karmas. When we have no karma left we are free and attain salvation. Now the question is how to exhaust our karmas? Scriptures say that every being has been incarnating in this world for countless births in the past and has been performing countless actions in every life and this has built a massive pile of karmas which bind a person to this world and hence everybody is caught in this cycle of infinite births and deaths and per force have to face the grim struggle of life. Karmas pile up because we perform motivated actions which means actions performed with a desire for fruits and rewards of actions. Now therefore, we must distinguish between karma and action. Karma is not only actions but also effect of actions. These effects of actions cause and condition our future actions and they are called Sanskaras. Sanskaras develop whenever we perform an action and its main cause is the motive or desire to do it. The cause of this desire is the similar actions we must have performed in the past and in previous births. The intensity of such actions form impressions in our mind and create sort of grooves in the mind which never leave us and condition us in the future births to perform similar actions. Thus we develop psychological tendencies to automatically obey this pattern of cause-effect which goes on increasing and resultantly, strengthens a person's bondage to Prakriti. Scriptures and experienced ones offer great effective remedies to shatter the shackles of karmas. To secure release from the effects of karma the *The Bhagawad Gita* suggests that it is necessary to properly understand the subtle nature of karma. Therefore, the nature of Karma, Vikarma and Akarma is to be known 4/17. Karma, according to the *The Bhagawad Gita,* means good and creative actions which can lead us to the attainment of higher spiritual ideals and thus enable us to earn the merit to go to the heavens. Vikarma are a usual mixture of motivated actions based on sanskaras which bind us to this world and subject us to rebirth. Akarma are the highest moral and spiritual actions which liberate us from bondage to Maya (this world) and inspire us to attain salvation because performance of Akarma causes no binding effects and their cause is not any personal motive or desire. These actions are called *Nishkam karma* and must be performed to attain spiritual heights for salvation. The main question, now here, is how to perform Nishkam karma? The concept and practice of Nishkam karma is under attack from various quarters. It is alleged that to perform actions without desire or motive is not only impractical but also alien to human nature and even if practiced, it may create a society of non-innovative, inactive and lazy people.

It must be pointed out that the concept of Nishkam karma is not a theoretical principle. It is based on the experience and practice of great people. The ideal of karma Yoga to attain success and peace in this world and salvation at death, as revealed in *The Bhagawad Gita* ,is based on the performance of Nishkam karma. Chapter after chapter in *The Bhagawad Gita*, the theme of Nishkam karma is inspiringly preached by lord Krishna as the only secret to success and salvation in this world. The essence of Nishkam karma is contained in verse 2-47, "human right is only to act, not to lay claim on its resultant fruits, be not the cause of the fruits of your actions and never forsake action" this verse contains four principles :

1. Human right is only to act or perform duty.
2. Human right is not for the fruits of actions performed.
3. One should not consider oneself the cause of the fruits of actions.
4. One should not run away from action or duty.

The conclusion of *The Bhagawad Gita* that human right is only to work and not for the fruits of actions is based on the knowledge and experience of the fundamental spiritual truth that whatever action is performed by any person, its correspondence result or reward is inevitable and the extent and quality of reward depends on the quality of actions performed. For example, when coriander and lime are mixed properly, the colour will be red and when hydrogen and oxygen molecules are mixed then the result will be water. Therefore, a person should concentrate on the quality of work and not dilute ones energy on the resultant fruits. Secondly, man has no option but to work because no person ,healthy or unhealthy, can remain even for a moment without action because his physical survival, psychological behaviour and thinking process depends on action as is laid down in *The Bhagawad Gita* 3/8. Definition of action as mentioned in *The Bhagawad Gita* 18/15 means thought, speech and gross action; therefore it is obvious that even unhealthy person cannot run away from action.

The theme of karma Yoga, due to its importance, must be properly understood because it is the centre of gravity of our spiritual and mundane lives. The main requirement of Karma yoga is that our actions must conform to the principles of Nishkam karma (detached action) which is the very essence of karma Yoga and the secret of success and salvation. Now it is necessary to understand that what Nishkam karma means? It means Akarma, the action that liberates the actor from prakriti and leads to God, because such action being detached (done with attachment and love for God) does not cause any binding and is above the cause- effect nexus. Therefore, one must plan action to attain the state of nishkriyata (the state of action-lessness). This state cannot be attained either by not beginning action or not giving up action. It must be attained through performing action, (*The Bhagawad Gita* ¾) and also not by running away from action which in any case is not possible and so the best way to perform an action is to perform it as a yagya which is both automatically rewarding and liberating-*The Bhagawad Gita* 3/9. But those people who do not have active disposition and are given to do desk, indoor or meditative work, they must work with the equanimity of mind which can be attained with both meditation and pure action. It is the equanimity of mind which liberates a person and in ultimate analysis; Yoga is nothing but the equanimity of mind- *The Bhagawad Gita* 2/48.

Performance of pure action is the basic condition of good life and the fundamental essence to achieve peace, honour and excellence in life. To attain this sublime goal a person has to rise above the effects of three gunas of nature and the pair of opposites which is possible by understanding and acting upon the fundamental principal of guna-karma-vibhaga. This means that all actions in the lives of all people in this world are performed by nature (prakriti) and the indwelling soul performs no action at all. Every person basically being the soul is always pure and above the effects of actions born out of the three gunas; therefore it is important to realize this truth as mentioned in *The Bhagawad Gita*.

The concept of three gunas, due to its centrality in life has been properly explained in various chapters. Here it is enough to mention that these three gunas are the forces which bind people to motivated actions. The three gunas are integral to prakriti; therefore prakriti invariably attracts and binds every person to perform actions (God created man and karma together, 3-8). Hence the need that the concept of guna-karma-vibhaga which is the liberating power from prakriti is to be realized and practically lived in life, is attainable through the practice of Nishkam karma.

The main power attracting or binding people to the charm of various goods and services of this world is Maya (mool prakriti). Therefore, it is necessary to understand what Maya really is. Basically there are two prime powers or forces in the world, God and Maya or the cosmic spirit or cosmic nature. Maya is God's creation to run the world and its domain is the entire cosmos called the phenomenon universe. It also includes all living beings except the divine and the divinely realized. Therefore, it means that all people living at the Rajsik (dynamic) and Tamsik (self-centred) levels of existence are at the mercy of Maya. But Maya being the creation of God is not a demon. Maya also performs the role of cosmic mother to feed and care for the worldly oriented masses, because Maya performs two roles, bhog and moksha. This theme is discussed in Patanjali's Yogasutra as well as the Katha Upanishad. Maya guides the satvik people towards God and looks after the rajsik and tamsik masses of people to provide for them, the facility of various goods and services to live in this world, which they think to be the end rather than a means to higher end.

Nishkam karma being an important way out to lead balanced life must be performed with due sense of responsibility by willing and intelligent people to uplift themselves and others by pursing the path of worldly actions with detachment. This process is to be started gradually. Teachers, parents and social groups; all have a role to play in this important responsibility, which could make people mutually friendly and help them to develop a sense of service and feeling of love. Simultaneaously, young people could be guided to develope cosmopolitan outlook. Human development is an evolutionary process which begins and is promoted both at home by parents and in academic institutions by teachers. Both have to teach by personal examples and not by precepts alone.

The basic theme of the theory of karma Yoga is to perform all actions; thought, speech and overt acts with the spirit of devotion and detachment to enable us to retrace our steps to go back to God, who is the only real home and true destination of all of us. To facilitate and accelerate this homeward journey, spiritual masters, with the blessing of God have prescribed within the domain of karma Yoga to follow three-fold path of Yoga, Yajna and Kartavya, which respectively means meditation, pure action and duty. These themes have also been discussed elaborately in other chapters. The path of Yoga is mainly based on the practice of scientific meditation which no doubt is the path of purest action because it entails no trace of motivation. Every breath (Pranayama) inhaled and exhaled is offered by a yogi as oblation to the cosmic spirit on the altar of his spine and soul. Slowly, it becomes an enjoyable experience as the practice advances. The best description of this practice is illustrated by God Himself in 4/29 and 5/27-28 of *The Bhagawad Gita*. But Yoga meditation is for very few to follow and even for fewer to accomplish. Easier for more people to perform and pursue is the path of yagya or pure action. It lays down that whatever action we perform is to be done for God and its fruits are to be surrendered to God; which means forsaking greed and imbibing the spirit of service and sacrifice through our daily activities. Once started consciously and pursued faithfully for a few months, it becomes a good habit and goes a long way to purge the heart of its negativity. This practice requires no spare time and extra energy or rituals. In fact actions performed in this spirit are the best illustrations of yagya as is laid down in verses 3/9, 3/14-15, 3/19 and 18/45 of *The Bhagawad Gita*. The crux of these verses is that in this world, yagya not only pleases God but God Himself remains present in it. And when a person acts with the spirit of service and sacrifice (yagya), he/she is serving and interactive with God even if unknowingly.

The third feature of karma Yoga to worship and realize God is the path of the performance of duty with devotion. The sphere of duty covers all functions performed in government, corporate and private sectors. It is the element of sincerity which counts and which is why in *The Bhagawad Gita* 3/19, God clearly declares that "he worships Me the best who performs ones duty the best." This theme of devotion to duty is mentioned by God even more emphatically in verses 45/46 of the 18th chapter. To qualify this test, the actor must act undeterred by dangers and difficulties are to be faced, which is why God tells Arjuna in *The Bhagawad Gita* 2/37, "Rise and fight the battle. Killed you go to heaven and winning you will rule the kingdom." Metaphorically, battle here does not only mean the battle of Kurukshetra, it equally implies the battle of this life which every person has to fight in this world. Human mind and heart are the inbuilt hell and heaven of every person. In this world even if one loses to challenges and adversaries fighting valiantly, he will have the honourable feeling of having fought well and will be free from qualms of the conscience which is the agony of cowards. Winners of battles in life become the masters of their mind and heart and can enjoy their life creatively. Here lord Krishna is making the point that only the brave hearts indifferent to victory and defeat can relax eloquent in life.

It is said about karma Yoga that it is the best option to lead a successful life with peace and honour. For a karmayogi, the gates of heaven are always wide open. It is said in *The Bhagawad Gita* that karma Yoga is an ideal means to attain the *Vyavsayatmika buddhi* (single pointed inner determination-centred in the self), *The Bhagawad Gita* 2/41-45. A karma yogi entrenched in the virtue of *Vyavsayatmika buddhi* valiantly fights the battles of life unfettered by the three gunas of nature and the pairs of opposites. Karma yogi is a great asset to society because his objective vision and commitment to serve all can inspire others to work for better future. According to *The Bhagawad Gita*, Karma Yoga so central to the glory of human life, is the base of Jnana Yoga because it purifies the mind and a pure mind is a precondition to excel in Jnana Yoga.

World famous yogi Paramahansa Yogananda, among other suggestions, advises two methods of Yoga for karma Yoga aspirants to detach themselves from lures of worldly attachments:

1. The reality of this world is like a dream which lasts as long as the dream lasts but on waking the dream realities end. Similarly, the reality of this physical world (the world of waking state) ends on waking in spiritual realization.
2. An aspiring yogi should believe that this world is his temporary home rather a camp-house, where he has come to learn a few useful lessons. After some time he must quit it and go to his astral home in the astral domain of God, which is the real home of us all. There

life is hassle free, beautiful and full of higher knowledge. However, it must be said that only those who have performed well during their worldly sojourn have better chances to understand and enjoy the beautiful subtleties of higher astral life. In his lessons and many books Gurudeva has prescribed appropriate ways and exercises to be performed in this life to attain eligibility to make the grade to enter the finer regions of astral worlds/heavens.

BHAKTI YOGA

It has been said in the concluding lines of the preceding chapter that Jnana Yoga cannot be achieved without Karma Yoga. At the same time, it is equally true that without Bhakti Yoga, even karma Yoga is not possible. Therefore, it is a simple inference that without Bhakti Yoga neither Karma Yoga nor Jnana Yoga is possible. Obviously Bhakti Yoga is the basis which lends spiritual essence to the two other forms of Yoga because without Bhakti (the force of love) there can be no Yoga, because people with devotional leanings can make quicker progress in Yoga to achieve the highest spiritual ideal of God-contact. According to Hindu spiritual heritage and culture, there are two paths that is generally followed by all people in life: the path of Nivritti and the path of Pravriti. The people having spiritual learnings follow the path of Nivritti and the people of non-spiritual dispensation and material orientation follow the Pravriti course of life. However, individual karmas of every person always work as an effective catalyst to effect the movement of these basic trends either way in everybody's life. Therefore, in this world, there are fewer followers of this path of nivritti but these people live a more contented and balanced life. The followers of the path of pravritti, being materially oriented, are exposed to hassles and drifts and unless they tilt towards nivritti path they lose right direction and suffer. Ony the followers of nivriti path make the spiritual grade in life. The magnet of Yoga attracts them and with regular and sincere practice, they enjoy the vibration and soothing sensations of yoga practices. Their devotional intensity draws such devotees deeper in their saga of devotion and through such dives, they succeed to grip the ever-elusive God.

Undoubtedly, Bhakti Yoga means deep love for God and the zeal to attain God-realization through the path and force of love. A Bhakti yogi is a 'divine lark', who is deeply drunk with the thought of God, he/she lives and dies solely for God. It is through such pure and deep love for God that a Bhakti yogi can succeed in manifesting the divine in his heart. However, to love God is not an easy experience. Infact it is difficult even to attempt. We may pray to God but to love God is a different matter. We love objects and people that please us or the ones we can see, but God is an invisible power which no senses can cognize. So as long as human mind is attached through senses to their worldly objects, it is rarely possible to withdraw and attach it to the invisible God.

Even on the worldly plane, of social life there is no regular way to fall in love yet there is nobody who does not love something or somebody but love for God, He, being a sense opaque essence, is so different. Therefore, it is Bhakti Yoga, which knows the avenue of love to God through the practice of self-surrender.

The best and most compact discourse on Bhakti Yoga is

described from chapter's seventh to twelfth of *The Bhagawad Gita*. In this section, Lord Krishna through the medium of his dialogue with Arjuna assures people of the world that the path of Bhakti (Divine love) though difficult to begin is simple, easy and the best to commune with God or realize the cosmic spirit (*The Bhagawad Gita* 8/14, 9/22). Simultaneously commenting on the obstructive role of the all-powerful Maya, which deludes and diverts people from the path of God realization, Lord Krishna explains that Maya cannot dissuade the sincere lovers of God because before the love force maya is always helpless. The intensity of love force needs no armour to defeat the onslaught of Maya, *The Bhagawad Gita* 7/14. Maya being God's creation, though extremely powerful, is unaware of the divine subtlety rendering it ineffective to delude great lovers of God who are deeply committed to seek God. Even otherwise, Maya being God's creation cannot be utterly devilish, as some would believe. It is said as is also mentioned in their commentary on Katha Upanishad by *The Bhagawad Gita* press Gorakhpur that Maya performs two main functions; bhog and moksh, therefore, only those people who are of rajsik and tamsik nature are prone to Maya's delusion and not those of advanced sattvik nature. Infact Maya is the cosmic Mother, God's own creation to serve and protect the overwhelming majority of population of the world who are not spiritually evolved. Maya or Prakriti, as cosmic mother, rules over the mundane worlds. Everything in the world, be it animate or inanimate, is fettered by prakriti's three gunas to the domain of Maya. It is Maya, which looks after all, eons after eons, until spiritual elevation is attained by the spiritually oriented. Divine grace never lacks to show the path of Bhakti to the spiritually committed to attain spiritual liberation. Devotees' love for God and His love for them is the central theme of important Hindu scriptures, mythologies, puranas and the epics, Mahabharata or Ramayana. The basic theme of *The Bhagawad Gita* is God's assurance to people through Arjuna that no path is simpler and surer to attain salvation than the path of deep and pure love for God. Ramcharitmanas is a unique example of the depiction of love for lord Rama not only by human but even by other non-human species. The devotion of pure and infinite love for God is illustrated by the examples of Vibhishan,Tulsidas, Sugriva and many others.

Devotional ethos through the ages has remained the prime plank of Indian spiritual culture. Shreemad Bhagawad Purana (sprawling volume of twenty-five thousand verses on divine love) begins with a story of the legendary ever young mother 'Bhakti', whose two sons Jnana and Vairagya, at the end of Dwapar-yuga and the commencement of Kaliyuga, had become older than their mother; but they regained their youth by devotionally listening to the love essence and devotional substance of all the verses of Shrimad Bhagawad Purana for eight days. It must be noted that unlike other important cultures of the world, whose glory is based on the acts of heroism, mundane feats, sacrifices, path breaking discoveries and inventions, Indian traditions are surfeit with the glory of unique feats of divine devotion. Legendary devotional feats of Hanuman, Shukdeva, Dhruva, Prahalada, Kabir, Mirabai, Nanak, Tukaram, Ramakrishna Paramahansa, Swami Yogananda and many other living saints and devotees of the past and present are only a few examples, who attained God realization through divine love.

The theme of divine love is so deep and widespread in the Hindu ethos that it permeates all forms of living beings. Therefore, it is befitting to say that the force of love reigns supreme in Indian culture covering the domains of various life forms, be it plants, animals, humans and angels. The Divine love force acts as a magnet to attract God and His lovers to each other.

Not only scriptures, yogis and Yoga-based texts alone, even God Himself (lord Krishna) declares that "omnipotent God's only Achilles heel is His lovers and worshippers." If there is, anything that God needs or rather anxiously looks forward to; it is His desire for human love; not as much for His own sake as for the sake of the worldly people who can find everything through the panacea of God-love. That is why lord Krishna reveals to Arjuna in Chapter 7 of *The Bhagawad Gita* (the opening chapter on Bhakti Yoga), "Arjuna be My devotee and I will reveal Myself to you in Toto; body, mind and soul in mundane, immanent, transcendal and absolute aspects knowing which you will know everything and will be fully blessed." No doubt, God is well aware and vigilant about His devotees and therefore declares that there are four types of his sincere devotees: the afflicted, the curious, the power seekers and the love addicts. God loves all of them because all are sincere devotees, but He loves and literally runs to embrace His love addicts *The Bhagawad Gita* 7/16.

The discourse on Bhakti Yoga beginning in the seventh chapter, culminates in the twelfth chapter where the two-fold nature of Saguna and Nirguna devotion is explained. In this enlightening and highly revealing discourse, lord Krishna declares that His constant concern is to liberate people from the deluding domain of Maya based on its three qualities (gunas) i.e. Sattva, Rajas, and Tamas. Lord Krishna preaches that the wise must perform yagya and Yoga to ignore and detach themselves from the ensnaring charms of nature, which are elusive and deluding. It is by mastering Yoga that the wise will learn to remain unaffected by Maya and treat its panorama as a snare of fleeting entertainment. Lord Krishna tells Arjuna in the opening verses of eighth chapter that practice of Bhakti Yoga reveals to its sincere practitioner the nature of *Brahmn* (the imperishable God), Adhyatma (presence of God as the soul in all beings), Karma (performance of actions to eliminate ego and experience God), Adhibhuta (bodied beings and objects), Adidevas (angels and astral beings), and Adiyagya (the supreme God who lives in body as soul and in the cosmos as spirit, for the benefit of the creation and He is therefore the supreme sacrifice maker.)

A perfected Bhakti yogi knows the deep mysteries of nature including the mystery regarding the day and the night of Brahma and at the end of life follows the Uttarayana path to realize God, *The Bhagawad Gita* 5/24-25, 27-28, 8/24-28.

On the other hand, God Himself is so abundantly fond of His Bhakti yogi that He breaks all bonds to meet and embrace him. Infact God wants all the people to seek Him through the path of Bhakti (devotion and love) because it is an easy method to understand, simple to follow and sure of success *The Bhagawad Gita* 8/14. It is for the benefit of true devotees that God has revealed His various powers in the tenth chapter of *The Bhagawad Gita*; to convince people that He is the only supreme and sovereign power in this universe that can shower the greatest benefits including salvation on the true lovers of God. Therefore, the sincere seekers of God should not waste their time and energy in their love and devotion on other gods and natural forces. No wonder, it was because of such deep concern of God for His devotee Arjuna that Lord Krishna revealed His cosmic form, the wonder of wonders, in the eleventh chapter of *The Bhagawad Gita*. This unique gesture by God was to convince and inspire all devotees that He is the only supreme God, so full of love and mercy for them and therefore they should unconditionally surrender to Him and worship Him with all their power, of body, mind and soul because no other power could bestow salvation on them. As if this was not enough, the all-merciful and gracious God so concerned for His devotees, in the twelfth chapter of *The Bhagawad Gita* (The Yoga of Devotion) explains for their benefit; the concept of Bhakti in simple terms. Explaining both aspects of Bhakti; the Saguna (worship of God with form) and Nirguna (worship of the formless spirit), Lord Krishna out of his love and concern for the simple worshippers, assures that the Saguna worship being simpler and easier is better than the nirguna worship and therefore must be performed even though the spiritual rewards of both are the same. To inspire the devotees Lord Krishna takes pains to explain the four methods of worship of the Saguna Bhakti; (i) Devotees must fix the mind and thoughts on God alone. (ii) If this is not possible then one should practice Abhyasa Yoga. (iii) Even if Abhyasa Yoga is not possible devotees should perform all actions for God and surrender all fruits of actions to God. However, if the worshipper found any one of the three earlier ways of worship difficult to do then he must perform worship in the fourth way i.e by controlling the mind and intellect and abandoning the fruits of action to God, infact this method is scientific meditation like Kriya Yoga.

It is further revealed by Lord Krishna that sincerely following the path of Bhakti Yoga, the yogi is blessed with intuitive knowledge, peace and inner fulfilment. Such a person develops evenness of mind, treats all foes and friends alike, remains unaffected by pain, pleasure, honour, dishonour, heat, and cold, and is ever free from attachment. Such an advanced state of devotion can be attained by an ardent devotee whose centre of attraction is only God. 'Vaishnava school of spiritual faith', particularly believes in Saguna Bhakti to worship God through love and deep devotion. A devotee's blind love is the best way to find God. This is the central message or core of Gita. Infact the very base of *The Bhagawad Gita* is that God himself is always vulnerable to the magnet of a devotee's love. The mutual power of pure and deep love between the two of them produced this priceless spiritual gift of *The Bhagawad Gita* for the greatest benefit of humankind.

JNANA YOGA

Jnana Yoga, also called *Gyana Yoga* in Devnagri script, begins with the basic inquiry into the quest of, "What am I? What is my purpose? What is God? What is soul? What is the purpose of life? Is there life after death? What is the universe and how did it come into being?"

These fundamental questions have been exercising great human minds ever since the dawn of civilization. Infact the main branches of human knowledge like religion, philosophy and science are the prime human endeavours to answer and explain these questions. The role of religion and philosophy in relation to these questions has been discussed in various chapters of this study. However, the contribution of science to fathom these truths is still in hot pursuit. Scientists from a few centuries in the past are working overtime to know the mystery shrouding the cause and evolution of the universe and about the origin and nature of life and energy. The latest example of their earnest pursuit to find answers to the origin and evolution of the universe is the recently conducted 'Large Hadrons Collider Project'. On the borders of Switzerland and

France, a twenty-seven mile long and one hundred metre deep tunnel has been dug and equipped with the latest scientific equipment and expertise costing trillions. This tunnel has become a mega-machine and some of the best scientists and physicists are working hard to know the truth about how the universe was born. The purpose of this herculean experiment is to create a high-energy particle collision, as is assumed to have occurred at the epochal event of the Big Bang. The release of this high-speed energy particle will simulate a Big Bang like situation, which may after further verification, lead to answer many fundamental questions about the origin and evolution of the universe. At present, scientists believe that the age of the universe is about fourteen billion years. This conclusion is not very different from the views of Hindu scriptures. Computing on the basis of vast time spans of the day of *Brahma* and the night of *Brahma,* the Hindus have calculated durations of time and cycles which almost tally with the calculations of the scientists. Through this great adventure scientists are hoping to gain latest knowledge about new forms of energy, forces, dark matter and about 'God Particle'- the imaginary "Higgs meson" that is believed to be the source that gives substance to all matter in the universe. This is one of the costliest experiments to be undertaken in the field of scientific inquiry but we know that in science without such trials, path-breaking results are not possible. The basic question about the origin, nature and evolution of the universe has been a constant concern of all thinking and inquisitive minds. In India, these basic questions were probed long time back by great *rishis*; whose creative passion kept them constantly engaged and their tireless efforts resulted in convincing answers to these basic questions.

However, these *rishis* of India adopted a different method to probe these great mysteries. Their method to probe these basic questions was based on a different knowledge- the knowledge of Yoga based intuitive insight.

The common answers, which various schools of Yoga discovered through their yogic and intuitive probes, were that the Self (cosmic spirit within) is the basic cause and origin of the animate and inanimate universe. This theme has been well explained in other relevant chapters of this book.

The Yoga system of education, as has been explained in another chapter 'Yoga as a Medium of complete Education', is a direct intuitive knowledge, which can be developed by scientific methods of meditation. The power of intuition evolves from within unlike reason, which comes from without. It does not need intellect and mind, and in fact pure intuition only emerges when the mind has been transcended. It reveals the Self, the only source of supreme knowledge; and to the seeker it reveals whatever is desired to be known. However, the attainment of such high degree of intuition, which leads to self-realization, is a difficult achievement. This highest knowledge dawns only in *Samadhi*- the supreme state of God-contact. In this state of super consciousness, the Self is the self-revealing font of the highest knowledge where intellect and mind do not figure. It is through the *Samadhi* born intuitive knowledge of Spiritual realization that Indian *rishis*, hundreds of years back and modern yogis even now, know the answers to various mysteries of the universe including the position and fate of man. *Jnana* Yoga is the sublime source of this rare and the highest spiritual knowledge. There are various sources of *Jnana* Yoga. In the nineteenth and twentieth centuries, great yogis like Lahiri Mahashya, Swami Yukteshwar Giri, Sri Paramahansa Yogananda, Swami Pnanavananda, Ram Krishna Paramahansa and many others have written volumes themselves; or have been written by their close followers about their *Samadhi* born intuitive experiences and knowledge, related to the origin and cause of the universe and also about the self (soul), human species, other forms of life and also regarding energy and matter. A lot of spiritual literature is being published by various important spiritual organisations like, *Yogda Satsang Society*-Ranchi, Self Realization Fellowship-Los-Angles,*The Bhagawad Gita* Press-Gorakhpur, Ramakrishna Paramahansa Mission-Kolkata, and a host of other reputed spiritual centres.

The important sources of *Jnana* Yoga, on which I have drawn, apart from literature published by Yogda Satsanga Society are *The Bhagawad Gita, Upanishads, Brahma Sutras* and *Patanjali Yogsutra.*

In *The Bhagawad Gita*, the core subject of *Jnana* Yoga commences from the thirteenth chapter and continues up to the eighteenth chapter, which is the last chapter of *The Bhagawad Gita*. This part of *The Bhagawad Gita* deals with the origin, evolution and dissolution of the universe. It reveals with intuitive brevity yet not discounting clarity, about the universe, life, consciousness, energy, matter, the reasons for bondage of man and the ways to attain salvation. The contents of these chapters being the words of God Himself (Lord Krishna) are therefore deeply inspiring and hence there would appear little need to fend for additional facts and evidence to support these divine revelations. However, it must be understood that divine revelations and scriptural versions are esoteric statements and are therefore beyond understanding of common masses.

Such revelations satisfy the spiritual curiosities of people but cannot fulfil the intellectual, material and physical needs of people. To fulfil these basic needs, the role of science and technology is imperative. It is science and material knowledge, which serve humanity and other species to live their mundane lives comfortably. It is to improve the material conditions and intellectual lives of people and to fulfil their insatiable intellectual curiosity that great scientists are always afire with; the passion to probe the myriad mysteries of the universe. Great adventures like the 'Large Hadrons Collider' projects are examples of such creative passion. Although these adventures being necessary and important, cannot satisfy the spiritual hunger of people so essential for peace, harmony and spiritual emancipation of people.

God being aware of all facets of human life and of the constraints of the un-initiated to know the secrets of spiritual life has therefore taken on Himself to reveal to people the spiritual mysteries, so essential for balanced human growth in this world, teeming with material and emotional complexities apart from other myriad pressures.

It is therefore with this purpose in view that in the thirteenth chapter of *The Bhagawad Gita*, Lord Krishna answers and explains the fundamental issues with a poetic insight: This chapter opens with the basic question that what are Kshetra and *Kshetrajana* i.e. *Prakriti* and *Purusha* or matter and the spirit and also which is ought to be known. The self or spirit (*purusha*) is explained as the absolute reality; birth-less, deathless, omnipresent and omniscient. *Prakriti* (energy or matter) is explained as the phenomenon universe, which has two forms, un-manifest and the manifest. *Prakriti* is described as having 24 evolutes i.e. *chitta,* intellect, ego, mind, five senses of knowledge, five senses of action, five *tanmatras* (astral forms of the five elements) and the five elements i.e. ether, air, fire, water and earth. Human body and mind are parts of prakriti and have seven modifications i.e. desire, hatred, pleasure, pain, the aggregate, intelligence and firmness. These constitute the human body and its modifications. That which ought to be known is the *Parma Brahmn. Brahmn* can be known through spiritual knowledge *antargyan* i.e. intuition because *Brahmn* is unknowable through intellect, mind and senses. Every being and object moving or unmoving in the world is the consequence of the union of *kshetra* and *kshetrajana* i.e. *Prakriti* and *Purusha.* As one sum illumines the world, so the lord of *kshetra (purusha)* aluminises this body.

Scriptures reveal that *Mahat Brahmn- Mool prakriti* or un-manifest nature is the womb of God in which God deposits His seed the *kutastha chaitanya* (the cause and essence of consciousness) which is the cause of birth of all beings (Gita 14/3). It means that Mahatbrahm or Maya, the cosmic nature by itself is a sterile power. It is the creative will of God which impregnates the Prakriti and thence begins the evolution. Therefore, in the process of creation three forces are at work: God, His seed (Intelligence- *Kutastha chaitanya*) and the *Prakriti.* The prime power in creation is God Himself; His seed (Intelligence) and *Mahat Brahmn (Mool Prakriti)* are God's reflection and creation, they have only their earmarked roles to perform. God as cosmic spirit is pure consciousness un-create and beyond the vibratory power and region. However on becoming desirous to create, God wills- *"Eko Aham Bahushyama"*, meaning 'I am one I will become many'- Then

He reflects Himself as the intelligence-*Kutastha* and through *Prakriti* starts the operation of creation which begins with the causal thought process. Spirit is the source from which evolves consciousness, life, energy *(Prana Shakti)* infinitely microscopic particles (sub-atomic parts) and the consequent matter. All these forces and objects are the components of *Prakriti*- the cosmic nature. The *prakriti* comprises three *gunas* (three basic qualities or basic materials). These three *gunas* being inherent in the *prakriti* bind the soul *(Jiva)* to the body. Due to body consciousness, *Jiva* remains a prisoner to the body, believing himself to be the body, and is ignorant of his real nature as the pure blissful soul. The three *gunas* are the three modes of *Prakriti- Sattva* (creative), *Rajas* (dynamic) and *Tamas* (inertia). *Sattva* binds the soul to body by attachment to happiness and knowledge. *Rajas* binds *jiva* through material activity and *Tamas* binds *jiva* to ignorance. Besides these three *gunas* (three strands of a rope), there are five sheaths as has been discussed in the chapter 'What is Yoga', which skirt the soul: *annamaya kosha, Pranaamaya kosh, manumaya kosh, jnanamaya kosha and anandmaya kosha.* Man's spiritual evolution or struggle for liberation entails successively ascending of the mind above the effects of these three *gunas* and transcending the five sheaths (*koshas*). The way to spiritual liberation is through *sadhana*, scientific meditation and pure action. Due to *sadhana,* as the effects of three *gunas* start shedding simultaneously, consciousness starts rising from its bondage to body towards astral consciousness; with deeper meditation an ascetic transcends the astral and causal bodies and merges with the spirit (the soul inside).

As has been discussed in other relevant chapters, the

journey of spiritual ascendance is evidenced in the three states of our body; physical, astral and causal. Our physical body is active during our waking state and it works and operates through the five senses of knowledge and action. In fact, all our senses, body and mind are operated by our astral body, which is made of the *Prana Shakti* (cosmic energy). During the waking state, our astral body enlivens and activates our physical body and during sleep, the astral body manifests itself as our dreams. Our worldly desires and experiences in sleep materialise as dream images, which are seen, and experienced by our finer astral or five sensory powers. During waking state, our gross sensory powers are at work and during sleep state; the finer astral sensory powers come into action. The third deep sleep state (causal body) is the source of consciousness and thoughts and it exists in deep sleep, it neither dreams nor works, it experiences joy. It reminds us of the existence of the fourth *Turiya* state- the state of super consciousness.

This highest state can be realized by cutting the sprawling worldly *Asvatha* tree of attachment with the strong axe of non-attachment as is mentioned in *The Bhagawad Gita* 15/3-5. Unless the tree of worldly attachment is uprooted with the double strategy of renunciation and mediation, spiritual liberation- the highest state of *jnana* Yoga cannot be realized.

The other important sources of jnana Yoga, as mentioned earlier, are Brahma-Sutra and the various Upanishads. These sources form the joint source of *Vedanta*, which is the pinnacle of the supreme knowledge of jnana Yoga. *Vedanta*, which has been discussed in other chapters also, is being discussed here in connection with jnana Yoga. *Vedanta* is the highest source of spiritual knowledge acquired through deep devotion and

Guru's grace. It embodies all the three branches of knowledge viz philosophy, Yoga and spirituality. It has three schools of thought: *Dvait* (dualist), *Vishisht Dvait* (qualified dualists) and *Advait* (monism).

According to *Vedanta,* human body and the cosmos are made of two forces, *Akasha* and *Prana*. The whole of physical and astral universe is made of these two forces but the soul or *jiva* is distinct and above *akasha* and *Prana.* Every being is an entity of three forces i.e. gross body, astral body and the soul; at death, it is the gross body that dies and not the astral body, which lasts for aeons. It is made of seventeen astral elements, ten senses, five *Pranas* and mind and intellect. Soul or *jiva* being the reflection of God is eternal. The dualists hold that the omniscient God is the creator and controller of this nature comprising trillions of forces and beings. Nevertheless, under the inscrutable plan and power of God called the powerful Maya, all beings are under its sway. The powerful *Maya,* which with its three *gunas* keeps all embroiled in the turmoil of worldly life. It is only by performing good karma and prayers that beings can avoid suffering and attain salvation. The conclusion of qualified dualism is that God, soul and nature *(prakriti)* are not three separate forces. God is the prime power and souls (*Jivas*) and the physical nature are His body. For example, if we treat our soul as God, our body as nature and all body cells as *jivas,* that will approximately explain the qualified unity of God, nature and the souls, as held by this school. Dualists and qualified dualists believe that God is the material and sentient cause of the universe.

The third step in *Vedanta* is *Advait* (monism). It is the highest reach and the most difficult to understand intellectually. *Advait* theory also believes that God is the absolute material and intelligent cause of the universe but its teachings are based on a very different approach. Advait, unlike the other two schools of Vedanta teaches that God is neither cause nor effect but is an absolute unity called *sat-chit-anand* meaning Existence-consciousness-bliss. If God as spirit or soul were the cause and nature or body the effect, this would mean that God as cause has become nature as effect, because without cause there cannot be an effect. Therefore, if God as cause has become nature as effect, but nature is always changing and it also dies and takes new birth then how can absolute God be subject to change and death? *Advait* therefore explains the absolute unity of God in a very subtle way. It states that this phenomenon universe with its angels, human beings, energy, matter and all the rest is not the real existence. It is a mere appearance, a seeming reality like the reality of a dream, which lasts as long as the dream lasts and on waking, the dream reality ceases to exist. The experience of a person's spiritual progress is confirmed when one feels that the reality of the material world is no different from the unreality of dream state. When an individual spiritually wakes up from the long lasting dream of mundane existence, he/she will realize the supreme reality of the divine essence which every *Jiva* infact is. The test of spiritual progress of a person pursuing Jnana Yoga is, when in the waking state he/she begins to feel that the reality of the waking life is hardly different from reality of the dream state. On spiritual realization a person loses ego and discovers inseparable oneness with the spiritmerging in the absolute God and yet retaining the individuality. It is the state of real existence, real knowledge and real bliss. All constraints of relativity, duality and multiplicity, which exist in the universe of time and space, vanish. Nevertheless, the supreme state of jnana Yoga cannot be known through reason or intellect. It has to be realized through *darshana, shravana, manana* and *nididhyasana* (the steps integral to *jnana Yoga sadhana*) following the long course of *neti-neti-neti* (not this-not this) until by repeatedly reflecting on the core thesis of Upanishads, when the self is revealed within leading to the source of the highest knowledge, from which flow all other branches of knowledge. However, none of the branches of terrestrial education has the power to impart complete and flawless knowledge that would simultaneously bestow peace, harmony and enlightenment. The source of this highest knowledge is Jnana Yoga as is laid down in *The Bhagawad Gita* 4/37-38, which reveals that Jnana Yoga is the highest purifier, which burns all impurities and reveals the Self to the seeker.

In conclusion, it may be said that Jnana Yoga is realization of the truth that the pure soul does not perform any action. All actions are performed by *Prakriti* (nature) called Maya which includes human body, senses and the mind. It is this theme which is integral to the reality of spiritual realization through jnana Yoga. This context is explained in *The Bhagawad Gita* in various chapters. Some of the relevant verses are 3/25 and 28, 4/18 and 34, 6/1, 13/24 and 29, 18/46 and 66. Now I may wind up the concept of Jnana Yoga with the conclusion that the test of progress made in gyan Yoga or spiritual life is when a seeker starts realizing that the reality of the life of waking state is comparable with the reality of a dream state, which vanishes on waking and so will vanish the so called reality of the waking state when we wake up in spiritual consciousness – the Kutastha chaitanya.

KRIYA YOGA

Kriya Yoga is an inclusive and advanced science of Yoga. Its prime purpose is to provide quicker spiritual progress to its practitioner. Therefore, it contains some of the useful and essential tenets of Karma Yoga, Bhakti Yoga, Jnana Yoga and Tantra. It has been designed by great spiritual masters as is explained below, to help mankind to lead a successful, peaceful and balanced spiritual life, which is so necessary for spiritual progress; and is under threat from hyper material orientation of modern man's own waywardness.

Kriya Yoga, through a set of specialized techniques, uses consciousness, energy and will to purify and spiritualize human behaviour by creatively changing the mindset. It is an effective spiritual dispensation that gifts its sincere follower with a rare reward of inner fulfilment, which the modern man misguidedly believes to be attained from the outer world of senses. In this world every person craves for comfort, luxuries, recognition, power, position and wealth and the growing belief is that money will fetch them all of this. Strangely enough even educated people fail to see that if it were so, the materially powerful in this world would not have been victims of delusion and unhappiness. Great spiritual masters know that the cause of this cosmic delusion is the pervasive Maya, which is formidable and cannot be neutralized except through Yoga. The yogis have, therefore, thoughtfully devised the ethical and spiritual discipline of Kriya Yoga, which is an ancient yet ever new science that can help sincere followers to outwit Maya and lead a balanced life replete with good health, peace and happiness. Kriya Yoga is a great spiritual art, which teaches the technique of reversing inward the usually outward flow of energy and consciousness, which disconnects the mind from deluded fallible senses and make it firm and steady to realize the truth. With deeper concentration and more advanced meditation, strictly following the brief given by the guru, a committed practitioner transcends the mind and begins experiencing some 'siddhis' – spiritual powers – on the long and illumining path of spiritual journey.

According to Kriya masters, Kriya Yoga is a science which if ardently followed and mastered can train one to control the heart, stop the breath, still the mind, liberate the soul and attain bliss. It is a unique spiritual science which has been gifted to this world by the great God-realized spiritual master Lahiri Mahashaya and has been popularized extensively across the globe by the great modern yogi, Paramahansa Yogananda. This science of Kriya Yoga, as briefly explained below, is a great secret and its techniques can be taught by an authorized monk to a registered member of the Yogda Satsang Society of India. To be precise, Kriya Yoga is a spiritual rite to spiritually activate the spinal centres (chakra) by activating the Kundalini Shakti, which is lying locked in the coccyx centre.

Kriya means 'activity' and Yoga means 'attainment of spiritual consciousness'. Therefore, Kriya Yoga is a spiritual activity, which can connect a faithful person to the spirit through his/her soul. But spiritual action also includes thoughts and speech. Therefore, a Kriya yogi, through practice, must discipline ones thoughts and speech too. Only then can one purify and spiritualize his/her actions without which it is difficult to withdraw from the whirlpool of material craving. Consequently, regular practice of Kriya Yoga creates a sincere sense of service and deep feeling of love towards all. In its practitioner, Kriya Yoga generates a duty consciousness to reach out to the needy and to improve and uplift them physically, mentally and spiritually. As a result, a Kriya yogi attracts the affection and following of people. Therefore, Kriya Yoga has been introduced in this world to produce creative and selfless individuals to serve people and orient them towards the spiritual destination.

Looking at the worldly involvements and duties of a person and his/her spiritual aspirations, Kriya Yoga is a well thought-out and carefully designed scientific method of meditation, practical action and devotion, to enable a person to lead a devotionally pure and socially successful worldly life culminating in divine union. Briefly put, it is a divinely ordained essence of spiritual science to liberate one from the bondage of Maya or the body consciousness and uplift a person to the blissful plane of soul consciousness. It is based on an effective and simple scientific technique of meditation. Its practice if faithfully done, expands human consciousness and enables its ardent practitioner to counter the imprisoning influence of the life of body and senses, enabling one to experience the sublime auras of higher spiritual life. In comparison to spiritual life, the mundane life of body and senses is full of pitfalls and shortcomings, because disease, trauma, boredom and age factors are its constant afflictions. No doubt to some, life offers various finer and better avenues for progress and prosperity and they feel that life is full of opportunities which offer physical pleasures, exciting experiences, mental joys and happiness. But even for them all these things and experiences are subject to change; they are never lasting and ultimately death swallows them all. We should know that no science and worldly knowledge can save our body and assets against the ravages of time. The spiritual science of Yoga teaches divine secrets which impart the power to defeat the ruthless of nature (Maya) in its game to delude man and finally saves him from the jaws of death. Only a spiritual science like Kriya Yoga can guard people against delusion, unhappiness, fear and even death by practically teaching them the supreme art of spiritual realization, which enables a yogi to attain permanent happiness and the power to even outwit death. Several such instances are recorded in a great book 'Autobiography of a Yogi', written by the world famous yogi Paramahansa Yogananda. No doubt such perfection in Yoga is for a few select, but the fact is that such masters exist and always will.

Such yogic feats, to a modern man involved in material pursuits and even to a sizeable section of the modern global society indulged in consumerism, may appear incredible or even mere tell-tale but during the last hundred and fifty years, several Kriya yogis have performed wonders not only in individual yogic achievements, but even more by extending selfless service to the afflicted, the ignored and the deprived and have preached this highest spiritual knowledge of Kriya Yoga in several countries of the world. It may be pertinent to point out that the science of Kriya Yoga has already unleashed spiritual awakening among a sizeable section of well-educated people in the United States of America and several parts of Europe where hundreds of Kriya Yoga centres have been functioning effectively.

Kriya Yoga teaches that the main cause, which binds every individual to the bondage of body is one's own breath. The cord of breath is a fetter, which life after life ties down a person to his/her body consciousness. By body consciousness is meant the consciousness of a person that he/she is this body, senses and mind. One is unaware of the soul which is the real self and realizing which would mean an end to one's all troubles. When somebody has realized the soul experience, such a person alone knows that how and why the life of body, senses and mind is a mere bondage in comparison to the supreme life of soul consciousness, which is the real bliss and eternal freedom. Therefore, it is important for a yogi to regulate and control his breath through the techniques of Kriya Yoga because the keynote of Kriya Yoga is that 'breathlessness is deathlessness'. Kriya Yoga, by regulating breath, controls the mind which is always restless due to the continuous flow of the process of modifications. The flow of modifications from the mind and its restlessness are caused by the inhalation and exhalation process of breathing. In fact, the process of breathing is caused by the opposite pulls of the Prana and Apana currents in the spine. Prana current, causing inhalation, also energizes and interiorizes the system. On the contrary,

Apana current, causing exhalation, externalizes the mind and makes the system restless and it is this restless mind which is a constant obstacle in the life of a person to attain lasting peace. As already said, if the mind is to be stilled the priority is to still the breath, which can only be done by controlling the heart. It may sound astounding but Kriya Yoga is the wondrous science which achieves this unique feat.

According to medical science and the science of Kriya Yoga, the main function of breathing in our body is to purify the blood. Our body has millions of cells and they need a constant supply of purified blood and oxygen. Without purified blood, these cells on which our survival depends, cannot live beyond a couple of minutes. Our blood in the body gets carbonized due to various toxins and impurities in the system. Our network of veins and arteries draws in impure blood from various cells of the body and supplies it in purified form back to the various respective parts. This vital function is performed by our lungs and the heart, which collectively constitutes the cardio-vascular system. This function is activated and operated by our involuntary nerves. This is an autonomous function on which our mind and will have no control. A special Kriya Yoga technique (which being a secret cannot be discussed here and can be revealed to a kriyavan- one who is properly initiated in Kriya Yoga, by an authorized Kriya Yoga teacher) prescribes an esoteric method to decarbonize contaminated blood in the lungs and oxygenize it with more supply of additional fresh oxygen. This technique also recharges the spinal centres (plexuses) and the brain cells with Prana energy. The technique, therefore, spares the labour of lungs and heart by itself taking over their functions.

This technique of Kriya Yoga is based on verse 4.29 of *The Bhagawad Gita* which reads: "By offering the incoming breath of Prana into the outgoing breath of Apana and by offering the outgoing breath of Apana into the incoming breath of Prana, the yogi renders redundant the process of breathing by the esoteric practice of Pranayama and liberates oneself from bondage and slavery to the body." This verse of Bhagwad Gita is a symbolic seed of the great liberating science of Kriya Yoga. It is very difficult to understand the essence of this verse, which preaches the attainment of mastery over the breath. The technique of Kriya Yoga, which is based on a special breathing method, correctly interprets it and scientifically applies its essence to attain a state of breathlessness so essential for spiritual liberation. Gurudeva Paramahansa Yogananda, with his personal experiences and experiments has evolved and perfected this technique of meditation for the spiritual liberation of a Kriya Yoga practitioner and it has already unleashed a Kriya Yoga-based spiritual revolution in several countries of the world, where lacs of educated devotees have taken diksha in Kriya Yoga.

Prana (life force or vital energy) is the cosmic energy, which permeates and sustains the entire universe. It activates and operates the body-mind system of every person at the individual level and the universe at the cosmic level. It emanates from Ishwara at the cosmic level and from the soul at individual level. It is the basic energy, called the mother source of all forms of energies, which exists in the world. In fact it is the Prana shakti which binds an individual to his body or the world of senses. Prana is the prime weapon with Prakriti (the un-manifest cosmic nature) with which it keeps each person fettered not only to one's body but also to its vast cosmic realm covering the earth, heavens and the astral universe, because the writ of Prakriti runs all over the universe, including its astral forms.

Yogis say that according to the divine scheme of creation, Prana Shakti (life force) flows continuously outward. Since our voluntary, involuntary systems, all senses and mind are operated by the power of Prana, which always flows outward from inside, therefore, all our senses and the mind are outwardly disposed. Our mind and senses are always attracted towards the world of senses like gravity attracts all the objects. Therefore, yogis say that unless the flow of Prana energy is reversed inwards, there can be no success in Yoga.

The technique of Kriya Yoga, therefore, effectively targets the Prana force in our body and through its esoteric methods, reverses the flow of Prana energy inwards through the correct use of Pratyahara and Pranayama techniques. There are two prime nerves in the body - the voluntary nerve and the involuntary nerve. We use the voluntary nerve through our will and initiative to do what we want. The Pratyahara method of Yoga is based on this principle. We withdraw our attention from the sense objects wilfully and concentrate it on our heart centre or Agya Chakra and perform our meditation. Our success level in meditation depends on our will power and concentration, which is why will and concentration are so important in meditation.

The great secret and uniqueness of the Kriya Yoga technique lies in its power to control wilfully the functioning of the involuntary nervous system of the body which is fully autonomous and works incessantly day in and day out during the entire length of our lifetime. It operates our cardio-vascular system (working of lungs and heart) and all other autonomous systems like the central nervous system, digestive system, circulatory system and several other body-mind functions.

It may be mentioned that Kriya Yoga is a unique science, which has succeeded in controlling wilfully the functioning of cardio-vascular system operated by the involuntary nerve. This difficult achievement is preceded by a long practice of Kriya Yoga Prana Sadhna and therefore, this process needs a brief explanation.

It has already been mentioned that Prana Shakti (cosmic energy or life force) operates and sustains the universe and our bodies too. It exists in the whole universe. Kriya yogis reveal that this Prana Shakti enters our bodies through the medulla oblongata and gets stored in the brain and spine centres from where it is used by everybody as per his/her requirement and ability to tap it. As already said, of the two main Prana currents (life currents) in our body, Prana current flows from coccyx (Mooladhara) to medulla (Agya Chakra- a point in between the eyebrows) and the other, Apana current flows from Agya Chakra to the Mooladhara. These two opposite currents (Prana and Apana) are the cause of our breathing. Prana current, when it moves up from Mooladhara, pulls in the breath into our lungs and Apana current, when it moves down from Agya Chakra to Mooladhara, pushes out the breath from the lungs. This autonomous process goes on till we live. It has already been explained that the purpose of this process of breathing is to purify the blood through decarbonization and it is then that the circulatory system distributes it to the entire body.

Kriya Yoga Pranayama, through a special esoteric technique,

uses Prana and Apana currents to stop the decay and mutation of growth cells in the body. Through this technique a yogi extracts more Prana energy from the breath, which is pulled into the lungs and is required to purify the blood and then divert it, to charge the spinal plexuses and the brain. This additional Prana energy reinforces the spine centres, which are the centres of life and consciousness, and provides additional energy to rejuvenate the cells in the brain. Thus decarbonization and oxygenation of the system and supply of additional energy by the Prana current renders breathing redundant. The lungs and heart, which now need not purify the blood, stop functioning at their usual pace and the yogi's body consciousness ends because it is breathing, which is the cause of mind and body consciousness. This process stills the mind and dissolves the thought waves. In this tranquillity the yogi can realize his/her soul. The cessation of breathing is called Kumbaka. Kumbaka is the state of soul and spiritual realization in which a yogi establishes spiritual contact. Through Kriya Pranayama, will and concentration, a yogi spiritualizes his consciousness and qualifies for higher ascension, which is said to be a state of ecstatic bliss.

There is another way to explain the science of Kriya Yoga practice. There are three main nerves in our spine – Ida, Pingla and Sushmna – which are related to the cardio-vascular system.

Sushmna nerve is a subtle nerve and runs from Mooladhara to Agya Chakra. Parallel to it, to its left and right, run Ida and Pingla nerves. Prana and Apana life currents activate Ida and Pingla nerves, which cause inhalation and exhalation of breathing. Sushmna nerve is a subtle and silent nerve and its mouth is closed. Kriya Yoga Pranayama, through the use of Prana energy, activates the Sushmna nerve. It may be noted that only fine Prana energy can pass through Sushmna nerve, being subtle, and not the oxygen. When the Sushmna nerve is activated through Kriya Pranayama, Ida and Pingla stop working and the process of breathing also stops. The body and life of a yogi is sustained by Prana energy extracted from oxygen, which is pure, much finer and more energetic. Operation of Sushmna nerve releases the Kundalini Shakti and the practitioner of Kriya Yoga gets spiritually uplifted. In essence, both these principles are similar because their objective is to interiorize the mind and Prana energy through Kriya Pranayama, which supplies abundant additional Prana energy, to reinforce the spine centres and brain cells; consequently oxygen through the lungs and heart is not needed. When the heart stops, the mind becomes still and the process of spiritual realization sets in. It is then that the yogi feels uplifted to experience the bliss of spirit.

Kriya Yoga is a distinctly exclusive branch of the ancient spiritual science of Yoga. It is well known that the antiquity of the science of Yoga precedes even the invention of alphabets and the script; infact it is as old as mankind. When Lord Krishna revealed it to Arjuna, it was already an accomplished and a tried science for too long a time in the past. It was rather late in the day when Patanjali learnt this special spiritual art and formulated it in the third century B.C. in the shape of Sutras (aphorisms). These Sutras cannot be understood and practiced gainfully without the help of an enlightened guru. The science of Yoga including Kriya Yoga is a sacred, secret and an occult knowledge. This is why Lord Krishna says in Chapter

IX of *The Bhagawad Gita* that 'Yoga is the supreme science and the sovereign secret.' It is the supreme science because it can reveal the soul and God to its faithful practitioner and it is the sovereign secret because nobody can know it without mastering the secret techniques and even on knowing it, God reveals Himself only to those whom He considers spiritually dynamic as is mentioned in *Mundaka Upanishad*. Nobody knows the time of origin of the science of Yoga. Yoga as a method of God contact and spiritual realization is described in Vedas, Upanishads, Puranas and *The Bhagawad Gita*. Some of the Shrutis which pre-date the invention of writing describe the Yoga techniques of self-realization with scientific precision and acting on these techniques and spiritual briefs, great ones have benefited in their pursuits.

Even in ordinary daily life, practice of Kriya Yoga helps a practitioner to improve his/her physical health, mental capabilities and spiritual potentials. Recorded instances speak for themselves that how faithful practitioners have attained spectacular success through their Kriya mission in establishing God contact within one lifetime, which through other methods would have taken several incarnations. This is why Gurudeva Paramahansa Yogananda declared that the practice of Kriya Yoga is an aeroplane journey to the abode of the supreme God in comparison with the bullock cart journey of other conventional spiritual practices to find the cosmic spirit. The spiritual masters who are concerned with spiritual salvation of the deluded mankind, carefully plan appropriate spiritual practices and courses for people so that people, with devotional leanings and good karmas, benefit from spiritually liberating disciplines like Kriya Yoga. Even elementary practice of Kriya Yoga imparts such benefits to its practitioners, which remove mental tension, physical fatigue and treat some of the psychological and physical ailments. The practice of Kriya makes a yogi shock-proof, carefree, relaxed and happy. Some of the Kriya techniques are effective substitutes even for sleep. Using these methods a yogi may not sleep for several nights and yet feel fine. Therefore, spiritual masters have taken initiative to devise courses based on Yoga, to suit the different intellectual levels of people in each yuga. At this point it appears necessary to mention that the highly enlightened spiritual souls who surpass even Rishis, Devas and angels are always watching the various worlds of this universe ,both at individual and cosmic levels, to guide and marshal the course of evolution and involution. Scriptures reveal that at individual level, this responsibility is discharged by Vishva (spiritual power to oversee and watch the physical evolution at individual level). In respect of the individual astral bodies, this function is performed by Tejas (spiritual power) and in respect of the causal individual bodies, this function is performed by the Prajna (spiritual power), as is explained in the Mandukya Upanishad too.

Yogis say that on the cosmic level these subtle and important functions in respect of gross, astral and causal planes, are spiritually observed and performed by great spiritual powers like Virata, Hiranyagarba and Ishwara respectively. No wonder it is mentioned in the Holy Bible that not a feather moves without the will of God. This however does not absolve a person of one's karmic responsibilities.

It is in furtherance of this spiritual mission and to answer the divine call of duty that Maha-avtar Babaji (the eternal incarnation who is ever watchful and working for the spiritual salvation of mankind) introduced the age-specific remedy of Kriya Yoga in this world at the precise time.. Maha-avtar Babaji's Kriya Yoga is the most thoughtfully designed course for the present age to prepare people to earn their spiritual reprieve and salvation. The ever fallible man whose discomfiture is compounded by the handicaps of short life expectancy and bleakness of worldly struggle for existence, is always in need of spiritual guidance. It is therefore the greatness of Maha-avtar Babaji to have personally gifted the spiritual boon of Kriya Yoga to the spiritually parching mankind of our era. Maha-avtar Babaji is called so because he is always there unlike other Avatars who incarnate on earth for a specific time and purpose; he is said to be living for many years in the Himalayas around Badrinath, Kedarnath region but he visits various places all over the universe and appears in person before sincere devotees of God, who intuitively recognize him and feel deeply blessed by having his glimpse or a brief conversation with him. It is said that Maha-avtar Babaji lives in both astral and gross bodies and moves about various places frequently in the company of a small group of highly advanced spiritual yogis and ascetics as is also mentioned in the 'Autobiography of a Yogi'.

For modern age, Kriya Yoga is a many splendid blessing. Its introduction in the world around this time of high industrialization phase is a well planned measure. Let us talk of pollution which is a dangerous side effect of industrialization and has become a serious threat to human health. Pranayama system of Kriya Yoga offers an effective remedy not only to effectively counter the toxic effects of pollution through oxygenation and decarbonization of the system but through the abundant supply of Prana energy (life force) and additional oxygen reinforcing the cardio vascular system, making it proof against various hazards of pollution and other harmful carbon agents.

Due to the great importance of Kriya Yoga in our modern times and due to its unfailing effect in transforming an ardent spiritual aspirant into a yogi within a short span of time by strictly following its ethical and spiritual regimen; it is necessary to say a few words about how Maha-avtar Babaji who introduced this great science of Yoga to this world. It is mentioned in the Autobiography of a Yogi that in the year 1828, on the 30th day of September, a highly spiritually advanced soul incarnated in a simple but devoted religious Brahmin family of village Ghurni, in Nadia District of Bengal. The boy's name was Shyama Charan Lahiri. His mother's name was Shrimati Muktakashi and father's name was Gaur Mohan Lahiri. It is said that even in his early childhood, Shyama Charan was often seen in yogic and meditative postures in secluded places. When the child Shyama Charan was barely five years of age, the family house was washed away in floods. His father Shri Gaur Mohan Lahiri along with all the family members shifted to Banaras and settled there. From early childhood Shyama Charan started studying and receiving lessons not only in Bengali, Hindi, Urdu and Sanskrit, but also in English and French. However, his absorption was in Vedic, Puranic, Epic and yogic literature. After his marriage and studies, Shri Shyama Charan Lahiri took up the job of an accountant in the Military Engineering department of the government in which his working efficiency earned him quick promotions.

It was in the year 1861, when Shri Lahiri was 33 years of age that a miraculously great spiritual event occurred in his life at Ranikhet. It was miraculous for many reasons. Shyama Charan Lahiri was transferred from Danapur to Ranikhet, five hundred miles away, where Maha-avatar Babaji revealed himself to Shri Lahiri and showed him the gufa (cave) where he was meditating in his previous life, created a golden palace for Shri Lahiri and initiated him in Kriya Yoga. These details make an absorbing reading not only in the great book, Autobiography of a Yogi, but in other pieces of literature too, published by the Yogda Satsang Society of India and the Self Realization Fellowship Centre located in Los Angeles, U.S.A.

In the annals of mankind introduction of the rare science of Kriya Yoga is an epoch making event. Since its introduction, Kriya Yoga has generated a silent spiritual revolution in Asia, Europe and America transforming thousands of people's lives physically, psychologically and spiritually. Then it is slowly continuing to transform the mindset of people. Revolutionary power of this landmark event lies in the fact that it was gifted by the great Maha avatar Babaji for the spiritual upliftment of mankind. This great event is comparable to the bringing of the Ganges to earth from heaven by Bhagiratha and to the astounding feat of bringing the fire to earth by the Greek hero Prometheus. This comparison is being made appreciating the great spiritual relief and enlightenment, which the technique of Kriya Yoga meditation has already provided to many people in numerous countries of the world within less than 150 years of its introduction. The wonder of Kriya Yoga, its scientific approach and quick spiritual effects have extensively inspired the informed segments of our global society. It is said that Maha-avtar Babaji was the guru of Lahiri Mahashya for several births in the past. He was waiting for Lahiri Mahashya to incarnate on earth because to introduce a great liberating spiritual mission, there had to be a great spiritual master of the stature of Lahiri Mahashya for Babaji to generate spiritual enlightenment for comforting and enlightening the arid hearts of the world.

Kriya Yoga, in its present form, is scientifically designed by Babaji and updated by Sri Sri Paramahansa Yogananda to suit the scientific temper of our inquisitive modern age. As already explained, the thrust of Kriya teachings is to radically regulate the cardio-vascular system by the process of decarbonization and oxygenization. It decarbonizes the system by prescribing proper food habits and a regimen of appropriate yogic energization exercises, both physical and psychological. The use of carbon based agents like drugs, tobacco, fats, alcohol, red meat, pork, beef, certain cereals, vegetables, and alcohol are not allowed. Decarbonization is done not only by taking more oxygen but by extracting Prana energy from oxygen with a special Kriya Yoga technique . The technique of Kriya Yoga, when scientifically performed as is explained in Kriya lessons, transmutes the atoms extracted from breath into life force which supply additional life force to the six spinal centres and the brain. The six spinal plexuses and the brain, which are the centres of life and consciousness, get charged with Prana energy and feel rejuvenated. In due course of time, with more concentrated meditation and with the additional supply and absorption of Prana Shakti, the spinal plexus and brain become reinforced and spiritualized. Resultantly, the yogi starts enjoying spiritual experiences in his spine and in the agya chakra (the point in-between the two eyes at the base of the nose). With advancement in practice of Kriya Yoga and with deeper concentration, the joyous feelings experienced by a yogi become deep and long-lasting. It is said that a yogi starts visualizing beautiful subtle lights and hearing delightful sounds. These astral lights and sounds are said to be deeply absorbing, highly refreshing and etherealizing. With longer and deeper Kriya Yoga meditation, the yogi succeeds in attaining samadhi – the state of indescribable bliss and God – experience. The first stage of samadhi is Savikalpa. It is said that in this samadhi a yogi experiences deep joy and even an occasional and brief feeling of bliss but does not fully rise above the body-mind state of consciousness. The higher state of samadhi is the Nirvikalpa samadhi. In this state a yogi fully transcends the body-mind consciousness and merges in the shoreless sea of divine bliss. In other higher states of Samadhi a yogi is face to face with the creator and at this stage the seeker's soul merges with cosmic spirit of the cosmic consciousness. The seeker becomes the sought and yet retains individual consciousness, enjoying the bliss and highest knowledge of the supreme power which no mind can ever comprehend. This fact is mentioned even in the commentary and translation of *The Bhagawad Gita*, 'God Talks with Arjuna' by Gurudeva Yogananda.

This wondrous science of Kriya Yoga is an advanced and more scientific version of the ancient system of Raj Yoga (meaning the 'Royal Yoga' or 'Complete Yoga'). The conventional form of Raj Yoga is elaborate and in the past its use was restricted to renunciates and ascetics. It was projected as difficult and beyond the reach of common householders. On the contrary, Lahiri Mahashya recommended Kriya Yoga practice for all working and earning self-respecting individuals whose temple was their own house and God was the chosen destination of their spiritual mission. Despite its easy approach and simple nature, the technique of Kriya Yoga taught by Lahiri Mahashya contains the basics of other three main Yogas, viz. Karma Yoga, Bhakti Yoga and Jnana Yoga, which is evident from its emphasis on purity of action, depth of devotion and divine quest.

It was by Lahiri Mahashya, under the guidance and spiritual brief given by Maha-avtar Babaji that Kriya Yoga was presented as a brief and simple spiritual rite to discover the human soul and through it gain access to the supreme God. Lahiri Mahashya straightaway dismissed traditional impressions that Yoga was a mysterious science, not easily accessible to common man. He practically proved to his disciples that Kriya Yoga was not only simple to understand and easy to practice but was a complete remedy to banish physical, psychological and spiritual problems of mankind. It made a person environment-friendly, human-friendly and God-friendly and that too in a comparatively shorter period of time. But it is to be borne in mind that Kriya Yoga is an article of faith and therefore its sacredness and secrecy must be maintained. It must be practiced with seriousness, regularity and depth.

It is a modern spiritual science for our new age unencumbered by theology and rituals. Its lab is only the human body and its key method is concentrated interiorization on the inner vibrations of astral sounds and lights through the mastery of breath, by an esoteric technique of Kriya Yoga Pranayama which only an authorized teacher like the monks of Yogda Satsang Society of India, Ranchi, can impart.

It must be pointed out that Kriya Yoga is not an entirely new invention of Yoga by Maha-avtar Babaji in which he initiated

Lahiri Mahashya. It is the same, imperishable and ancient science of Yoga suitably modified by Maha-avtar Babaji, to suit the modern age, which was revealed by Lord Krishna himself to Arjuna. The devotees of Kriya Yoga need no proof of this claim because the essence of Kriya Yoga Pranayama is the same as is explained by Lord Krishna in verse 4.29 of *The Bhagawad Gita*. The contents and meaning of verse 4.29 have been explained above.

Apart from *The Bhagawad Gita*, Patanjali also has written a good deal on Kriya Yoga and recommends Kriya Yoga as a means to spiritual liberation (Kaivalya) or God contact. In his prime treatise, Yoga Sutra, Patanjali has devoted its Section-II to Kriya Yoga. Patanjali defines Kriya Yoga as Tapa (austerity), Swadhyay (study), and Ishwara Pranaaidhana (resignation to God). Tapa (austerity) includes various observances such as fasting, pilgrimages, charity, chanting of incantations and Pranayama.

Study means both knowledge of scriptures and analysis of one's own self. Scriptures would mean mainly those religious texts which are recommended by the guru and would also include listening to Aum (Pranaava) in meditation by sitting in an isolated place, preferably at night.

Ishwara Pranaaidhana or resignation to God means unconditional surrender with complete self-abandonment to the supreme God. Thoughts, speech and gross actions all are to be treated as His gift and are to be performed to please God. Ego is to be controlled and the mind is to be completely surrendered to His will. Through such self-abandonment, the Kriya yogi rises above the polarity of attraction and repulsion, which aids and abets the process of the modifications of the mind which must be eradicated root and branch to attain Kaivalya. Ishwara or God is the omniscient power and its indicator is the Pranaava (Aum). Meditation on Aum by chanting it and by listening to it in silence leads a Kriya yogi to spiritual liberation or samadhi.

According to Patanjali, there are five Kleshas (distractions) which must be overcome before one may aspire to attain Samadhi through Kriya Yoga. Those distractions are Avidya (delusion), Asmita (ego), Raga (attachment), Dvesha (aversion), and Abhinivesha (the fear of death). Since a separate chapter has been written in this book on Patanjali's Yoga Sutra, it is not necessary to discuss these matters here.

In the wake of the foregoing discussion on Kriya Yoga, it appears necessary to compare the exposition of Kriya Yoga as formulated by Maha Rishi Patanjali in his Yoga Sutra and the scientific unfoldment of this spiritual dispensation as gifted by Maha-avatar Babaji to the modern world by initiating in it the great yogi Lahiri Baba, which now has been popularized extensively in several countries of the world by a dedicated endeavour of great modern yogi Paramahansa Yoganand ji.

In fact Kriya Yoga is a spiritual science which is based on the infallible experience attained by a yogi in Samadhi. Therefore, there is no scope for any major point of difference between these two expositions as is also obvious from the above discussion. A few points of difference which appear are due to the reason of time factor because for each age different emphasis and nuances are considered differently.

The first point of difference between these two Kriya Yoga systems is that while in Patanjali Yoga-Sutra there is no mention of the seven spine chakras, in Gurudeva Yogananda ji's teachings the seven spine chakras, coccyx to brain (sahsrara), occupy great importance for purification and enlightenment. Even the five sheaths skirting the soul are not mentioned in Yoga Sutra. But it may be said that these effects are indirectly covered by Patanjali by stressing the need to conquer five vritis and five basic distractions.

Patanjali Yoga Sutra opens with Samadhi section and at the outset defines Yoga as chitta vriti nirodya – cessation of all modifications of the mind which indeed is no mean challenge to grapple with. Stopping of the process of these modifications of the mind is a life-long trial and may even take many incarnations to master. To attain Kaivalya, the highest state of spiritual liberation, Patanjali lays emphasis on the observance of vairagya (renunciation), abhyasa (high degree of yogic exercises) and observance of Brahamacharya to attain high level of internal purity. On the other hand, the science of Kriya Yoga, as revealed by Lahiri Babaji and preached by Paramahansa Yoganand ji, is a scientific, gradual and a certain process, which does not begin with Samadhi but culminates in it. No sanyasa and Brahmacharya is a condition for its practice. It is for all householders, commoners, sanyasis and ascetics; of course, purity of character and devotion are the priority requirement.

Patanjali deals with Kriya Yoga in the second section of Yoga Sutra (Sadhna section) and prescribes it for beginners who are to practice tapa (austerity), swadhyay (study of self and scriptures), and Ishwara Pranaaidhana (surrender to God). The composite course of Kriya Yoga of Paramahansa Yoganand is not sub-divided into sections. It is one complete unified whole catering to transform three dimensions of man's personality –

physical, psychological and spiritual. Observance of Sanyam is integral to the advanced technique of Kriya.

Patanjali prescribes, like Parmahansa Yogananda, four types of Pranayama, aimed at stopping the flow of modifications of the mind, by purifying the mind and senses. A fifth type of advanced Pranayama system, "sanyamn", is prescribed to acquire various occult powers. On the other hand, the different Pranayama categories of Kriya technique, as preached by Paramahansa Yoganand ji, are a closely guarded secret, precisely designed to spiritualize the consciousness under the strict supervision of an authorised monk.

Patanjali prescribes in the third section of Yoga Sutra (Vibhuti section), a network of sidhis (occult powers) which empower a practitioner to attain various powers over mind, nature and other people. On the other hand, the Kriya Yoga of Paramahansa Yoganand, practiced for attainment of occult powers (sidhi), is not recommended.

It appears that Patanjali Yoga Sutra does not describe at length with the Divinity or the Supreme God. It only mentions Ishwara, as the source of supreme knowledge, the indicator of which is Aum in aphorisms 1/25-26-27. On the other hand, Kriya Yoga of Paramahansa Yogananda is a dedicated spiritual discourse albeit with secret techniques aimed at divine revelation of the Supreme God who is the source of all matter, life, knowledge, power and love. Faithful practice of Kriya Yoga is prescribed as a sure path to reach the Supreme God. Master yogis declare that both these Yoga expositions are divine revelations and can unfailingly lead an ardent yogi to spiritual enlightenment. Therefore, attempting any comparison between the two is an unrewarding exercise.

A brief and general explanation of the principles of Kriya Yoga, because its core techniques are guarded secrets, should enable an intelligent reader to envision that Kriya Yoga is a unique science to culture, sublimate and transcend the mind. It is through esoteric techniques of Pranayama and intuitive mediation that the highest goal of spiritual realization can be mastered. The mind so cultured and sublimated with special techniques and esoteric exercises develops in a Kriya yogi, the qualities and the will to serve, love and uplift others. Kriya yogis feel satisfaction and happiness to serve the needy. They are happy to educate raw people and to enlighten the educated. This they do for no material benefits and for no motive. When the mind has been transcended, which a few Kriya yogis can achieve, because it is a rare feat, a person experiences the unending abundance of happiness called bliss. In this state a person acquires the inner zeal and deep yearning to love and serve all. He lives to serve God and uplift others. Now it should need no more explanation to point out the unique power of Kriya Yoga to generate a new culture of love, harmony and enlightenment which the present world badly needs.

PATANJALI YOGA SUTRA

PREFACE

All students of Yoga know that Patanjali's Yoga Sutra is a masterpiece on the practice of ethics, Yoga and spirituality. It is not only a great book on Yoga principles requiring scientific practice of its each sutra, but each of its small aphorisms contains spiritual essence which holds the secret to unfold divinity to the seeker. Purification of body and mind is a precondition to attain progress in Patanjali Yoga to finally attain samadhi. In fact, Patanjali was not the discoverer or founder of the science of Yoga. Yoga as a spiritual science is as old as mankind itself. After experiencing and mastering it himself, Patanjali is said to have expounded and formulated this system to facilitate systematically its access to all ardent seekers. Yoga Sutra is a surprisingly small book. It contains one hundred and ninety-five small aphorisms, each of less than one line length, but each of its aphorisms is a spiritualized intonation that can enlighten the sincere seeker. The book contains four chapters, viz., *Samadhi paada, Sadhna paada, Vibhuti paada, and Kaivalya paada.*

The ultimate aim of Patanjali Yoga is to attain Kaivalya, the highest state of spiritual liberation which Vedanta calls salvation (moksha) or spiritual bliss. *Drashta (Purusha* or soul) is to secure his state of spiritual liberation from *Drishya (Prakriti);* therefore, *Drashta's* (soul) victory over *Drishya (Prakriti*) is the main theme of Yoga Sutra. *Purusha (Drashta)* in simple words means soul and *Prakriti* for our convenience may be called nature. This concept of *Purusha* and *Prakriti* is very well explained in the Sankhya school of philosophy of Kapil Muni. Briefly, Prakriti may be explained as a principle containing twenty-four evolutes and the twenty-fifth is the *Purusha* (soul). These twenty-four evolutes are *chitta* (the feeling principle), intelligence, ego, mind, five senses of knowledge and five action senses, five tanmatras (the causal forms of the five elements) and the five elements, viz., earth, water, fire, air and ether. These twenty-four evolutes of Prakriti are called evolutes because they evolve from the *Mool Prakriti* (the causal form of Prakriti). Prakriti is always unmanifest, which is why it is called the principle of twenty-four evolutes. This unmanifest Prakriti, having twenty-four evolutes, is made of three gunas the basic qualities or properties of the universe - *Satvik* (positive), *Rajsik* (dynamic) and *Tamsik* (negative or gross). In Prakriti these three gunas are always in a state of equilibrium. *The Bhagawad Gita* and Upanishads disclose that the Prakriti is an infinitely great power emanating from God. God has created Prakriti to operate, run and regulate the universe both at cosmic and individual levels. Evolution begins with disturbance or motion in the equilibrium state of Prakriti. Thus, through billions of years the *shrishti* (phenomenon nature or universe) evolves.

At individual level human being too, being a part of Prakriti, is made of the twenty-four evolutes and Purusha (soul), the twenty-fifth, is also present in every individual. The Purusha and Prakriti are inseparably together ever since the dawn of creation. Purusha inside Prakriti has only the mind level of consciousness and is under the power of Prakriti (nature) in all the three states of consciousness - waking, dream and also partly in sleeping state. Purusha (soul as Jiva) is unconscious of its spiritual origin and essence; being the seeing or sensing principle, it believes itself to be body and mind (ego) and identifies himself with whatever his mind and senses expose him to. Nature of man being ego and pain and pleasure being systemic to it, is the cause of three-fold pain (physical, psychological and metaphysical) of man. This Prakriti or the mind stuff is in a continuous state of transformations called modifications, keeping the Purusha (soul) engaged with itself due to its various varieties and attractions. Patanjali's chitta-vriti-nirodha (cessation of the modifications of mind) is a great remedy to stop the distracting process of modifications of the mind by decimating the five distractions through Yoga practices (sanyamn), non-attachment, surrender to Ishwara, observance of purity and samadhi.

SAMADHI SECTION

This opening section of Yoga Sutra contains fifty-one aphorisms. It defines Yoga and the ways to attain samadhi. Samadhi is the highest spiritual attainment which Vedanta, *The Bhagawad Gita* and Upanishads call Moksha and Param-ananda (the highest state of spiritual liberation). It is described as the state of bliss, which cannot be experienced by mind and therefore requires transcendence of mind. Samadhi has three major categories - Savikalpa, Nirvikalpa, and Nirbeej. In Savikalpa samadhi, the mind is not transcended fully and spiritual realization of the highest level (Moksha) is not attained. Nirvikalpa samadhi is a state of complete spiritual realization in which the seeker becomes the sought and fully transcends the body consciousness. In Nirbij samadhi, all seeds of worldly desires and impressions are burnt from consciousness, and the human consciousness becomes the pure soul (called the divine spirit). This attainment means no rebirth due to realization of eternity, which completely destroys the body consciousness. Patanjali calls this Dharammegh samadhi; the state of Kaivalya as defined in the fourth section of Yoga Sutra. The exposition of Yoga Sutra appears to be analogous to the pattern followed in Upanishad where a master explains the spiritual context to his disciple who is seated next to him. Yoga exposition, being an esoteric knowledge, attracts the attention of only a few ardent seekers possessing purity of conduct and strong spiritual quest.

In the second aphorism of this section, Patanjali defines Yoga as chitta-vriti-nirodha cessation of the modifications of mind. When modifications of the mind stop, Drashta (the soul or the cognizing power) becomes pure and blissful, otherwise Drashta thinks and believes himself to be exactly as the modifications reveal. Therefore, Drashta is subject to constant experience of change, pain, pleasure and even boredom. To attain poise, peace and enlightenment, it is necessary to stop the process of modifications of the mind through Yoga practice.

These modifications are countless and constant in their flow. Patanjali has, therefore, arranged them into five categories. Each one of these vritis (modifications) has two characteristics - one is helpful in Yoga practices and other is obstructive.

The five vritis (modifications) are:

Pramana: It means knowledge of any object that mind and senses know, perceive and cognize directly.

Viparyaya: It means mistaken knowledge when the unreal is mistaken for real. Silver may be mistaken for pearl or yellow metal may be mistaken for gold.

Vikalpa: It is fancy or imaginary knowledge such as an ascetic may imagine the form of his chosen God whom he has not seen or a tourist may imagine the beautyof a place he has not visited.

Nidra-vriti: It is a feeling of the effect of no knowledge, because in deep sleep we (the mind) have no knowledge of anything. However, on waking up we experience the feeling of freshness.

Smriti-vriti: It means appearance and feeling of the experienced objects and situations in the mind.

Looking at the extent and nature of these vritis (modifications of mind), it is obvious that their scope is very wide leaving hardly anything uncovered that comes or may come in contact with human intelligence, mind and senses. Obviously, to control and stop this vast and unending process of the modifications of mind is no mean challenge. Man's antah-karna (the mind stuff), activated by the Prana energy, which never stops working even in sleep, is ceaselessly in a state of modifications. As long as man's breathing continues his mental modifications will continue too. This means there exists a direct cause-affect link between the breathing process and modifications of mind. After carefully diagnosing this deep and subtle truth, Patanjali has discovered a remedy which can stop the incessant flow of modifications of the mind and can arm a yogi with various occult powers and finally lead him to the attainment of Kaivalya (spiritual liberation).

Pramana-vriti, the first of the five vritis mentioned above, has three forms:

(1) Pratyaksha (2) *Anuman* and (3) *Agama*

Pratyaksha Pramana means the right knowledge of all objects due to direct contact of the mind and senses with them.

Anuman Pramana means inferred knowledge like existence of smoke must indicate fire.

Agama Pramana means knowledge based on conviction, unsupported by material evidence like pronouncements of Mahapurusha and contents of great scriptures.Being unquestionable truths, they need no supportive proof.

To permanently stop the modifications of mind, Patanjali prescribes the use of practice and renunciation (abhyasa and vairagya).

Practice can be of meditation, Pranayama or any other esoteric technique but it is to be done regularly, carefully, with full concentration and deep devotion as taught by the guru. It must be done for a long time and may even take the whole life course.

Renunciation is complete non-attachment to all objects of mind and senses, whether seen or heard. Nothing worldly should be the object of desire of a Yoga devotee except the will to attain Kaivalya. Desire and worldly attachment are deep-rooted in the human psyche for many births in the past. Therefore, the requirement is to uproot them completely from the system, both from conscious and subconscious levels. To attain this level of non-attachment, there are special techniques which must be observed regularly and strictly. After mastering Apara Vairagya, Patanjali says that to attain Kaivalya, complete spiritual liberation, observance of Para (supreme) Vairagya is necessary. This follows the vision of the Divine in samadhi (trance); unless Purusha (soul) is experienced in Samadhi, Para Vairagya (supreme renunciation) is not complete. This stage can only be attained through complete detachment, observance of Brahmacharya, rising above three gunas and completely transcending the mind, senses and intelligence, as is revealed in aphorism 3/35. Controlling all senses fully, observing purity, mastering abhyasa (Yoga practice) with full concentration and devotion, only such a yogi attains Nirbij samadhi or Kaivalya (full spiritual liberation). To attain Nirbij Samadhi, the end purpose of Yoga, deep concentration must be practiced in meditation.

This preparatory exercise in meditative concentration to banish root and branch, the modifications from consciousness, is called Sampragyata Yoga (samadhi). Its purpose is to uproot all feelings of the elements of logic (vitarka), reflection (vichar), deliberative faculty, joy (ananda) and ego (asmita). Its practice is performed in two stages. In the first stage the difference between the thinker and the thought is felt but in the second stage of deep concentration, the consciousness of the knower and known disappears. Observance of Vairagya, as explained above, is important during the practice of Sampragyat Yoga. It is only when the supreme non-attachment sinks deep into consciousness that all longing and impressions of the world of senses (sansara) disappear. The performance of Yoga with energetic vigour, observance of purity (Brahmacharya), faith and the right sense of discrimination lead the yogi to attain Samadhi quickly. With vigorous pursuit, faith and purity, the intelligence of a yogi becomes ritambra (sharp, pure and truthful).

Ishwara Pranaaidhana (complete surrender to God) is prominently recommended by Patanjali as an effective way to attain Nirbij samadhi. Unconditional surrender to God helps because God is omniscient and merciful. He has special weakness for his pure devotees, as is also declared by God in *The Bhagawad Gita* 7/17. In aphorism 1/24, the characteristics of Ishwara are defined. Ishwara is one who is unaffected by kalesh, karma, vipaka and ashya. These terms are explained in the next part (Sadhna section). Kalesh means affliction of distraction.

Distractions are five as mentioned in 2/3: (1) Avidya (delusion) (2) Asmita (ego or the sense of being) (3) Dvesh (aversion) (4) Raga (attraction) and (5) Abhinivesh (desire). Actions are of four types: good (punya), bad (paap), mixed and above good and bad. Due to the powers of omniscience, non-attachment, detachment from rewards of action, above-ness from afflictions and His supreme state among Purushas (the supreme Purusha), is called by Patanjali Ishwara as the Supreme Guru, even the guru of Brahma because Brahma is subject to the command of time but not Ishwara. It is apparent that Patanjali is of the view that Ishwara is the supreme power. In aphorism 27, it is mentioned the name or indicator of that God, which is Pranaava (Aum). The divinity of Aum and its cosmic creative power is well explained in Mandukya Upanishad. Aum is the wonder word revealing four dimensions of existence and consciousness, viz. waking, sleep, dream and turya (spiritual consciousness).

Patanjali says that by performing Japa and meditation on Aum 'word', all the nine distracting agents like ailment, laziness, doubt, carelessness, lack of concentration, lack of non-attachment, etc. are vanished and the yogi succeeds in attaining Nirbij samadhi. Nirbij samadhi also destroys such other causes of distractions as pain, trauma, despondency, inhalation and exhalation and bestows peace and poise.

In aphorism 32, the importance of the power of concentration is emphasized both for the destruction of obstructive and distracting agents and for success in attaining Nirbij samadhi. Purity of heart (complete observance of Brahmacharya) is the key factor for success in Yoga. To purify the heart systematically and psychologically, Patanjali lays down precise exercises and important measures which are illustrated from aphorism 33 to 40. In this regard, the main emphasis to keep the mind in even state, is laid on maintaining happy disposition, observance of sympathy, compassion and indifference to vice and virtue. Pointed mention is made to breathing techniques, improvement in concentration, analysis of dreams and sleep and equanimity towards aversion and attachment.

The acid test of the highest level of purity (when no seed or vestige of desires and their impressions are left in mind) is the attainment of Ritambra. In Ritambra, the intelligence of a yogi becomes pure and cognizes the essence and reality of an object and all chances of illusion and delusion are banished from consciousness. This is not a state of vacuum but an abundance of the radiant delight of purity. All impressions and desires and their seeds are burnt permanently in this stage. In this state of supreme purity, Nirbij Samadhi (Kaivalya) dawns as if automatically.

SADHNA SECTION

Samadhi section, the first part of Yoga darshan, is a complete theory to attain Kaivalya (final illumination). It requires mastering Yoga practices (abhyasa), non-attachment (vairagya),purity (Brahamacharya), devotion (shradha), Ishwara Pracaidhana (surrender to God), and Aumkar Japa (meditation on Aum). This presupposes that the Yoga ascetic should already be well advanced in his Yoga effort and must have attained purity of heart; otherwise, it is not possible to master these Yoga practices and acquire Kaivalya. Obviously, attaining Kaivalya through this discipline is not possible for a beginner. For the beginners, who possesses shradha (devotion) and are keen to become yogis, Patanjali recommends the practice of Kriya Yoga. Kriya Yoga is defined in the first aphorism of Sadhna section as Tapa, Swadhyaya and Ishwara Pranaaidhana.

Tapa means austerity and asceticism. It also requires rigid physical, psychological and spiritual discipline by observing fasts, penances and observing all canons of dharma (duty irrespective of difficulty and danger involved). Keeping in mind that detachment from world and devotion to Ishwara are necessary to achieve purity of heart, which is the basic purpose of Tapa.

Swadhyaya means study of the scriptures and self study through self analysis. Even knowing the opinion of others about one's own life can help in swadhyaya. Faith in guru's words is very important because guru knows the disciple and also the discipline he is following. Therefore, his advice is useful. Keeping company of saints, performing Japa (incantations) and listening to Aum sound contribute to swadhyaya. Swadhyaya basically means what I must do.

Ishwar Pranaaidhana means unconditional surrender to God and to love God with all the purity of heart and mind. But loving God is a difficult exercise because one always wonders how to love the unseen. Therefore, the best way to love God is to perform all actions for him with devotion. Whatever we experience or perform by doing, seeing, listening and thinking should be surrendered to God. Slowly, the feeling to love God starts growing and it develops into intense devotion for God. We must remember that love is a magnetism which God cannot resist.

The biggest threat to success in Samadhi is from five basic Kleshas (distractions) which are mentioned below:

Kriya Yoga is the most effective weapon to destroy these five distractions. In this section (sadhna), Patanjali explains the prime necessity and methods to destroy these distractions, clearly emphasizing that without uprooting each vestige of these Kleshas (distractions) from the system no progress is possible in Yoga.

The five Kleshas (distractions) are: *Avidya* (ignorance), *Asmita* (ego), *Raga* (desire), *Dwesha* (aversion), and *Abhinivesh* (blind attachment).*Avidya* is the basic ignorance or cosmic delusion. At individual level, it is called Avidya and at the cosmic level it is called Maya. Avidya is the basic delusion due to which we feel that we are this body and our blind attachment to it .

Its role is to bind the individual to body, the transitory world of senses (the nature) by entertaining him with its varieties and unending diversities of colour, light, sound, form, etc.

Asmita is the basic ego due to which man thinks himself to be intelligent and not the soul that he in reality is.

Raga means desire, which conditions man's liking for particular objects and experiences.

Dwesha means aversion, which is the opposite of Raga, and therefore conditions man's dislike for some experiences and objects.

Abhinivesh means blind attachment of fear and love instinct. The ever-existent feeling of the fear of death and love of body life are due to the cause of Abhinivesh.

Among the five distractions, Avidya is very powerful and is the basic cause of other four distractions. This Avidya (ignorance) is deep rooted in human psyche. Patanjali defines ignorance as taking the unreal to be real, impure to be pure, bad for good and soul to be non-soul. It is obvious that due to Avidya (ignorance), man is unable to know that he is basically soul and not the body and mind that he always believes himself to be. Avidya makes people totally ignorant and helpless to distinguish between good and bad, pure and impure and between the right means of happiness and wrong pursuits which lead to unhappiness. Due to ignorance, people waste their lives in superficial existence of this transitory and artificial world. The reason for this is Avidya, which blinds peoples' spiritual vision and binds them to the world of senses.

The five distractions are so potent and powerful that their destruction should be undertaken with effective strategy. After their gross forms have been eliminated, they persist in their astral forms because their impressions are too deep in the mind. Unless Kriya Yoga is performed for a long time with deep devotion and complete concentration, the vestiges of these distractions will reemerge. Therefore, Kriya Yoga with deep meditation is the effective remedy to destroy the poison from the fangs of these distractions.

Patanjali says that non-destruction of these five distractions (Kleshas) cause and condition rebirth, quality of life and living conditions in the future life. Not only this, these distractive agents are so powerful and far-reaching in their effect that in future incarnations they become the cause of people's good and bad (paap and Punya)actions. They even affect the quality and life span of each person and thus unleash an array of pains and pleasures as if unendingly parading and multiplying themselves in successive births.

Patanjali says that the basic cause of all these problems of life is the union of Drashta (purush) and Drishya (Prakriti). Unless this union of Drashta and Drishya is broken, there is no possibility for Drashta's (soul) freedom from Drishya (Prakriti). In fact, Drashta (soul) is basically pure and free but due to its contact and association with intelligence (mind stuff), it loses its originality and sees as the mind sees.

Basically the cause of loss of awareness by Purusha of his original nature is the fact of Drashta's (Purusha or soul) contact and connections with Drishya or Prakriti. It is obvious that Purusha is both in and above Prakriti. In fact, he is in and not of the Prakriti. In fact the basic design of creation is that Prakriti is made for Purusha. Prakriti has two-fold purposes to serve the Purusha through its various forms, products, services, varieties, powers, attractions and diverse ingenuity. Despite this, the Drishya or Prakriti is unable to provide lasting happiness and spiritual joy because Prakriti itself is incomplete and spirituality is none of its constituents. When ultimately Drashta is exhausted with nature due to his failures and follies and is convinced that Prakriti lacks the power to provide him lasting peace and happiness, he starts looking inside himself. The second function of Prakriti is to provide Mukti (salvation) by withdrawing itself from Drashta's path, after performing the first function of serving the Purusha. Prakriti therefore, performs both the functions for Purusha: (1) service and (2) salvation. At this point the inseparable union between Drishta (soul) and Drishya (Prakriti or nature), which has been continuing since times immemorial, breaks and Drashta becomes free. Simultaneously, all desires along with their seeds are destroyed which cannot sprout in future; therefore, Drashta attains Kaivalya.

Patanjali says that for final Kaivalya,Vivek-gyan (enlightenment) is necessary. Vivek-gyan means actual realization and not just intellectual knowledge of the truth that Drashta (soul) is essentially different from Drishya (Prakriti). There is no relationship and similarity between the two. Drishta (soul) is bliss and exists above the ravages of time unlike Drishya (Prakriti), which is impermanent, always changing and is meant only to serve and delude the Puruha (soul) in the world. At final Kaivalya, when Purusha (Drashta) attains freedom, Prakriti (chitta, the avyakta and mind) revert to their causal form – the Mool Prakriti.

The real nature of Prakriti (its swarup) is the unmanifest state of equilibrium, which is made of allpervasive three unmanifest gunas--Sattva (positive), Rajas (dynamic) and Tamas (gross or negative). This is the causal form of Prakriti. Evolution commences with motion in gunas, which is started by Rajo-guna and continues endlessly through millions of years, ultimately culminating in evolution of the phenomenon universe.

Basically this Prakriti (Drishya) is made of the following twenty-four evolutes, as described in aphorism 19 of the Sadhna paada.

The five basic elements – earth, water, fire, air, ether

Five senses of knowledge and mind

Five senses of action. Three gunas of Prakriti manifest and act through these sixteen elements. They are called vishesh.

Five tanmatras of sound, touch, light, taste, smell and ego. Ego is the cause of mind and senses. They are called avishesh.

Mahatatva, which is called Budhi (intelligence), in Vedanta and Chitta in Yoga.

Alinga – Mool Prakriti, which is made of three gunas which *The Bhagawad Gita* and the Upanishads call avyakta.

From aphorism 29 to 55, Patanjali describes in detail the eight-fold Ashtang Yoga with declaration that mastery over these eight vital steps of Yoga places the enlightened soul irreversibly far above the Prakriti in complete disassociation from chitta, intelligence, ego, and mind, where the soul remains eternally blissful in its divine splendour of spiritual consciousness.

The eight parts of Yoga are:

- Yama (forbearance)
- Niyama (observance)
- Asana (posture)

- Pranayama (regulation and control of breath)
- Pratyahara (interiorization of mind or consciousness)
- Dharna (concentration)
- Dhyana (meditation)
- Samadhi (trance or soul and God-realization).

Niyama (forbearance): It includes non-violence, truth, abstinence from theft and greed, and observance of Brahmacharya.

(i) Non-violence: It means complete restraint over the instinct of violence, i.e., using no violence despite provocation. Basically it means love for life as a whole. A yogi who succeeds to master the instinct of violence, is loved even by the most dangerous animals like cobra and lion.

(ii) Truth: It means not telling lies, not even in self-defence, and stating the facts truthfully as known to mind and senses. When a yogi masters truth, what he speaks becomes true.

(iii) Abstinence from theft: It means not to own dishonestly the things belonging to others. It also means not cheating. Theft also includes taking and giving bribes and tax evasion. When a yogi completely banishes the feeling of theft from mind, even hidden gems appear before him.

(iv) Abstinence from greed: It means not to acquire or collect, with a sense of attachment, any material objects selfishly for personal benefit. When a yogi banishes the greed instinct, he starts knowing his earlier births.

(v) Brahamacharya: It means complete inner and outer discipline, not only to sublimate the sex instincts but also to feel joy in ethics and creative thinking. After mastering Brahmacharya, a yogi attains super psychological powers.

Six Niyams;

(i) *SHAUCH* (purity): Externally it means purity of the body, dwelling and surroundings. Internally it means purity of thoughts, to remain above attachment and aversion. It also means friendly mind-set and eating pure (sattvik) food. Purity generates a feeling of detachment and purifies the senses of a yogi which result in deep inner peace.

(ii) *SANTOSH* (contentment): It means performance of duty sincerely irrespective of motive for rewards. It also means entertaining no desire and attachment. It lays stress on cultivating a feeling of deep inner satisfaction. Mastering this quality fills the heart of a yogi with immeasurable joy.

(iii) *TAPA* (austerity): It means exposing the body to various severities and performing all duties with dedication despite the danger and difficulties involved therein. The main purpose of tapa is to purify the ten senses, mind and the body. Performance of tapa adds to the fitness of body and efficiency of senses. Its regular observance with devotion for a long time spiritually enlightens the consciousness of a yogi.

(iv) *SWADHAYA*: It means studying scriptures and performing self analysis to know who I am, what I must do and what is the purpose of life?

(v) *ISHWARA PRANAAIDHAN*: It means complete and unconditional surrender to God and to have full faith in His sense of justice and love for all. The prerequisite is to love God unconditionally and to be at His command. Regular performance of daily prayers with full devotion is a necessary requirement to attract God's grace. Faith in Ishwara destroys all distractions which can obstruct the yogi's course of sadhna.

(vi) *AASANA* (posture): It means a firm, steady and comfortable seat and a motionless body posture for meditation. It helps avoid pain and facilitates in concentration and Prana. In Hatha Yoga there are different 84 asana which cure several psychological and physical diseases.

Patanjali reveals that perfect Yoga posture not only makes a yogi impervious to effects of hot and cold conditions, but eliminates the feeling of Dwandvabhava (feeling of the opposites) from the system of a yogi, which is a distinct step on the way to achieve success in Yoga.

After successful observance of yama, niyama and asana (posture), Pranayama begins. Pranayama is the cessation of the process of inspiration (inhalation) and expiration (exhalation) of breath. This definition of pranayama is given in aphorisn 2/49.

Patanjali cautions that the pranayama principle must be understood and performed carefully because Pranayama is regulation and control of the life force. The aforesaid definition of Pranayama is elaborated by Patanjali in the three following forms:

- *Bahayabriti:* It is also called Rechak Prana. In this Pranayama, breath is exhaled and comfortably kept out as long as possible. Time is to be counted on the basis of seconds. Longer the breath remains out, it must be followed comfortably, the lighter it feels.
- *Abhyantarvriti*: This is also called Poorak Pranayama In this Pranayama, breath is taken in and kept inside as long as it is comfortable. Mind must be concentrated on breath. It is to be seen how much deep the breath goes. Time count in seconds is to be kept. By performing these two Pranayama the body becomes light and comfortable.
- *Stambvriti*: This is also called Kumbak Pranayama. In this Pranayama there is automatic Rechak and Poorak (exhalation and inhalation) and flow of breath is not to be disturbed. The natural pause of breath between exhalation and inhalation is to be counted in terms of seconds. With perfection in this Pranayama flow of breathing stops automatically and the yogi feels etherealized.
- Bahaya-Abhyantravishya-Kshepi Prana (2/51): In this state a person becomes unmindful of the inner and outer objects and experiences no feeling of the incoming and outgoing flow of breath. When his breath and heartbeat stop, the yogi experiences deep peace and inner upliftment. This is the fourth Pranayama. With the performance of these Pranayama

the yogi's worldly attachment is distinctly reduced and his ignorance (Avidya) declinessteadily; he progresses towards Kaivalya because Pranayama has the power to deplete and then destroy the cover of Maya (nature). Pranayama practice qualitatively contributes to the yogi's interest in concentration because the ascetic starts feeling the joy in its practice.

- *Pratyahara:* This means withdrawing the mind and consciousness from their external objects and concentrating on the inner self with full absorption. After mastering pratyahara, all the ten senses and mind come fully under the control of a yogi.

  Pratyahara practice can only succeed when with the regular practice of Pranayama mind and senses have been purified. To exercise complete control over senses is very difficult as is declared by God in *The Bhagawad Gita* (2/67). Only perfect performance of Pranayama can control and de-capacitate the senses because practice of Pranayama generates a feeling of deep joy inside before which the pleasure of sense and sense objects is inconsequential. Therefore, the yogi can dissolve the outer pleasure of senses in the inner joy of the heart. It is at this stage that Pratyahara, complete absorption in the inside, is accomplished.

VIBHUTI SECTION

In Vibhuti section, spiritual or occult powers are described which are attained as a result of Sadhna (the spiritual endeavour).

In the preceding Sadhna section, Patanjali has described the five basic steps of the eight-fold path of Yoga with their consequential benefits. These five steps are Yama (forbearance), Niyama (observance), Asana (posture), Prana (breath regulation), and Pratyahara (interiorization of mind). These five basic steps of the eight-fold path Yoga are the external or outer parts of Yoga and are therefore called Bahiranga. The main purpose of these five steps is to attain the highest level of purity because without purity of chitta, sublimation to (Purusha) soul level is not possible. Ordinarily these five steps can lead a yogi to attain Savikalpa Samadhi, which is not the highest samadhi called Nirvikalpa or Nirbij Samadhi. To attain the highest samadhi the practice of inner Yoga performed with dharna, dhyana and Samadhi is necessary. The three final steps of the eight-fold path Yoga, which constitute the inner Yoga called Antrang, are Dharna, Dhyana and Samadhi.

- *Dharna or concentration*. It means fixing the mind on any internal or external part of the body. The mind can also be concentrated or fixed on any pure object outside the body such as a picture or idol of a deity, the sun or the moon or a flower, but the concentration must be single-pointed and complete. The object concentrated upon must be associated with holiness and purity. Chaste purity and undiluted concentration are the hallmark of Dharna.
- *Dhyana or meditation.* It means concentrating the mind at one point or object for a long time, so completely that there occurs no modification (transformation) in mind. No other idea or image should enter the mind;

the mind must be conscious, during dhyana, only of itself and the object of dhyana as if nothing else exists. Dhyana (meditation) is the most important aspect of Yoga. It is preceded by other six steps which are preparatory to this important Yoga sadhna. Samadhi is not possible without correct and long meditation.

- *Samadhi.* When there exists only one consciousness of the meditated object and even the self consciousness is non-existent, that consciousness is samadhi. It is complete absorption in the object of meditation as if the consciousness and mind is one unit. The awareness of one's own self is lost and only the consciousness of the object of meditation prevails.

  Sanyam: When the three steps of dharna, dhyana and samadhi are practised together continuously at one place and at the same time for spiritual cause and to acquire any occult power, it is called sanyam. To attain spiritual benefit sanyam is to be practised very carefully. It must be ensured that to begin with, sanyam is practiced on gross objects and slowly the yogi may move to finer and subtler objects of meditation. But performing meditation in this way, yogi attains victory over sanyam. By practicing sanyam on any idea or object the yogi attains full power over it because his intelligence becomes pure (ritambra), as explained in Yoga Sutra 1/47-48.

It must be noted that to rise from the lower level of samadhi (Savikalpa) to higher level (Nirvikalpa or Nirbij samadhi) is a very difficult process. Careful practice of sanyam is therefore important while performing this spiritual exercise. The mind, which is made of three gunas, is always in a state of modifications which cannot be completely stopped in Savikalpa samadhi. Unless the mind is fully sublimated, Nirvikalpa or higher Samadhi is unattainable. The practice of Sanyam, when carefully performed, is the only way to move up the spiritual ladder to the summit of Kevalya.

From aphorism 9 to 15, the fundamental principle of evolution is explained that how a substratum or object is transformed differently at each successive stage into different forms, like raw earth is changed into various different forms like pots, toys, dwellings, etc. and raw cotton is changed differently at successive levels, i.e., cotton into thread, thread into cloth and so on. Just as water changes into ice and steam, subject to temperature and attendant conditions, similarly this universe too from unmanifest Prakriti to various successive forms is a succession of transformations in its properties due to different conditions. It is with the performance of sanyam that a yogi can attain various occult forms of knowledge and powers and create the desired results. Now, obviously if an individual yogi, by the practice of sanyam can gradually create desired results, to a limited extent, why can't the omnipotent Ishwara do it on a universal scale? No wonder, the yogis say that this world is a dream of God.

From aphorism 16 onwards, Patanjali describes that by performing sanyam on any chosen object, a yogi gets the desired results. Therefore, he should be careful to select his object which will help him in his spiritual progress; otherwise digression can cost delay and frustration.

By performing sanyam (dharna, dhyana and samadhi) on

an object, its transformed properties, its transformed character and transformed consequence are revealed. The idea is that when a yogi wants to know the basic nature or cause of an object, how it has assumed its present form in how much time and how and what the object will become in future; this will be revealed to the yogi after performing sanyam on the object ., This means that by performing sanyam in this manner, a yogi can have the knowledge of the past and the future. When a yogi performs sanyam on his desires and aspirations, he knows about his previous births too.

By performing sanyam on the mind of another person, the yogi can know the state of his mind and by doing sanyam on that subject's mind (what may be engaging the other person's mind), that too will get revealed to the yogi.

If a yogi practices sanyam on his body, his body becomes invisible to others and similarly doing sanyam of his sound and touch senses renders the yogi's speech inaudible to others and his body intangible to others. But his sanyam does not change or affect the sight, touch, or sound sense of others but makes his body and senses invisible, intangible or inaudible to others.

By scrutinizing his Sanchit karmas (the affect of which has not started and will start in future) and Prarabdh karma (the affect of which is in progress), the yogi can know about his death. Inauspicious symptoms also are indicators of the death time.

By performing sanyam on fellow feeling, the yogi acquires the virtues of friendship, kindness and equanimity. As a result, he can make aggrieved people happy and remain himself happy and contented.

By performing sanyam on any animal or natural power, the yogi gets the power of that animal like lion and power of wind.

By doing sanyam on the inner light, the yogi gets the power to know distant things, hidden objects and inaccessible things. Inner light means the astral light (Brahma jyoti) seen in samadhi.

By performing sanyam on the sun and the moon, the knowledge of various regions in the cosmos is revealed.

By performing sanyam on the navel point, knowledge of the body systems such as anatomy, physiology, digestive system, nervous system, etc. is acquired. By doing sanyam on the base of the throat (pit), no hunger and thirst are felt.

By performing sanyam on the astral light in the Brahmarandhra, the yogi can see the angels and enlightened beings.

By performing sanyam on Pratibh (3/33), one knows all because it leads to the attainment of intuition. By doing sanyam on heart, one knows the mind which means that after mastering the heart knowledge, the modifications of the mind would stop.

By performing sanyam on Purusha and not on buddhi (intelligence or Prakriti), the soul knowledge dawns. In fact, due to Asmita, Sadbudhi (Prakriti) and Purusha are so indistinguishably inseparable that we can only reach budhi (intelligence) and not the Purusha. By doing sanyam on Purusha, the Purusha is revealed and the soul knowledge dawns. In fact, the yogi attains the power of intuition.

The knowledge that a yogi obtains by performing sanyam on the senses of sound, touch, sight, taste and smell, has been described in aphorisms 36 and 37.. These sidhis are not to be attained because these occult powers have the retrograde effect and keep the yogi bound to the worldly matters. Therefore, a yogi remains tied to the fetters of ego.

When a yogi successfully masters the cause of Karma (burns all seeds of his Karma and desires), he gets the power to enter, at will, into another body, be it dead or alive. The reason is that a being is bound to a particular body by the bond of action effects; when all actions along with desires are burnt in samadhi, the yogi attains the power to get out of his body at will and get into another body.

By mastering the udan current of life force, a yogi obtains the power to become light like air. There are five Prana vayu currents in the body: Prana (crystallization), Viyan (circulation), Samana (assimilation), Udan (metabolism) and Apan (elimination). These Prana powers or life force currents operate and regulate all our body functions and actions.

Samana Vayu: By mastering it, a yogi's body becomes effulgent (full of light).

By performing sanyam over the connection between sound (shabad) and ether (Akash), the yogi acquires supernatural power of hearing the inaudible irrespective of the distance and cover.

By performing sanyam on the relationship between body and space, the yogi acquires the power to walk in space.

By performing sanyam on the real nature (swarup) of mind and senses, the yogi acquires the videha (transcendent power) and completely banishes the body and ego consciousness. He no longer feels himself the body but the pure mind either thinking about the outer or inner objects. This videha power enables a yogi to know the description of anything and everything.

By performing sanyam over five states, viz., physical, basic elements, astral, universality and fruit-yielding capacity of the five basic elements (earth, water, fire, air and akash), the yogi acquires full power over these five elements.

With this achievement the yogi attains the eight forms of great occult power.

Anima: The yogi can become microscopic like an atom.

Laghima: This makes the body light and the yogi can move in space.

Mahima: This can make the body massive like mountain as Hanuman had done when Bhima obstructed his passage.

Garima: It can make the body immensely heavy as the yogi likes.

Prapti: It is the power to possess and attain any desired material object.

Prakamya: It is the automatic and unobstructed fulfilment of any material wish.

Vashitava: Full control over five elements. A yogi can bring anything under his control.

Ishitava: It is complete rule over the five elements and to produce any object and power through them. Thus, the yogi attains physical beauty, magnetic shine, force and toughness, apart from other tangible objects and intangible powers.

By performing sanyam over Grahan (cognition), Swarup (basic nature), Asmita (ego), Anvaya (universality), and Arthatava (fruit-yielding capacity), the yogi attains complete power over mind and senses. Having full control over the mind and the ten senses, amounts to conquering the ego because ego is the source of mind and senses. Conquest over ego is a spectacular victory for a yogi on the spiritual path to attain Kaivalya. With this victory the yogi attains the power to reach any part of the world instantly because he attains the speed of mind. The yogi can see objects and places in distant lands. This enables the yogi to have power over the Prakriti, which is the final victory over nature.

Consequently, the yogi knows the distinction between Budhi (Prakriti) and Purusha (soul); he attains supreme vairagya and becomes the knower of all. Finally by performing sanyam over the minutest units of time, Kshana and Krama (having conquered space and times), a yogi attains Param Vivek-gyana. He knows the difference between Prakriti and Purusha. Prakriti (Budhi) reverts to its causal state the Mool Prakriti and Purusha attains the Kaivalya.

KAIVALYA SECTION

Patanjali describes that in the preceding three parts of samadhi, sadhna and vibhuti sections, attainment of occult powers and Kaivalya have been explained on the basis of the methods described in these sections. In the first section 'samadhi pada', primarily the nature of Samadhi and the methods to attain it have been explained. In the second section 'Sadhana pada', mainly the means to attain Samadhi through Kriya Yoga have been described. In the third section 'Vibhuti pada', various powers have been explained which are attained through sanyama. In the fourth and final section, Patanjali attempts to explain analytically the concept of

Kaivalya stating that in addition to the factors described in the earlier sections there are other methods too to acquire occult powers. In Samadhi pada, the main methods to be employed to attain Kaivalya are concentration, meditation, practice of Yoga exercises, non-attachment, surrender to God and strict observance of Brahmacharya (purity) by complete sublimation of the sex instinct. In fact, Patanjali has prescribed the Samadhi section for devout and serious Yoga students whose aim is to be a perfect yogi by attaining Nirbij Samadhi.

Sadhna section is for beginners and common practitioners of Yoga who want to attain Samadhi, step by step and stage by stage, by gradually purifying their conduct and improving their practice. For such Yoga practitioners, important and specific methods and Yoga practices are explained in Sadhna pada. More important of which are tapa, swadhyaya and Ishwara-Pranaaidhana. In Sadhna sections, it is also prescribed that all Yoga students must overcome the five basic distractions without which the five modifications of the mind cannot be conquered.

In the Vibhuti section, various siddhis (occult powers) are mentioned along with the methods to attain them. However, the most important method to attain and master occult powers prescribed in it is the method of sanyam.

The five additional causes to attain occult powers or *sidhis* mentioned in the first aphorism of this section (Kaivalya) are: birth (janam), herb (aushdhi), incantation (mantra), austerity (tapa) and trance (Samadhi). Due to changes in the body, senses and mind of practitioners of these sidhis, they attain many unusual powers and in this process, body, senses and mind register changes in their form and capacity. Patanjali calls this process *"Jatyentraparinam"*. According to this principle, the changes in body, senses and mind which generate various powers are not caused by the aforesaid siddhis; birth, herb, mantra etc, they only remove obstructions from the path of spiritual progress. The spiritual progress being an innate power flows from within. Patanjali illustrates the *"Jatyentraparinam"* principle with an example, as a peasant while irrigating his land from one field to another does not cause the movement of water, which is innate to water, but merely removes obstructions from the course of its flow. Similarly, the above mentioned siddhis are not the causative factors but external aids that facilitate changes in the body, senses and mind which attain various powers. Mind is changed (transcended) by Samadhi and not by siddhis. This is explained by Patanjali in the beginning of this *pada*.

Through sadhna due to changes in the body, senses and mind of the Yoga ascetic, supernatural powers are attained by him which appear to be caused by the factors of birth, herb, incantation, austerity or asceticism and trance, but basically the factors of birth, incantation, etc. per se do not change the nature of the ascetic, lifting him to a higher plane; they only remove obstructions from his path. Change being the innate characteristic of Prakriti, it automatically effects changes in the mind of the ascetic resulting in attainment of occult powers for Yogi. In fact, attainment of occult powers or Kaivalya is not an easy or a simple exercise. It is an adventure of adventures which is difficult to continue and hard to achieve. It is not only full of pitfalls but is time-consuming too for which even one life span may prove inconsequential. Cumulative effect of several births may show the ascetic the light of inner illumination and such an experience is indeed a great event for the yogi. This certainly explains that every input in Yoga is an investment in the gold mine of divinity because no effort is ever wasted in Yoga, as is clearly pronounced by God in *The Bhagawad Gita*. But we must always remember that spirituality and Yoga are not to be explained and understood with reason. Thus, the use of a herb or drug may illumine an ascetic 'A' but not the ascetic 'B' at the same time, not only because of the variation in the quality of their spiritual effort but also owing to the factor of Sanchit karma, which being based on individual karma, takes time to ripen for results, differently in each case.

Incantation is a very potent factor and a well tried cause of spiritual enlightenment. These incantations are mentioned in Vedas and Tantra texts. Some ascetics attain occult powers through these incantations. It is for this reason that meditation based on incantation occupies a priority position. Tapa (asceticism or austerity) as a means to attain occult powers is well known and widely experienced. Even in common life the duty performed with devotion and a sense of sacrifice, irrespective of the danger and difficulty involved, fills the heart of a person with unusual courage and satisfaction. Through asceticism, Yoga ascetics have always been attaining occult powers. Yogic asceticism creates supernatural powers in the yogi's mind, senses and body, with which the yogi can see the unseen and can superbly master the weakness of attachment. These four causes of birth, herb, incantation and tapa cannot by themselves bestow on an ascetic the great benediction of Kaivalya because they cannot destroy sanskaras (impression) from mind but can only bless the ascetic with various occult powers. Realization of Kaivalya is attainable through dharna and dhyana-based samadhi, which purify the mind completely. The changes brought about in the psyche and system (body, senses and mind) of an ascetic by the factors of birth, herb, incantations and tapa (austerity) are in the realm of Prakriti (mind, senses and body being Prakriti) and even in this respect they (birth, incantations, herb and tapa) only act to remove the obstructions from the ever-moving flow of Prakriti. They cannot change the Prakriti because the constantly changing nature of Prakriti is its innate characteristic. Prakriti being made of three gunas is action-based and actions cause impressions which generate sanskars and therefore Prakriti being in a perennial state of flux generates a vicious circle of action, impression and sanskars.

Actions are of four kinds: (1) Good, which are of angels, (2) Bad, which are of bad people, (3) Mixed, which are of common people, and (4) Indifferent, which are of a yogi because yogis being spiritually realized are not motivated, bound and affected by actions. Common people are affected by actions which create corresponding impressions on the mind of the performer of every action. These impressions are called vaasnas which affect and condition the future actions, birth and quality of life of the people.

People who have not purified their minds through spiritual and Yoga practices, the impressions of their actions or sanskars remain stored in their minds. Of these actions, only those which are ripe and ready to yield their effects or fruits, create corresponding vaasna in peoples' mind to cause performance and enjoyment of similar action to the exclusion of other actions. Thus, people due to performance of their actions are under the effect of these impressions or vasnaas.

These sanskars and vaasnas, along with their consequential actions, can take place in future at any time, in any incarnation and in any place or country. There is no chance for any omission or confusion in this concept of Karma theory due to time lag or change in birth or place because of the existence of foolproof link between memory and sanskar.

In aphorisms 13th to 24th, metaphysical description of time, matter, three gunas (qualities of Prakriti), mind and soul is explained. It is mentioned that vaasnas or impressions which create actions cannot be unrelated to objects (Vastu) or matter. Matter, being indestructible, is made of three gunas which are ever existent. Gunas, matter, impressions, or vaasnas and mind, all exist due to ego or ignorance – the basic distractive agent – which can only be destroyed in samadhi. With the destruction of ignorance, the rest of the properties of Prakriti vanish as if unsought.

Relationship between object, mind and soul (Purusha) is discussed saying that objects which exist independently exist for the mind only when they are reflected in it. Mind has the cognizing power due to soul which is the ever-conscious power and the ever-present witness. It is the consciousness of soul which is reflected in the mind. For convenience it may be said that soul has two powers – one is its own original divine power of consciousness and the second is reflected in the mind. The second power reflected in the mind, which makes the mind conscious, does not affect the purity of the original power of the pure soul. Mind is conscious and acts due to the magnetic effect of the soul on it just as at any place the mere presence of magnet activates the iron bits or iron files. The bottom line of this discussion up to the 24th aphorism is that action, impressions, vaasnas, matter and mind, all exist for Purusha (Drashta) or the soul because they are all compound, made of three gunas and not pure like soul. The compounds are meant to serve and the soul (jiva) is to be served. When the Drashta becomes soul he no longer needs the Drashya (mind or matter called Prakriti). When the Drashta knows the difference between the soul and the mind (Purusha and Prakriti) that the two are essentially separate and basically different, then it abides in him and becomes pure.

At this point, the highest knowledge of discrimination (Vivekgyan) born of samadhi dawns on the yogi. The yogi's mind disciplined with discrimination is gravitated towards Kaivalya. All seeds of sanskars, vaasnas and impressions are destroyed like the burnt seeds which never sprout. The yogi becomes pure and all knowing. He thus attains Dharammegh samadhi which follows the destruction of all the five agents of distractions, avidya, asmita, etc., the three types of good, bad and mixed actions along with their impressions. All limits end for the yogi and he becomes fully liberated. The ever-existent three gunas of Prakriti, which exist for the service and salvation of Purusha (Drashta), now beg leave of the illumined yogi. Thus, Kaivalya (alone like God) would mean attainment of bliss and eternity which for the human mind are mere dreams. At this pinnacle of attainment, the soul ascends to the spirit and chitta and its three gunas revert to the mool prakriti, their basic source.

HATHA YOGA

What a paradox. Lord Shiva, the creator of the science of Hatha Yoga, is the saviour of one and the destroyer of many! But this is no contradiction and points to the two different and distinct roles of Lord Shiva, who in one capacity is the destroyer of the world at the crucial juncture of cosmic dissolution (pralaya) and in other capacity is the saviour of the faithful follower who has mastered the science of Hatha Yoga. It is said that Lord Shiva created Hatha Yoga to empower its individual practitioners to acquire spiritual occult powers to defeat death in this life itself by mastering the Hatha Yoga techniques for attaining deathlessness. A perfect Hatha yogi, therefore, by mastering this occult art not only conquers death in one life but earns invulnerability even against the cosmic scourge of pralaya (the cycle of cosmic dissolution). To acquire such an advanced level of perfection, a Hatha yogi must master this occult art to such a pitch where he can move out of his physical body at will or dissolve it at his chosen time and place. Obviously, it needs no emphasis that to master Hatha Yoga, to attain that level of spiritual attainment, it must be an extremely challenging spiritual endeavour, which only a committed seeker may attempt successfully. No wonder, the two supreme sciences of Hatha Yoga and Raj Yoga are the divine gifts of Lord Shiva and God Vishnu respectively to mankind for their spiritual emancipation. Lord Shiva, therefore, in Shiva Samhita reveals, "The study of all shastras has convinced Me that no shastra is as important as Yoga-shastra." There are various categories of Yoga like Raj Yoga, Ashtang Yoga, Laya Yoga, Mantra Yoga, Bhakti Yoga, Gyana Yoga, Karma Yoga, etc. Most yogis class them into two categories: Hatha Yoga and Raj Yoga. Both these Yogas are interdependent and mutually supportive. Prana power (cosmic energy) is the prime basis of both Hatha Yoga and Raj Yoga. Yogis say that Prana is the vehicle of mind and is the basic energy which operates the human system, It is laid down in Yoga Vashishtha that experiences of the world, including its pains and pleasures, depend on the mind which is operated and can be controlled by Prana. Therefore, controlling the mind through Prana means to win the world. Prana is the basic power which controls and regulates the operations of our physical (sthula), astral (Sushmna), and causal (karana) bodies.

Hatha comprises two words: ha and tha; ha means the moon (Ida, the left nostril) and tha means the sun (Pingla, the right nostril) and they correspond to the breath flowing through the left and the right nostrils. Therefore, Hatha Yoga stands for the regulation of the breath for stopping the process of the modifications of the mind called chit-vriti-nirodha by Patanjali in the Yoga Sutra. The idea that Hatha Yoga is a dangerous practice is totally ill-founded and misconceived. On the contrary, it is the key to good health and cheerful longevity and, if perfected, even prepares a person to ward off the scourge of death. Hatha Yoga being the basic Yoga without which Raj Yoga cannot proceed purifies and transforms man's body, mind and moral nature. Hatha Yoga and Raj Yoga are supplementary to each other. Therefore, Yoga and Sankhya (Jnana Yoga) are not different but are identical as revealed by God in *The Bhagawad Gita*: "The ignorant think that Yoga and Sankhya are different and not the enlightened." Sage Vashishtha, the guru of Lord Rama says in Yoga Vashishtha: "O Rama! For controlling the mind only two ways exist: Yoga (action) and Jnana (knowledge). The former suppresses the mind and the latter sublimates it."

The Practice of Hatha Yoga

Those who practice Hatha Yoga should live alone in a small monastery (matha) located in peaceful surroundings. The matha must be clean, smeared with cow dung, should have only one door and no holes or windows. It should have a mandapa, water well and surrounded by a wall. Living in it a yogi, with carefree mind, should practice Yoga all the time ,as prescribed by the guru, by following the regimen of dos and don'ts which primarily include: commitment, firmness, fortitude, truth, faith, avoiding the company of unworthy people, avoiding over-eating, tiredness, over-talking, indiscipline, promiscuity and restlessness.

Strict observance of the ten niyamas and ten yamas which are more elaborately explained in Hatha Yoga than spelled out in Patanjali Yoga is strictly to be followed. Asana is the priority principle in Hatha Yoga and is its first stage. Asana makes a practitioner strong, firm, free, elastic, light and pure. They banish Rajo guna and Tamo guna elements from the system which cause disease, dullness and doubt.

Some of the important asana which are acknowledged by Yoga masters like Vashishtha, Matsyendra, etc. are described below. The four most important asana are: Siddha asana, Padma asana, Simha asana, and Bhadra asana.

Siddha asana: Pres the perineum with the base of the left heel and place the right foot firmly above the pubis. Keep the chin steady on the breast. Fixing the gaze in-between the eyebrows remain motionless, as long as possible – without strain. If performed regularly, it purifies the entire nervous system comprising 72000 nadis and makes a devotee after 12 years of correct practice, a perfect yogi.

Padma asana: Place the right foot on the left thigh and the left foot on the right thigh, cross the hands behind the back and hold the toes firmly. Place the chin on breast and fix the gaze at the tip of the nose.

There is another description of Padma asana. Place the feet on opposite thighs as explained above and place hands with palms upwards between the thighs. Direct the eyes on the tip of the nose and place the tongue at the root of the front teeth. The chin be placed on the chest, slowly raise the Prana upwards and contract the anus (rectum) at the Mooladhara. Padma asana destroys all diseases by raising inhaled Prana upwards and drawing Apana downwards to coccyx. It empowers a person to attain Kundalini shakti.

Simha azans: Place the ankles below the scrotum, on the either side of the perineum, the right ankle on the left side of it and the left ankle on the right side. The palms should be placed on the knees with the fingers spread out. With mouth open and mind concentrated, fix the gaze at the tip of the nose.

Bhadra asana: Place the ankles below the scrotum on the sides of the perineum, the left ankle on the left and the right ankle on the right side. Then firmly hold the feet with hands, which are on their sides and remain still. It is said that this asana destroys many diseases and is also called Gorak asana. Other useful asana are Kukut asana, Kurum asana, Matsyendra asana, Paschimatan asana, etc.

Kukut asana: Assuming the Padma asana posture, insert the hands between thighs and knees, rise in the air, supported by the hands.

Kurum asana: Assuming the Kukut asana position, put the arms round the neck, like a tortoise lie on the back.

Dhanur asana: Bend and clutch both toes, release one arm and raise it up to the ear in a posture while drawing a bow.

Matsyendra asana: Put the right foot at the base of the left thigh and the left foot outside the right knee and take hold of the right foot by the left hand and of the left foot by the right hand. Turn the body to the left. Its practice lifts the Kundalini shakti.

Pascimtan asana: Spread both legs, without bending firmly on ground. Clutch the toes of both feet and keep the forehead on the knees.

In the sequence of Hatha Yoga, after observing ten yamas and ten niyamas, asana are to be performed. Other important steps are Kumbhak and Mahamudra, followed by the Nada Kriya which means listening to the inner subtle sounds. The practitioner must take moderate diet (sattvik) and one-fourth of the stomach should be kept free. The food must be taken as an offering to Shiva. The beginners must avoid sex, long journeys and basking in the fire. Hard physical activity, early morning bathing and fasting are to be avoided. Nourishing diet like sweet, ghee and milk must be taken. The asana and diet regimen must be performed and observed strictly under the guidance of a guru.

Pranaayama and Kumbhak

In Hatha Yoga, Prana is prescribed as the remedy to purify and strengthen the nadis (nervous system) and to make the restless mind steady. To make the restless mind still and to control the senses, the use of moderate diet and use of Prana under the guidance of a guru, is necessary. The regular practice of Prana activates the middle nadi (Sushmna) which leads to the attainment of Unmani avashta (the state of spiritual poise). It is said that there is no asana like the Sidha, no Kumbhak like the Kewala, no Mudra like the Khechri and no Laya like the Nada. These four important Yoga features are explained below in their respective sections.

Pranaayama is to be performed as per the guru's teachings by assuming the Padma asana. The Prana should be drawn in through Ida (the left nostril) and after retaining it as long as possible, it should be exhaled through Pingla (the right nostril). Again draw in Prana through Pingla, retain as long as possible, and exhale through Ida. When Prana is drawn in by Ida, it must be exhaled by Pingla and vice versa (Prana is the life current and breath is its vehicle). The period of retention of Prana (breath) between inhaling and exhaling is called Kumbhak, which is very important to activate the Kundalini. Therefore, the duration of retention being a sensitive and strategic aspect of Pranaayama must be performed according to the guru's brief but never risking the discomfort. Not only the duration of retention (Kumbhak) is important but the frequency of Kumbhak is also important, which may go up to well beyond a hundred times daily. It is only through such strict discipline that the obstinate Prana can be tamed, which is said to be as hard to tame as a wild tiger. With the regular practice of Pranaayama and Kumbhak, the body becomes slim, emits glow, becomes disease free, the mind becomes pure and the nada (the inner peaceful sound) is heard.

Those who are flabby and phlegmatic should practice, before the practice of Pranaayama, the six following performances which also eliminate the wind, bile and phlegm from the system. These six practices are named Dhauti, Vasti, Neti, Trataka, Nauli and Kapalbhati.

Dhauti: According to the instructions of a guru, swallow a four-inch wide and 15 spans long piece of wet cloth and draw it out; do it again.

Vasti: Sit in water, navel deep. Rest on toes so that heels touch the buttocks, insert a small bamboo tune into the anus; contract the anus and draw in the water and then expel the water out. This washes the stomach.

Neti: Through the nasal passage, insert a clean and soft thread about 10 inches long and draw it out through the mouth.

Trataka: Look at a minute object with fixed eyes and with full concentration, till tears drop. It cures and improves the eye sight.

Nauli: Bend shoulders down and with the speed of fast

circling water or a hand-operated grinding mill, rotate the stomach to right and left.

Kapalbhati: This is performance of breath, inhaling and exhaling, very rapidly like bellows of blacksmith.

In Hatha Yoga the following eight Kumbhaks are prescribed.

Suryabedana: Assuming comfortable asana the yogi should slowly draw in the outside air through the right nadi (Pingla). Then he should practice Kumbhak (retaining the breath) to the utmost till it is felt (the breath) from the hair on head to the nails on toes; and then he should slowly exhale the air through the left nadi (Ida).

Ujjayi Kumbhak: Close the mouth and draw in air through both nostrils till the breath is felt to be sonorous from the throat to the heart. It can be practiced even walking and standing.

Sitali: Protrude the tongue a little outside the mouth and curl it (making a hollow) and inhale air through the tongue, and perform Kumbhak; then exhale and repeat. It will generate cool breath (while inhaling) and warm feeling (while exhaling) sensations.

Bhastrika Kumbhak: Assuming Padma asana keep the back upright, close the mouth and through nostrils throw out the breath with effort and gradual force till the breath resounds not only in heart and throat but also up to the skull. After this, air should be drawn in by rapidly inhaling till it touches the lotus of the heart. This process is to be repeated again and again rapidly and Prana must be flowing in and out through nostrils. This Prana must be performed under the guidance of a guru. Bhastrika Kumbhak helps in rousing the Kundalini.

Bhramari Kumbhak: Breathe in rapidly resembling the sound of a male bee after observing Kumbhak; exhale slowly making the humming sound of a female bee. This Kumbhak breeds the bliss feeling.

Murcha Kumbhak: After fully completing inhalation assuming Jalandhara bandh, exhale the breath slowly.

Plavini: Drawing in air to the full, completely filling the inside, the yogi, floats leisurely, even in deep waters, as if a lotus leaf.

Pranaayama is of three kinds (Purak, Recheka and Kumbhak) and Kumbhak is of two kinds (Sahita Kumbhak and Kevala Kumbhak).

Kevala Kumbhak: When breathing (inhalation and exhalation) is redundant or not necessary, it is called Kevalya Kumbhak. At this stage there is nothing unattainable in this world. The highest spiritual realization attainable through Raj Yoga (samadhi) dawns on the yogi. At this stage the identity between Hatha Yoga and Raj Yoga becomes indistinguishable. The body of a yogi becomes slim, face bright, eyes attain higher vision, disease disappears, and the yogi hears the nada (inner spiritual sounds).

Mudras

The regular practice of Mudras, which are ten in number, is very effective to awaken Kundalini (the goddess) which sleeps at the mouth of the Sushmna nadi, which is the Royal Road to Lord Shiva. The following are the ten Mudras:

Mahamudra, Mahabandha, Mahavedha, Khechri, Udiyana, Mulabandh, Jalandharabandh, Vipritakarni, Vajroli, and

Sakticalana. The mastery over these ten Mudras can conquer old age, time and death.

They were devised by Lord Shiva Himself to enable its faithful follower to attain eight sidhis and salvation.

Mahamudra: Pressing the perineum with the left heel and stretching out the right leg, touch and hold the toes with both hands firmly. Contact the throat (as in Jalandhara bandha) and hold the breath in the upper part, then slowly breathe out. Then it should be practiced on the right side. It should be performed in equal numbers on both sides and then ended. This Mahamudra should be kept secret. If devotionally done, it cures serious diseases and can vanquish five Kleshas and death. The five Kleshas are the same as mentioned by Patanjali in Yoga Sutra: Avidya, Asmita, Raga, Davesha, and Abhinivasha.

Mahabandha: Place the heel of the left foot on the perineum and place the right foot on the left thigh. Draw in the breath, press the chin gently on the breast (as in Jalandhara bandha), contract the anus (as in Mool bandha) and fix the mind on Sushmna. After retaining the breath as long as possible, exhale slowly. Then repeat on the right side.

Mahavedha: Assuming the posture of Maha bandha, draw in the breath with concentrated mind stopping the Prana movement (as in Jalandhara bandha). Place both palms firmly on ground; strike the ground slowly with buttocks. This unites the Moon (Ida), Sun (Pingla), and Fire (Sushmna) and opens the mouth of Sushmna, allowing the flow of Prana through it. Then exhale the breath.

Mahamudra, Mahabanda and Mahavedha are performed for best results together. There are said to be eight different ways to perform this joint practice under the guidance of a guru. Its mastery conquers both disease and death.

Khecheri: In Khechri Mudra, the tongue is rolled back to enable it to enter the hole in the throat, leading to the skull, and the gaze of eyes is fixed in-between the eye brows. In Khechri Mudra the tongue is subjected to special treatment and exercised to elongate it. The tongue is to be skilfully cut to a mere hair's breadth repeatedly with a special knife and is to be treated each time with the specially prescribed treatment. The tongue should be lengthened to touch the eye brows and is to be put through the cavity of the palate. He who knows Khechri,; there is no death for him and Karmas do not affect him. Mastering Khechri Mudra means complete control over life and death. That is why it is said in Hatha Yoga pradipika of Swatmarama that there is only one germ of evolution (Om); there is only one Mudra, Khechri; only one deity, not dependent on anything; and only one (spiritual) state, Mauonmani.

Uddiyana bandha: Uddiyana bandha when practiced, captures Prana and subjects its course through Sushmna, which activates Sushmna (the divine nadi). In this bandha, the stomach is completely drawn back below and above the navel, upwards the thorax.

Mula bandha: In this bandha, Prana vayu is drawn upwards by contracting the anus and by pressing the perineum with heel. This bandha reverses the natural downward flow of Apana by forcing its flow upwards through Sushmna. It is said that this bandha unites Prana and Apana with the nada and bindu and the yogi attains perfection (nada is the inner beautiful spiritual sound and bindu is the anuswara), the inaudible sound of the point in the sacred syllable 'Om' symbolizing the transcendent Shiva (Hatha Yoga pradipika of Swatmarama, Chapter three).

Jalandhara Bandha: In Jalandhara bandha, the throat is contracted and the chin is firmly held against the chest; this action contracts the Ida and Pingla nadis at the point of Visudha chakra and stops the downwards flow of the *Jala* (the spiritual liquid which flows through the cavity of the palate).

Viparitakarni bandha: This bandha stops the flow of the spiritual nectar emanating from the palate. It is said that the nectar that flows from the moon, the whole of that is swallowed by the sun and this is the cause of old age. Therefore, this bandha stops this process but its practice must be learnt from a guru because it involves the reversal of the roles of the moon and the sun.

"The Moon is situated at the root of the palate and pours down the nectar; the sun is situated near the naval and its fire consumes the ambrosial flow (Hatha Yoga pradipika of Swatmarama)."

Vajroli Mudra: It regulates the sexual activity by specializing in the skill of preserving semen by withdrawing it up internally through a tube inserted in the hole of male organ. The strategy and sanctity of this intricate practice is well described in the third chapter of Hatha Yoga pradipika of Swatmarama. Vajroli Mudra practice is prescribed both for male and female actors. It is said that Vajroli practice done for three hours daily can conquer death. In Vajroli Mudra the link between the preservation of semen, mind, longevity and deathlessness is well explained if performed as per the guru's brief.

Sahajoli and Amaroli Mudras are to be performed after sex activity for purification and treatment but it is said that it helps only the people who are virtuous and pure of the mind and remain always unaffected by envy. These three Mudras bestow the benefits of physical beauty, mental balance, attitudinal grace and spiritual emancipation. It is also said that Vajroli Mudra is a great spiritual performance and its physical aspect is a mere symbolism.

Satkticalana or Kundalini Mudra: The goddess (Kundalini) sleeps above the 'Kanda' (Kanda is the place between the navel and the scrotum from where spring the 72,000 nadis (Hatha Yoga pradipika of Swatmarama) and when awakened, it gifts enlightenment to the yogi. Kundalini, like a coiled-up serpent, closes the mouth of Sushmna which is the royal road to Lord Shiva. The sleeping Kundalini is to be awakened by following the process of paridhana, which only a guru can teach. It is to be performed by assuming the Vajrasana posture for a long time under the guidance of a guru and after the Kundalini is awakened, Bhastrika Kumbhak is to be performed. The performance of asana, Pranas, Kumbhaks and Mudras is the only way to awaken the pure goddess Kundalini and secure the release Sushmna from her grip which seals the mouth of Sushmna. Sushmna is the only yogic secret avenue to God.

SAMADHI

In Hatha Yoga pradipika of Swatmarama, samadhi is defined: *As salt in water merges and dissolves into it, a likewise of mind into self is samadhi.*

In Vedanta, samadhi is defined as the inseparable union of the soul and the spirit like the union of two waters (which cannot be separated).

In Hatha Yoga, Samadhi and Raj Yoga are synonymous and confer supreme bliss and destroy death. Samadhi can be attained only through the grace and compassion of a true guru by awakening Kundalini through the practices of asana, Prana, Kumbhaks and Mudras when the Prana flows through the Sushmna and the mind is absorbed in the void (*Brahmn*) who is beyond time, space and causation. Samadhi is not possible as long as Prana and mind are active. They can be rendered inactive only by awakening the sleeping Kundalini who closes the mouth of the Sushmna nadi. Of the 72,000 nerves of the body, only Sushmna is the chosen one of Shiva(Sambhavi Shakti); the rest of them, including Ida and Pingla, are not of great use for spiritual pursuit.

The purpose of Prana is to course the Prana through Sushmna; otherwise it becomes a mere physical exercise.

Prana and mind are inter-connected and mingled like milk and water and their operation is mutually inseparable. Only he, who suspends the breath at will, can control the mind at will and stilling the mind is the beginning of Samadhi. Therefore, the way to Samadhi is by stilling the mind which can be stilled by stilling the Prana and Prana can be stilled only by suspending the breath, which is possible through Prana, asana, Kumbhaks and Mudras. Now it is obvious that the secret to Samadhi is to control the breath because that alone can control Prana and still the mind.

That is why Lord Shiva tells Parvati, "Mercury and mind are unsteady by nature; if mercury and mind are bound nothing on earth remains unattainable. Mercury is made solid and inactive by the use of herbs and the Prana is made immobile, when absorbed in the Brahmarandhra by the use of Kumbhak."

Laya is the inner absorption which is caused by the nada

(inner blissful sound). It is nada which absorbs the mind. The mind is stilled by the still Prana and the Prana, in turn, is stilled by the suspension of breath. It is in this state that the indefinable bliss bursts, which is the state of spiritual emancipation. In this state of divine bliss, the body is motionless, there is no modification of the mind, no breath and no world of senses; such is the wondrous effect of Laya Samadhi.

Sambhvi Mudra: In Sambhvi Mudra, the yogi is deeply absorbed in the inner (spine) anahata chakra so completely that his mind is completely unaware of the senses and their objects. His pupils are still and cannot cognize the objects. It is the state of Samadhi in which the yogi feels, "I am *Brahmn*". The difference between Khechri Mudra and Sambhvi Mudra is that in the former the mind is fixed on the ajana chakra and in the latter on the anahta chakra. In both, the eyes remain half closed and fixed at the tip of the nose.

Khechri Mudra: In Khechri Mudra, the Prana flows through the Sushmna nadi and Ida and Pingla nadis stop working. Prana Shakti in Khechri Mudra is absorbed by Sushmna and its flow in Sushmna remains steady, keeping the yogi in a state of bliss.

Turya is the fourth state of consciousness, the other three being the waking, dream and the dreamless sleep. In this state of super-consciousness, there is no time (death). In fact, Khechri should be practiced to attain the Turya state because in this state of Khechri, Prana remains established in Brahmarandhra and the yogi gets completely absorbed in the *Brahmn*. The difference between the seeker and the sought vanishes.

The practice of nada and Laya: It is said that this great practice was taught by Gorakanatha and is suitable even to the unlettered. Lord Shiva is said to have expounded one crore and quarter ways to attain Laya Yoga but the devotion to nada is the most important of the Laya. To listen to the nada, the yogi should sit in Muktasna posture assuming the Sambhvi Mudra and with concentrated mind should concentrate on the inner sound heard in the right ear. The sound is of different kinds: buzzing of the bee swarm, flute-like sound, sound of bells, of ocean and the thunder. The eyes, ears, mouth and nose should be closed as in Pranamukti Mudra. Whatever is heard of the nature of mysterious nada is the shakti and in which all elements dissolve is Ishwara.

In all Yoga practices there are said to be four stages: Arambha, Ghata, Paricya and Nispati. During these practices, the above-mentioned sounds are heard in deep meditation.

In Hatha Yoga, the state of absorption generated by nada leads to the attainment of samadhi, which is the highest fruit of the effort of Hatha Yoga. It is called the Nispattaya avastha. In it, Rudra granthi in Ajna chakra is united and nada floods the being of the yogi who becomes blissful. This is the unrivalled reward of Raj Yoga (samadhi). Hatha Yoga teaches that pranayama controls the Prana and Pratyahara controls the mind which is followed by the eruption of nada. Meditation on nada must be performed daily. The mystic resonance of nada is deeply etherealizing. All practices of Hatha Yoga and Laya Yoga lead to Raj Yoga (Samadhi) in which all gunas are dissolved and the yogi is not affected by heat, cold, pain, pleasure, honour and dishonour. It is the supreme state of spiritual liberation. It may be mentioned that among other sources, I have found the study of "The Hath Yoga Pradipika" more useful both for knowledge and practice. For good results I recommend it to serious students of Hath Yoga.

YOGA AS A MEDIUM OF BALANCED EDUCATION

Education is the time-honoured source at human command to understand and unravel the mysteries of the universe and of life, by acquiring and disseminating knowledge through its various systems. Ofcourse there are many sources of knowledge and education but Yoga as a system of education is inherently different from all other systems. It is different because its source, nature, methodology and the purpose which the education of Yoga serves, are distinct from other fields of knowledge. We know that the source of conventional education is the human intellect and mind and reason are its main instrument whereas the source of Yoga as a system of education is the human soul and meditation, to attain intuition, is its prime medium. Similarly, the nature and methodology of Yoga system of education are different. It acquires knowledge from within by unlocking the mystical power of *Kundalini* (*Kundalini* is the secret source of cosmic energy-*Prana Shakti,* which is used to draw untapped energy from the spine and brain). The use of this power through *yogic Kriya*, on being taught by a Yoga master, can lead an ardent student to attain the supreme, secret and inexhaustible intuitive knowledge of Yoga.

But Yoga is not only intuitive knowledge, it is both intuitive and scientific. Because, without experience and experiment, Yoga accepts nothing. Which is why the theme of equanimity is essential to the preaching and practice of Yoga. It should be understood that the main feature of Yoga based education is to create the virtue of equanimity of the mind. Yogis believe that the equanimity of the mind is the prerequisite to perfection. It makes a person permanently objective and fair in outlook. The super structure of balanced education, which Yoga teaches is based on this foundation. The Yoga system of balanced education offers theory and action plan with a methodology to change the mindset and transform human values to generate a climate in which the virtues of selfless service, peace and love will thrive. Therefore, it is radically different from other theories of education and social approaches intended to improve social behaviour and human conduct. Yogic methods bring about systemic change in human outlook and behaviour by making the human mind a source of universal love and service.

In this esoteric pursuit human spine and brain are the fields to be cultivated through the medium of meditation to acquire the highest knowledge of intuition. To acquire this higher knowledge the spine and brain are as if to be reinvented through scientific Yoga techniques, exercises, intonations and renunciation. It is important to note that renunciation in Yoga means to renounce attachment but performance of detached actions is to be pursued vigorously. To allay misgivings it is necessary to mention that teachings of Yoga are easy to do, simple to understand, even though difficult to master, and take less time to be acquired unlike the general education which takes years to get even a degree. Yoga emphasises to build character and attain purity of body, senses and the mind. Purification of the system is the fundamental base of Yoga education because an impure mind is incapable of cognizing Yoga texts and the subtle effects of its spiritual progress. The process of purification is attained through specific asana; special Pranaayama system and proper observance of *yama* and *niyama* methodology.

Secondly, Yoga techniques emphasise on the need to build courage, endurance, patience and simplicity without which the qualities of selfless service and sacrifice cannot be cultivated; which are essential to generate the dynamics of peace and harmony, both at individual level and on the social plane in society at large. The ultimate purpose of Yoga education is to uplift the human mind into an instrument of love, i.e., the all-loving pure heart which will be a stepping stone to achieve soul contact; the acme of spiritual life. "In the spiritual life one becomes just like a little child- without resentment, without attachment, full of life and joy" — Sri Sri Paramahansa Yogananda, from the Spiritual Diary.

Yoga is an inclusive science and is in harmony with other forms of knowledge, be it the sciences, arts or technology, but it teaches what other branches of knowledge cannot and this exclusive field is the realm of spiritual super science. It is obvious that the knowledge which our educational institutions impart is incomplete because it mainly caters to the socio-economic sides of life whereas the spiritual dimensions of life remains ignored. We must learn that it is the spiritual knowledge acquired through Yoga texts and techniques which can promote peace and harmony in the world and unlock the vital force of love. In imparting knowledge, Yoga adopts a unique approach and a distinct methodology. Script and arithmetic are not its important media of instruction. Mind is not its main instrument to acquire or disseminate knowledge; in fact, ultimately Yoga system of education transcends the mind to ascend to the spiritual level. Through tried and tested occult and esoteric methods, Yoga uplifts the consciousness of a person to become the source of higher knowledge and virtues, to serve, educate and love others. Therefore, the prime purpose and focus of Yoga as a system of education is to uplift human consciousness to make it a source not only of moral and spiritual values but also the fount of human love and social harmony. To achieve this ideal Yoga uses a unique methodology.

Yogis know that the highest source of knowledge is the soul (human spirit). *'Aum'*- the vibratory power of creation called the pranava principle, flows from the soul. From Aum emenates the fifty letters of Devnagri script. The sound effect of these fifty alphabets is naturally transcribed on the fifty petals which exist in the six centers of the human spine. 4 petals in the coccyx, 6 petals in the sacral center, 10 petals in the lumbar center, 12 petals in the dorsal center, 16 petals in the cervical center and 2 petals in medulla (*Agya chakra*). These fifty petals (currents) and fity Devnagri alphabets are interrelated having common origin in the human brain. It is said that the Sanskrit language, which is said to be the language of devas, evolves from this combine. Yogis have esoteric techniques to tap astral spine centres and their petals to acquire the power of intuition. It is to be noted that only a Guru can teach the secret method to acquire the power of intuition from this esoteric pursuit. Yogis teach carefully the faculty of intuition through this methodology. The guru makes sure that thedeserving students should be chosen to learn the supreme knowledge of intuition knowing which a yogi becomes master and acquires unique, mundane and spiritual knowledge as is also mentioned in Patanjali Yoga Sutra— vibhuti pada. Yogis say that this proficiency takes long time and hard training. It comes with lot of patience and observance of purity. An impure heart can never master it. Intuition is the sixth sense, the only real omniscience in real sense of the term because it gifts a person with the power of omniscience to know what may happen anywhere. It is through this rarest of the rare knowledge that angels, saints and God know the things which are unknown to mortals. There are five forms of intuition; Anomaya, pranamaya, manomaya, gyana maya and anandmaya. After mastering these, the yogi becomes the spirit and is one with the supreme God.

We know that Yoga is neither a new concept nor yet popular with the academic world. It is old, rather ancient, but its uniqueness as a medium of higher education lies in its basic nature to remain ever new, to impart the highest and the best knowledge to genuine seekers, because it expands the consciousness to the widest horizons where pure love abounds. To deliver these basic qualities, yogis feel that the human mind and reason that are the main instruments of modern education, cannot go far enough, as is evident from the lack of these qualities in the prevailing system of education, and the same is reflected in deteriorating human behaviour and erosion of the value system. This deterioration is pervasive and is causing ethical decline of the modern generation. The existing system of education has not adequately addressed itself to the moral and spiritual dimensions of human life. It has therefore failed to uplift human consciousness above body consciousness and an average person remains hypnotized by his/her physical interests. A person wastes his/her precious life mainly in improving and fulfilling ones bodily concerns. Man remains self-centred and unconcerned with what is happening next door and in the society at large. Basic values of love and service towards others to alleviate their sufferings rarely attract their attention.

The quality of Yoga-based education lies in its priority to generate and inculcate in its students, through well-prescribed lessons and methods of special meditation, a sense of deep responsibility towards others. The prime concern of the basic Yoga instructions and training is to serve and love others. It is carefully taught that when moral and spiritual services are rendered to others with love, the good effects of such services flow back as if unsought to the performers of such selfless services. These basic qualities cannot be ingrained in the behaviour of students by the existing teaching methods, because the existing system of education mainly concentrates on the mental faculties of students and has no syllabus to teach the spiritual basics which promote values of love and sense of sacrifice. A Yoga-based system of education, having identified inadequacy of the mind to cope with this challenge, therefore uses intuition as the main medium of instruction. This highest knowledge is acquired by targeting the spine and brain. Six centers of the spine and brain which are the source of life and consciousness are scientifically harnessed to yield the supreme and secret knowledge of intuition. As already mentioned, intuition can be developed and acquired by special methods and practices by targeting the spine and brain. It is to be noted that the six centres of spine and brain are the source of life and consciousness, which when scientifically harnessed can reveal the true knowledge of intuition. Intuition, due to its enlightening effect, promotes virtues and eliminates the vices of greed and selfishness. Slowly it makes a person creative, innovative, self-reliant and an ever-willing agent of love and service to all.

The fundamental base and medium of instructions of Yoga-based education is the traditional, divinely inspired, eight-fold path of Raj Yoga (Royal Yoga), which is suitably amended by great Yoga masters to suit the changing cycles of different ages. Therefore, for our modern age, Kriya Yoga is the best dispensation to spiritually liberate mankind from ignorance. It could not have been without a divine design that the venerable Maha Avatar Babaji, introduced this great knowledge to the world in the 18th century.

The main thrust of Yoga-based education is to improve character and change the mindset of an individual to transform his social behaviour thereby making him love and service orientated towards others. Its focus is on inculcating such moral and spiritual values, which transcend the narrow self-centered life approach. For this, a distinct mental field is to be prepared. To achieve this fundamental task, the methodology of Yoga uses the powers of energy (Prana-shakti) and consciousness directly, by harnessing them through Yoga practices and techniques suitably designed to serve this end. One of the important techniques to regulate and control the power of Prana and consciousness is a spiritual method in which a particular form of Pranaayama and pratyahara methods are used to reverse the natural role of energy and consciousness. The natural role of energy and consciousness is to externalize the human mind by permanently connecting it to senses, which in turn bind it permanently to the outer world of sense objects. Yogis, through a masterstroke (a secret technique), delink the senses from their objects, and reverse the flow of energy and consciousness inwards. This theme along with its varied aspects is developed and discussed in the following pages, particularly in the chapter on Kriya Yoga which for the modern time forms the anchor sheet of Yoga-based system of education. If carefully developed and intelligently pursued Yoga knowledge can be a great source of creative and innovative knowledge.

It is important to mention that to impart quality education to the students of modern age who face grave challenges on various fronts, Yogabased education is an ideal amalgam of the oldest and the latest knowledge that human endeavour can achieve. It is said to be an infallible and interesting learning adventure by pursuing the journey of yoga, to move beyond the ultimate potentials of the mind and to see what lies beyond the mind. Yogis know that the real knowledge lies beyond the mind which is to be accessed through a different research method, based on a distinct experiment. It turns the mind into a lab to intuitively verify its experiences. On knowing its limits, the mind is transcended to ascend to the higher realms of knowledge; which means not only to know the mundane and relative truths but also to venture into the imminent, transcendental and the absolute. However, before describing the nature, feasibility and scope of Yoga-based system of education for proper understanding, it is necessary to examine at length the different aspects of the prevailing system of education, which has helped mankind to evolve despite dangers and darkness through the ages.

The modern system of education which is widely followed for learning and teaching has benefited students to acquire knowledge and information to develop the mind and build character. Broadly speaking, in most countries the modern system of education centers around the proverbial axis of three Rs – reading, (w)riting and (a)rithmetic to impart knowledge at three levels; primary, secondary and higher. However, in advanced countries, the purpose and ideals of education have improved and it is being used to acquire knowledge and technology to improve governance, standard of living and boost creativity. Therefore, the emphasis is on producing through education, good citizens and creative men. A good citizen from the perspective of establishment is one who obeys the laws of the land, made to maintain public order and to promote prosperity. However, the nature of a creative person is different. His conduct is rooted in wider awareness and moral principles. He likes to obey the laws of the land but such laws should promote freedom and general welfare. Violation of this principle evokes a strong reaction from such a person who struggles to set things in order. Such a person does not sit quiet even if he is not personally affected, because he knows that bad laws and bad implementation degrade individuals and societies, which result in degeneration of values. Degraded values contaminate cultures and civilizations and societies lose direction. Therefore, the main purpose of education is to create creative people to promote basic human values that are the essence and substance, which breed creative cultures to produce good and great people. But the existing system of education has not been able to respond to this prime responsibility.

Now the question is how can values be promoted? The answer to this is 'Education.' Here we may note that education is not only learnt and imparted in schools, colleges and universities, though these are the time-honoured centers of learning to educate humanity. There are other subsidiary centers, which are key performers in teaching values. Parents, social groups, public environment, the company a student moves in and above all the role of media and the combination of indoor and outdoor pursuits and curriculum, all contribute to educate an individual.

Against this background we may reflect that how our modern education system is performing. If we first talk of the west, the education system that they are following looks good. It has provided employment, security, prosperity, means of entertainment and knowledge. It may not be flawless but that aspect I will touch later. In comparison, the condition of education system in our country leaves a lot to be aspired. Quantitatively we are far behind and qualitatively the condition is no better. Despite explicit directions of the Constitution, the field of education has been denied its due. The teaching communities at lower levels are irresponsible and its higher level suffers from low self-esteem syndrome. It is the taught who are on the receiving end. Efforts are afoot to improve the situation but there is dire need to reconstruct the system. Ethics, science and technology need priority and attention and there is need for genuine teachers with passion for teaching. It is tragic that we could not improve this paramount resource, which would have revolutionized our individual and social lives. The reason why education has done wonders in the west is mainly due to the fact that it has evolved from their socio-cultural milieu. Their native needs, native languages and encouraged flair for research have resulted in this creative wonderment. They have learnt that education is the best means to improve life in all respects and is a life-long pursuit because learning and teaching are a never-ending process.

However, this does not mean that western system of education is flawless. Here we may recall our description of a creative man. A creative man's forte, apart from intellectual and moral qualities, is his spiritual spark. In this regard even western democratic countries have not done their best to serve this ideal. Admitting that it is difficult to tackle the spiritual dimension but appreciating its key role in human development, it deserves proper response from state and social elites because the purpose of good education is to draw out the best from the student. Examination of western system of education shows that its secular stance has resulted in sheer neglect of the spiritual dimension of human knowledge. We should know that beside intellectual and moral qualities of good citizens and creative men, there is the higher power of spirituality which forms the core and climax of the process of human evolution. Such a spiritual master is whom the Hindus call a 'yogi'.

Therefore, the real purpose of education in the modern world which stands threatened by grave dangers is to promote, apart from science and I.T., cultural, moral and spiritual dimensions. To achieve palpable results in these areas, revolutionary steps are required by all organizations operating the education system.

Because the need is to produce higher knowledge and spiritual quest. Unfortunately, the prevailing education system and its operators appear unaware of the magical effect of yoga power to generate spiritual consciousness. Talking of our country, where squalor and hunger are major concerns and greed and corruption are assuming dangerous proportions, it is of utmost importance that a revolutionary education policy is framed to serve both, the alleviation of poverty and inculcation of moral and spiritual values. In the modern world, there is pressing need to develop both the basic faculties of human nature; scientific outlook and spiritual quest. Therefore, we need a discipline which will address both. Though it may appear paradoxical that metaphysical science of Yoga-based system of education may produce scientists but it is a tried reality that Yoga system can produce highly creative individuals, who can well serve both mundane and spiritual planes. The purpose of this endeavour is to discover the source from where science and spirituality both emanate and that source lies in the Self which can be reached by Yoga practices. Therefore, Yoga is a panacea to promote science and spirituality to ensure balanced growth both at individual and social levels. Ofcourse, the problem of poverty being a priority concern and a major challenge, it can be tackled by proper planning and technological programmes and projects.

Besides generating a deep desire to serve others and love all, another distinct and useful feature of Yoga system of education is that in its curriculum, medical and health care systems are fully integrated. Through scientific methods and exercises it caters to keep the body fit, healthy and agile to the optimum level. It offers comprehensive and compact medical teaching and training programmes with emphasis on making the body strong and the mind pure. It minutely caters to basic bodily requirements, mental conditions and spiritual profiles to train and transform these parts of the human system to imbibe the subtleties of Yoga. The prime concern of Yoga training and education is to purify the body and mind. Without full purity, success in Yoga remains a dream. Therefore, it can be assumed that besides ethical and spiritual aspects, Yoga students and scholars are also a proficient practitioner of health concerns, as far as medication and treatment according to Yoga system are concerned.

Yogis declare and its beneficiaries acknowledge that Yoga as medical science is a great healer. It caters to treat and cure all the three dimensions of human life; physical, psychological and spiritual. Some of the incurable diseases like AIDS and some cancers if detected early are also claimed to be curable by Yoga methods. It is said that some of the Pranayam, used in Kriya Yoga, make the body's defence system so strong that such diseases cannot affect the system. There are some Pranayams which make nervous system and cardio-vascular-systems so strong that many diseases cannot attack the vital organs.

It is important to note that mind is the main subject and object of Yoga education. To train, culture, control and transcend the mind is the crux of Yoga teaching and training. Yogis know that mind is the door through which most of the physical and psychological diseases enter the human system. Therefore yogis seal this entry point through special yogic affirmations, intonations, preventive practices and exercises.

Yogis know that soul is always pure and no disease can ever touch it. The only challenge which the soul faces is that of delusion caused by Maya (cosmic delusion). In fact, on entering human body at the time of conception the pure soul becomes jiva. It is the jiva who is the permanent victim of Maya, which is a formidable power and a kind of permanent affliction that nobody can escape. No power can ever defeat Maya and its writ runs over earth, heaven and nether land, as is mentioned in *The Bhagawad Gita* 7-14. Men, devas and angels, all are its victims. Maya is the cosmic delusion which projects the real as unreal and the unreal as real. Therefore, every person life after life remains in the dark about reality and is permanently deluded about the truth. Thus, basically it is Maya which is the real cause of peoples' physical and psychological ailments. Once Maya has been defeated, a person rises above the body-mind consciousness and all diseases vanish because then the person attains spiritual consciousness, which is a disease-free state. Yoga is the only weapon which if deftly used is sure to defeat Maya and liberate man from its slavery.

The uniqueness about Yoga education is that it is the only knowledge system which specializes in the art to withdraw consciousness from senses and directs it to activate the spiritual centers in the spine and the Kutastha (the spiritual centre in between the eye brows and the brain). These features exist inside the astral body and can be accessed through deep meditation accompanied by deep devotion (shraddha). Yoga education, which leads a yogi to this great spiritual discovery, can be achieved through the intense pursuit of self-purification by following the systematic esoteric course of interiorization, which manifests the astral body, in which exist the seven spiritual astral centers and spiritual astral light of the Kutastha which revolutionizes the personality of an individual by opening his/

her spiritual dimension which is the only panacea to solve our problems, pains and challenges and attain full liberation.

Therefore, there is a pressing need to introduce Yoga system of education because the challenges confronting of the modern world are too deep and diverse to be answered by science alone. Countries highly developed in science are experiencing that science and technology, which have done a lot to revolutionize their lives have created some of the worst dangers also, which have become their nightmares. Therefore, science and technology are a mixed blessing. We need an education system which will produce balanced culture which can be produced by balanced individuals, therefore we need an educational system capable of producing balanced individuals to create balanced societies. Now let us examine how far the western education system has produced a balanced outlook and in turn balanced societies.

The basis of a balanced society or a state is that it provides security and prosperity on the one hand and peace and harmony on the other, both at intra and interstate and society levels. Looking at the conditions around and the mounting challenges, which the world is facing, the answer is obvious that the western education partly fulfils the first test but not the second, therefore it is an incomplete system of education. Now let us take up a preposition whether there is any education system, which can fulfil both the above-mentioned pressing needs of the contemporary world? Yoga texts and yogis say that if science and spirituality, as is taught in Yoga, are made the basis of a new system of education, the world can enjoy and experience both prosperity and peace in an ample measure. The reason that yogis and spiritualists advance in support of their contention is that the modern education system based on the western system is lopsided. It does not include Yoga and spirituality as important subjects in its curriculum. It has not realized that spiritual education is a key component to impart universal values to create a balanced mind. On the other hand, yogis claim that Yoga syllabus is essentially designed to create a balanced mind to cater to three levels of human personality; the physical, psychological and the spiritual. A beginning in this important and sensitive adventure is made through well tested training methodology based on eight-fold path of Raj Yoga and Kriya Yoga with special emphasis on yama, niyama principles, Pranaayama/pratyahara system of meditation and concentration techniques to effect improvement in an individual mindset, through a special training course to improve his/her physical, psychological and spiritual dimensions. Secondly, it lays emphasis on creating group consciousness through special training courses to serve others and thirdly, to develop universal understanding by teaching that humanity is one race, has one source, have common needs, common goals and common destiny to be realized through spiritual methods.

Before embarking upon the elaboration of Yoga and spiritual system of education it is necessary to identify some of the constraints in the modern system of education and see what options and improvements yoga offers. The test of the quality of education is reflected in the knowledge and happiness of an individual and the society at large. We know that happiness of an individual depends on his health, income, knowledge and moral, social and spiritual values. Similarly, the harmony level of a society too depends on the attainment of these basics by more people of a given society.

Now let us examine as to how much useful the role of education has been through the centuries to develop and improve individuals and societies in respect of their prosperity, security, knowledge, happiness and social harmony? During the last two thousand years, the record of our journey on earth has been a mixed adventure, showing areas of sensational progress and depressing failures. Our health has improved and our knowledge increased, recording quantum leaps in several fields. On the other hand, security, happiness and harmony are the segments where human performance has remained quite dismal. The knowledge acquired through education of science and technology has progressively added to the prosperity of mankind, and of late has even created material bonanza for the so-called advanced countries of our world. The material prosperity has been acquired through landmark discoveries, revolutionary inventions and feats of management, but these achievements have been used for aggrandizement, acquisition, territorial conquests through aggression and exploitation by trade cartels and industrial monopolies. The march of civilization throughout has largely been characterized by display of aggression by man to exploit and subjugate external nature and co-human beings. From Alexander the Great up to the 18th century, our annals are full of the exploits of kings and generals with scant concern for the common man. Then started the age of wars for territorial conquests, followed by wars for political creeds and ideologies, succeeded by cold wars and then followed by star wars between global power blocks. Now the orgy of human violence has shifted from international wars to intra-nation and international terrorism. The dangers of nuclear weapons and global warming have become worrying concerns, which are defying solutions. Through the ages, even religion has been exploited to fulfil atrocious barbaric ends.

The moral of the story is that the system of education that the world has been following has proved deficient to ensure balanced growth of human individuals and societies. Even a cursory view of human history through various ages reveals that the phases of creativity, virtue, compassion, peace and harmony have been occasional events in the common drama of savagery, violence, war, frenzies of hate and attrition caused by selfishness and greed. Unfortunately, greed has been a constant factor drying up the vestige of virtue from human heart and filling it with vices to make man impervious to the cause of common good. It can be summed up as a saga of neglect of core values.

Knowledge explosion, which is the biggest achievement of modern education, apart from expanding human vision and depth of understanding has generated a surfeit of goods and services, but this bonanza has been arbitrarily exploited to their benefit by the power lobbies. Science and technology, the main vehicles of modern education ,if fairly pursued, could transform our planet into a paradise on earth, but the fangs of human malice and meanness are un-relented and there is no decency around to hone these edges. It is the vice of greed, which is calling the shots. Since a few centuries in the past, the virus of greed is threatening to become an epidemic. Its tide in our country is submerging the very traces of integrity as is well reflected in the behaviour of power circles. Even globally, the major cause of current global recession caused by the sub-prime factor, which is threatening to swamp the world economy, is a dangerous consequence of the poison of greed and selfishness.

All over the world, greed for money and more money for the sake of power and pride has doomed many families and institutions. Like a social cancer, human greed has devalued social ethics and ruined moral standards threatening collapse of economic stability and social security. Black money, illegal trades, tax evasion and the boom of tax havens are prospering due to the evil of greed. The global scenario is becoming grimmer as if iron is entering the human soul. Explosion of drug trafficking, smuggling and economic crimes are breeding an unholy global fraternity of white colour criminals, which is targeting the youth of the world. It seems as if the menace of greed is spreading like wild fire and has captured the core of human heart. Little wonder the scriptures say that greed is the seed of the ruin of man. Among the six proverbial inner enemies of man; lust, anger, attachment, greed, ego and fear, at the present juncture of human history, greed has assumed dangerous proportions. If remedial measures are not adopted this lapse can dampen our aspirations to work for a better socio-economic new world order.

We must remember that education system bereft of its spiritual strand and deficient in moral content cannot boost the strength of character and develop new outlook in peoples' minds to produce balanced people and societies. Therefore, there is a need to overhaul the modern education to root it in morality and feed it with spiritual élan. Yoga and spirituality are the founts, which will unleash new dynamism to promote harmony and peace. Spiritual sciences like Yoga based on tested experience have the techniques to root out from human mind, the seeds of such vices as greed, hatred, ethnicity, violence and vengeance instinct. Nobody can deny that terrorism, global warming, nuclear arsenals, star-wars and militarization of the world are consequences of the short-comings in the system of our education which has been promoting aggressive patriotism and unethical aspirations of different ethnicities and nations blinded by ignorance, selfishness, greed and antagonism. Introduction of a revamped system of education aiming to develop ethics and spirituality based on Yoga methods and techniques, which change psychological and physiological nature of human mind, is the need of the hour.

Well meaning people around the world are awakening to the fact that an economically inter-dependent and technologically advanced and united world but culturally and ideologically divided, is a bad omen. To progress peacefully in the modern world which has become a globalized society we urgently need a new system of education; a system which will spiritually and scientifically teach that all human beings are one race and there is only one source from where all have evolved. Colour, castes, ethnicity and religious divisiveness are false notions fed on prejudices. Human beings share common genes and common destiny. Political ideologies are passing phases and freedom is the only ideology to be lived for and protected. True meaning of globalization is to believe that entire world is our country and our home, which we must learn to preserve and promote.

Nevertheless, despite being aware that our freedom and aspirations are under threat (from without and within) our responses are slow and inadequate. There is a need to change the traditional mindset to evolve new values and beliefs to introduce change in our aspirations, sentiments, emotions and feelings. For centuries people in different societies and different lands have been taught different beliefs and ideologies, which have been deeply rooted in their egocentricity and have hardened their prejudices. To uproot people from their rigid mindset is a herculean task. It is worse than calling an angry liar a liar, in a bid to make him agree with his rational opponent. Fortunately, with the growth of knowledge and development new vistas are opening on the horizons of human experience. With the evolution of science and technology, ground realities have improved. This has happened, as yogis say, due to the advancing process of evolution as is described in one of the chapters of this book.

Now many people have started realizing that in the wake of prevailing global challenges, unless we learn the art of co-existence and plan for it, we may perish. To change this necessity into reality there is aneed to find institutions manned by eminent people to teach and train at least a few selected women and men to usher in new movement to change human thinking to suit the changed dynamics of the new world order. The existing education system despite the ideals of philosophy, religions, literature, art and science has not succeeded in preventing antagonistic nationalism, divisive ideologies, religious fanaticism, terrorism, and wars fuelled by ignorance, greed and selfishness.

Obviously, there is an urgent need to evolve and recast the new education system aimed at evolving a new global mind set. However we know that changing human thinking and introducing the new mind-set through the existing system of education is an extremely arduous and time consuming process. However, yogis declare that they have a method, which is effective and time-saving in producing the desired results. Their approach is based on scientific and spiritual methods which plant within an individual, a deep sense of love, service and sacrifice for others. This is the basic theme of their education because the yogis know through experience that the real purpose of education is to bring about inner perfection in a person. Unless man is changed from within, his mind cannot change. For this, yogis pick up a few selected individuals for training who will work as dynamos of change to fan the theme of this new education based on scientific spirituality.

It has been said in the beginning that Yoga as a means of education and as a source of highest knowledge is unique. Dealing with the mind as mentioned earlier, is the speciality of Yoga because it trains the mind primarily for spiritual benefits. Its precise techniques culture, train, control and then transcend the mind. Originally, mind's domain is the phenomenon world. Practically everything in this world has been created by man with the mind power, of which great discoveries and inventions are a proof. However, spiritual plane is an unknown realm which human mind cannot handle. It is said to be an ecstatic enigma full of bliss. In this field, human mind is not only like a stranger in a foreign land, unaware of its language, but even runs counter to the magnetic love field of the cosmic spirit. Therefore, for spiritual gains, mind is to be controlled and cultured because the uncontrolled mind is an obstruction to access the subtle spiritual realm. It learns little beyond the mundane events of birth, growth and death. Upanishads say that to cleanse the mind it is to be drowned in the depth of deep meditation so that 'the consumer is consumed in the process of consumption' otherwise, it is very difficult to control and transcend the ever obstinate mind. No wonder, Arjuna expressing his helplessness, tells Lord Krishna in *The Bhagawad Gita* that controlling the mind is as difficult as controlling the wind (breath), but God offers the remedy in *The Bhagawad Gita* verse 6/34-35, where it is said that mind can be controlled through practice and renunciation. God being the creator of this powerful mind also knows the method to humble it. God, therefore, has Himself preached in *The Bhagawad Gita* 3/42-43 that mind must be controlled through intelligence to reap spiritual gains. To illustrate this theme God further explains the use of right Yoga methods and the subtle art of renunciation to achieve spiritual realization. Therefore a yogi knows that the new education based on esoteric practices and scientific renunciation are the effective means to train and transcend the mind, but such Yoga practices and renunciation required to control and transcend the mind are challenging endeavours. There are special Yoga practices, which are an ideal mixture of will, energy and consciousness. These practices and exercises first store in and then transmit the cosmic energy from the brain through the Yoga techniques and will power to charge and rejuvenate different cells, tissues and nerves in the body, not only to decarbonize and oxygenize them but enliven them with the fresh inputs of life force. A God realized guru gifts these exercises to his disciples, which help to control the mind along with the practice of renunciation, but the guru bestows these rare gifts when he satisfies himself of the sincerity and dedication of the seeker to master the art of Yoga-based education. The guru intuitively knows the potentials of his disciple for love, service and faith in God, as an ordinary person cannot transcend the ego and commit himself to the cause of unconditional service to God and humanity. Similarly, the standard of renunciation required to become a yogi is of a high order. True renunciation is possible after conquering the six inner enemies of man, i.e., carnal desire, anger, attachment, greed, ego and fear. However, renunciation of a yogi never means non-performance of action. On the contrary, to attain purity, a Yoga disciple must perform all duties with full vigour and dedication but with no trace of selfishness or motive. Non-performance of action is the antithesis of yogic renunciation. Perfection in renunciation is acquired through performance of action with detachment, which is the real acid test. As laid down in *The Bhagawad Gita* 2/47, 2/48, 3/9, 3/19, 4/18 - The crux is that renunciation attained through action is the real yogic achievement because it is only pure action, which exhausts the stock of sanchit karma, which binds a person to the world. This great achievement can be mastered by following the eight steps of ashtang Yoga as updated for the modern age by Kriya Yoga techniques that Sri Sri Paramahansa Yogananda has gifted to the world. These spiritual techniques are advanced yogic methods to channelize energy and consciousness, to control and transcend the mind and to lift consciousness to the super conscious level. In fact, this esoteric method of Yoga is for a few selected individuals. Different Yoga schools prescribe useful and practical methods for higher Yoga attainments. These methods and techniques within permissible limits have been discussed in different chapters.

In the wake of the prevailing surcharged scenario, our concern is twofold to bailout the present and guide the future. Therefore, our priority is to spell out briefly the ways and means to transform modern education and to introduce new Yoga knowledge basics to serve the changed scenario of the prospective world order to ensure a conducive atmosphere for the global society to prosper peacefully. The challenges facing the world being grave and the time being short; therefore, half-hearted measures cannot work. Therefore, an all out endeavour is the need of the hour to ward off the challenges. In the presence of various challenges staring at the world in the face, this new education system based on Yoga techniques and methods, deserves a chance. Yoga teachings are basically different, as they target the mind internally. Books, tutorials, lecturing and discussion are useful but only as a subsidiary.

To secure the future and protect new generations of our children, we must introduce with proper planning, scientific Yoga lessons of education to develop love and people friendly feeling tempered by the desire to serve. It has already been said that Yoga is a science rather a higher science because it deals with life, consciousness and the super-consciousness, unlike the natural and conventional sciences, which deal only with energy and matter. Therefore, its approach and methods are different. The approach of natural sciences, broadly speaking, is based on observation, prediction and experiment or the use of inductive and deductive methods. But Yoga science as it is intended to be taught by modern enlightened yogis to attract and benefit more people is based on two streams of knowledge. One is conventional knowledge and the other is intuitive knowledge. In the modern world, conventional knowledge, which is based on the study of arts, sciences and technology, is important even for yogis because it provides the understanding of the conditions of life in the everyday material world. With this understanding, a yogi can have a common base with common people to understand their daily problems. Therefore, due to interaction on this plane he can command better respect and following among people. This approach will also correct the impression about yogis that they are not interested in ordinary day-to-day life of people, which in fact they are not, but for this there is different reason. It is the reason of inner renunciation, which yogis practice for joy and spiritual progress. Therefore, they are not interested in the things of the world but they are interested in the worldly things for the benefit of others, because they know that Yoga, being a progressive discipline moves gradually.

The intuitive aspect of Yoga knowledge is a gradual process. First, it is to train beginners to slowly detach not from possessions but from greed and selfishness by inculcating the values of sharing and service. Slowly Yoga moves up to train and discipline the mind through special techniques and practices. It is towards the end that a student is initiated into the spiritual aspect of intuitive meditation and higher Yoga techniques.

Being a tried and well-experienced science, it can be learnt even by a non-believer. Therefore, people of different religions may show less resistance to accept Yoga science as a mean to improve their life. Once the good results have surfaced, Yoga education can spread. As already said Yoga is the quickest and the most effective method to change people from inside and save them from false pride and prejudices, and equip them with a sense of deep love for all. Consequently, it develops cosmopolitan outlook, which breaks many barriers and brings people together.

To have satisfactory results of this method of education it is necessary to start it with young children – as it is proverbially said, "Catch them young". It will attract children because Yoga has its distinct aura to attract the youth; it combines physical, recreational and spiritual aspects. This combination of teaching is displayed with demonstrations and personal involvement. In various school functions the most often quoted advice in the speeches delivered is, "the main purpose of education is to draw out the best from within the students." However, hardly anybody spells out and identifies what is this best, which is to be drawn out. Only a few know that the only hidden power present in all and which must to be drawn out and manifested is the self – the unmanifest soul. It is the soul manifestation which has the power to transform a person, though slowly but certainly, into a genius or at least a disciplined person equipped with higher values rooted in ethics and spirituality which enable a person to serve and love all. This transformation can be accomplished by Yoga-based education, which has ready techniques and methods to impart to the serious students. Once serious students have attained the benefits, others will follow suit because moral and spiritual ways produce values, which generate spontaneous following unlike other text-based studies, which largely produce lopsided introverts.

The core of Yoga education is meditation and development of intuition. Meditation is concentrating the mind on God, the cosmic spirit, which is present inside all of us as soul and it involves no religious rituals. Mind also can be concentrated on any non-religious fixed point. Intuition means direct and correct knowledge of the natural and supernatural facts and forces, which human intelligence, mind and senses as already discussed cannot discern. Yoga meditation is a scientific discipline. Raj Yoga and Kriya Yoga systems of meditation involve eight-fold steps. Yama, niyama, asana, Pranayama, pratyahara, dharna, dhyana (meditation) and samadhi. Dhyana (meditation) occupies the 6th position in Yoga practice. This means that for spiritual benefits the preceding five Yoga stages must be mastered before real meditation is started. How Yoga meditation is to be started and accomplished has been discussed in a separate chapter. The point to be remembered here is that after success has been achieved in meditation, it uplifts the consciousness. The person transcends mind consciousness and attains the spiritual consciousness which of course is a time consuming process involving strenuous effort.

These two levels are poles apart. Mind consciousness is what we all have from a manual worker up to a scientist, diplomats or even a poet; of course, difference in degrees between each class and individual is natural due to karma theory and the vast spectrum of mind and intelligence. But the super-conscious is basically totally different. There man does not use senses, mind or intelligence to know what he – she wants to know. The yogi knows everything through intuition. An intuitive person ascends to a higher plane. Mundane beauty, pleasures, positions and fortunes appear superfluities. Such a person lives on the astral plane where service, sacrifice and love are his natural pursuits and passions. Obviously, attainment of the super-conscious is for very few dedicated souls. Even other serious and committed people, on being inspired by spiritual leaders, will contribute to promote the cause of Yoga-based education, which aims at heralding a new peaceful global order.

New world order cannot grow only on suitably changed economic, political and military institutions. These areas to some extent have already started changing in the right direction conducive to the evolution of new global needs and aspirations. Leaders of economic and political organizations, media and academia are well aware of the inevitability of the evolution of a global order and also of the hurdles confronting the growth of this evolution. However, our need is to produce leaders who will lead from the shoulder with spiritual force. Yoga is a new type of education, which teaches the techniques to lead with the power of service and sacrifice. The nature of this education has been explained in the chapters on 'What is Yoga' and 'Why Yoga Education'. Here it may be briefly re-emphasized that Yoga teaches a student through meditation and concentration techniques which are mentioned in Yoga texts, *The Bhagawad Gita* and The Upanishads but these techniques are to be learnt from a master yogi. These techniques help a student to go deep into meditation to the base of consciousness where senses, mind and intelligence appear mere objects different from the observing faculty. Then a yogi realizes that he is not the senses, not the mind and not the body. Going still deeper, he sees the Self – the same soul in all. This spiritual marvel, it is said, unfolds a sea of ecstatic experiences before which the heavens may appear husks. This being the source of highest knowledge is the only source of highest value, which must be cultivated to avoid violence and tragedies and to experience love.

The basic thing to be realized is that a new world order apart from other factors needs for its solid foundation, a set of new values rooted in ethics and spirituality. Here we are to note that spirituality is the core and crux of Yoga. Yoga is not a rigid organization like religion with its rituals, beliefs and authority. It is an individual pursuit for getting connected with the spirit (soul) because according to Yoga, human nature is already a reflection of the divine within, therefore, it is a matter of identification rather than an effort to acquire it. The priority to access the soul is to purify the mind from the debris of ethnicity, pride and prejudice and from the craze for power and position. It is only the purity of human minds which can generate the new consciousness to struggle to provide equality and freedom for all. Yoga therefore emphasizes the creation of a new vision grounded in spirituality and re-enforced by morality. Yogic spirituality is a syncretism of the secular and sacred yet ensuring that secular is to serve the sacred i.e. the spirituality because spirit is always superior to the mind. Yoga can generate the basic network of new values enshrined in universal love, universal service and spirit of sacrifice. How Yoga can generate, propagate and activate such a shift in consciousness, to some extent has been hinted in the above lines but more is explained in the following pages.

To some readers this thesis may appear utopian or even speculative. In fact, it is far from that. The reason is that due to its spiritual magnetism and scientific insight Yoga knowledge can resolve socio-cultural tensions and emotional frictions of various classes and groups and thus fuel the engine of evolutionary process to move unhindered on the path of building a progressive and balanced new world order. An outline of new world order has already been drawn by security concerns, trade interests, technology factors and forces though mainly for economic and social aspirations. To ensure tangible results these must be strengthened and accomplished by moral and spiritual values. These values can be created by following Yoga practices and philosophy, which must be integrated in new education system designed for universal education.

To counter resistance to Yoga teachings from certain religious and communal forces, the scientific and secular nature of Yoga must be understood and explained. Its practice and results are demonstrable. Its physical, psychological, recreational, medicinal, moral and spiritual benefits are there for all to watch and experience. Yoga benefits all alike whether a believer, non-believer, atheist, a worshiper, a Hindu, Muslim or a Christian. The only condition is to sincerely learn its lessons and to assimilate its practice in the system. One of the most important benefits of Yoga practice particularly of Kriya Yoga, is its effectiveness to counter the effects of pollution. Toxic gases and carbon agents daily attack our body's respiratory and cardio-vascular system. We know that the menace of pollution is threatening to be an epidemic. Pranayama system taught in Kriya Yoga is the most effective remedy to counter pollution and cleanse the system. It not only decarbonizes the system with oxygenization but also abundantly recharges the system with Prana energy (life force).

We know that the evolution of all cultures has advanced by countering confrontations. There is no smooth sailing for big movements. All enlightening and revolutionary movements have had humble beginnings but the latent creative power in such movements supported by the vigour of inspiring personalities works wonders to affect the course of history. We also know that the present civilization and its culture of science has not been created by turning many people into students of science, neither the democratic culture, despite other severe challenges, is growing by every body's knowledge of democratic values. Socio-cultural evolution and revolutionary movements emerge from inherent seeds ingrained in evolutionary forces. The creative people read such trends and vigorously push forward such movements. Great things are the creation of creative people who are few. Their knowledge, conviction and social compulsions all assemble to usher in the advent and emergence of new orders. Similarly, Yoga culture should be fine-tuned intelligently into a movement because the spiritual imperative of Yoga has the power to galvanize and stabilize the dynamics of new global order due to its scientific credential and spiritual power. The yogic culture need not be based either on material foundation nor its want should be a constraint. Its students and teachers should be sincere and devoted people and better still if they are from different backgrounds. Once creative values of Yoga have been realized by students of foreign lands like U.S.A. and European countries where some people are already showing interest in Yoga, its dissemination to the learning centers of other countries will get momentum. The scientific base of Yoga techniques and the evidence of desired results experienced by Yoga students will lend concrete support to disseminate and popularize Yoga--based education.

Therefore, it is necessary that Yoga be started as a subject of education in a few selected schools, colleges and universities. Its good effect to improve physiological and psychological health and behaviour of students when seen by others will spread in academic and media circles. After critical examination of the positive effects of Yoga, schools and vocational institutions that are affected by indiscipline and plagued by violence can benefit from Yoga remedies.

To illustrate the benefits of Yoga; ancient history, Yoga texts, scriptures and achievements of modern yogis can be used as good evidence in support of Yoga to inspire response. In the past, in ancient India the great rishis and yogis founded big universities and great spiritual centers to enlighten and educate people. It is no exaggeration to claim that even today, despite the neglect of Yoga, the world recognizes us because of our spiritual attainments based on the credentials of Yoga. I think it is high time in our country we rise to the occasion and take the right decision to introduce Yoga as a subject of study in carefully identified schools, colleges and universities. After trials, Yoga must be enlisted as one of the subjects for state and national level government service competitions and for entry into corporate bodies. Yoga should be made a compulsory subject of study in health and medical vocations.

The world knows that India is the biggest successful democracy despite the diversity of communal, religious, linguistic, socio-cultural and ethnic factors. The main reason for the continuity of this sub-continent as a vibrant society despite our plurality lies in the underlying unity of its spiritual power. The spiritual power of Indian culture has been the powerful binding force to keep us together despite eddies and drops of various hues. Our spiritual culture has absorbed alien invaders, conquerors and hoards of attacking tyrants. Our spiritual resilience is rooted in the reality of Yoga, which enabled rishis of the yore and yogis of the present to realize the cosmic spirit, which is an infinite source of consciousness, life, service, sacrifice, truth, knowledge and love. No wonder the science of spiritual realization and the methods to acquire it which Yoga teaches is the permanent source of universal values, which can be the solid substratum to build a better new world, to provide security and freedom to all.

To suggest that Yoga-based education is the best option to impart substance to the creation of new harmonious world order and ensure its qualitative evolution calls for re-capitulation of the important aspects of the aforesaid discussion. Human knowledge and capability to perform depend on mind and intelligence. Through intelligence and mental power, we have created our great civilization, its flagships are the material opulence and nuclear power. Now as already said both have backfired. It happens because mind being a polarity produces both the positive and the negative forces. In fact according to Yoga mind is made of both these forces. It is a unit made of two opposite forces: positive and negative both are mutually inalienable. Removing one will cause it to cease. Our thoughts, feelings, imagination and will are the mind powers and mundane education being their product has no permanent remedy to purify the mind.

On the other hand, yogis claim and have proved with personal examples that it is possible to purify and control the mind. Some of these Yoga practices and techniques have been mentioned and are dealt with in the chapter "What is Yoga". Here it may suffice to mention that yogis know that mind is always restless and is made of thought modifications, which are countless and are always at work both in waking and dream states. These modifications form a barrier between the all-knowing human soul and sense based mind. When the unending process of modifications is stopped, man realizes his soul and thus transcending the mind becomes one with the all-knowing and blissful self. Yogis have known through intuition and gained through Yoga practices that restlessness, and modifications of the mind are caused by the non- stop breathing activity of the cardio-vascular system. The action of cardio-vascular system is jointly performed by lungs, heart, veins and arteries. Lungs breathe in oxygen to purify the blood, heart pumps it to the brain and other body parts, veins and arteries transmit forward and backward the blood supply to enliven and activate cells, tissues and other parts and most importantly the brain cells, which are the key performers to keep the body-mind machine alive and working. Yogis have confirmed with experience the fact that when breathing is scientifically regulated and then stopped, cardio-vascular activities stop and consequently, modifications and restlessness of the mind stop and the mind becomes still.

This great feat of Yoga is performed by controlling and directing the Prana energy. Yogis have intuitively realized and practically proved that it is the Prana energy (the life force) which enlivens, activates and operates the human body and mind and not only the food and oxygen directly. The food when digested becomes energy, which sustains the body, but the finest form of energy to sustain the body and mind is Prana energy. Oxygen also contains this fine and vital Prana energy. This Prana energy, present in oxygen drinks and food, sustains life. Yogis know the techniques to distil this Prana energy from oxygen and store its added supply in the brain. When through yogic techniques breathing is stopped or reduced to the minimum, the operation of cardio-vascular system nearly stops and also the supply of blood to brain and other body parts. At this stage, the Prana energy already stored in the brain takes over in a subtle but scientific way to keep the body and brain alive. Restlessness and modifications of the mind stop and the supply of subtle Prana energy feeds the vital organs with the life force. This state in Yoga is called *'kumbak'*. *Kumbak* is said to be the state of wonderful spiritual experiences unimaginable by the mind. With more practice, the Yoga practitioner can ascend to attain *Samadhi* – the highest spiritual experience. Yogis say that kumbak and samadhi expose Yoga practitioner to unique supra mundane spiritual sights, sounds, experiences and visions. It is said that a yogi sees the infinite vastness of the causal universes, incredible sources of knowledge, infinite beauties, peace and bliss and ultimately with higher yogic Kriya, yogi meets God i.e. cosmic spirit. No doubt such attainments and experiences are for the few but that should not be accepted as the basis to brand Yoga discipline impracticable because even different religions which promise similar experiences are not labelled impracticable at least not by their followers.

Yoga being scientific and its practices and results being observable and demonstrable are different from many religions. The essence of Yoga is purity of body, heart and mind. Its practice begins with basic exercises to make body healthy and mind clean. Some yama, niyama, asana, Pranayama and pratihara exercises performed under guru's guidance produce the desired effect to purify the system. The point to understand is that these techniques discipline and control the mind by generating psychological and physiological effects. Only these scientific and spiritual methods can control, culture and transcend the mind unlike the reading and lecturing methods, which produce only short time effects to improve thinking and behaviour. In situations where personal stakes are involved, non-Yoga methods do not work to discipline and restrain people but in such conditions, Yoga is effective because its base is equanimity. Yoga opens a new dimension in consciousness and through that a successful yogi attains the super-conscious state. Yoga education, if started in education institutions, may not transfigure quite a few into yogis, which is a question of individual karmic effect, but its purpose being attainment of peace, brotherhood, love and universal service can generate an atmosphere of healthy co-existence. Yoga being a pragmatic and scientific pursuit and being rooted in the concept of simple living and high thinking, can contribute to the growth of a conducive environment for a violence free, peaceful and prosperous better world order.

It is important to mention that Yoga education lays stress on performance of duty. It prescribes a charter of duty for all age groups and different vocations as is also spelled out in the 18th chapter of *The Bhagawad Gita*. In Yoga dispensation, every person's duty is to serve all without reservation and conditions. There is no mention of rights, but only performance of duty and service to all is its credo. The basic training of Yoga centers on the principle that selfless service sows the seed of social peace and individual salvation. Yoga implies that when people and state perform their duties, rights are automatically protected. Duties of human beings are not only towards each other but also towards plants, animals, angels and God. Yoga education is an elaborate discipline covering all important areas of life and caters to different aspects of important human responsibilities. Yoga education does not have a big syllabus for studies. The most important source of

Yoga education is the teachings of a guru. One's association and surrender to him is the key to master the knowledge of Yoga. Other important sources of Yoga, apart from various Yoga schools and texts are *The Bhagawad Gita, Patanjali Yoga Sutra, Hatha Yoga Pradeepika,* different Upanishads and a few select references to Yoga in Vedas. For example, the four *Maha-Vakyas* of four Vedas – (1) "Consciousness is *Brahmn"* – Rig-Veda, (2) "I am *Brahmn"* – Yajur-Veda, (3) "Thou art That" – Sama – Veda (4) "This *atman* is *Brahmn"* – Athar-Veda; reveal the prime concern of Vedas with the spiritual core of all beings which is the soul of all. Simultaneously, Vedas also spell out ways to promote socio-cultural well being through the performance of yagya-dana-tapa. Yoga education is not based mainly on its philosophy and literature, which is brief and precise; it is based on the practice of a spiritual brief imparted by the guru. The most important part of Yoga education is meditation. Meditation being the very centre and substance of Yoga education has been described separately in various chapters.

Meditation means managing the mind through concentration, which has different methods and different techniques. It may not be concentrating on the mind. Mediation means concentrating on consciousness; God or the spirit. Its techniques are given by the guru along with the meditation mantra (spiritual intonation) like Aum or aham, Brahamn, asmi, etc. When the art of concentration has been perfected after long practice with the guru given mantra, it leads to the rise of intuition. Intuition is the highest knowledge because it is the direct knowledge of the truth. To attain the spiritual level of acquiring intuition, high degree of meditation is necessary.

The duration of such high quality of meditation lasts for hours at a time. It is a different art based on different techniques but once intuition has been acquired, the person becomes a master or guru himself. Intuition is not based on reason but on the direct vision to see the truth without any proof or inference. In intuition, the soul is at work and not the mind and senses. It is a divine faculty and evolves from within unlike reason and thoughts, which are external to the soul because their field is the world of senses. In this world we perceive things with intelligence, mind and ten senses. However, a yogi who has developed intuition he/she uses the soul power to know whatever needs to be known. Soul does not need a mind and senses because soul is the source of all things including the mind and senses. It has its own sixth sense – the sense of intuition that feels, sees, smells, tastes, touches directly with this sixth sense. This sixth sense is called by various names – The Third Eye, The Spiritual Eye and The Shiva-netra. That is why it is said in scriptures that God has no hands, feet and other senses yet He is everywhere, does and knows everything which is due to His power of intuition. In *The Bhagawad Gita* 13/13 also the same theme is highlighted. With intuition, a person can see into the future and can recall the events of the past. Intuition, the highest knowledge, cannot be attained without deep concentration, as told in *The Bhagawad Gita* 6/19. By going deep in meditation when mind consciousness is lost and thought modifications cease, the Divine grace flows. At that spiritual base, polarity ceases and duality is non-existent. A yogi loses the sense of negatives and develops the force of love and a sense of service to all. He becomes the unit of God consciousness where love and bliss are experienced because at this level Maya (delusion) cannot operate as it is the realm of the spirit.

Only the attainment of Yoga knowledge (intuition) can banish violence, greed and ignorance from human psyche. It is this knowledge, which can generate the values of ethics, service, and sense of sacrifice, peace and love for all. Therefore, no effort should be spared to recast and overhaul the existing system of education. The new system of education should be designed to give opportunity to intuition-based education to flourish. It is true that very few people will be able to attain the high level of intuition called the sixth sense but when some committed individuals attain it, that will generate the ripple effect inspiring other to follow, as is mentioned in *The Bhagawad Gita* 3/21.

In the end, I may point out that the purpose of this chapter is not to build a case to project Yoga system of education as a substitute to the existing system. That would sound preposterous because most of the distinct contributions of modern education to promote civilization and transform cultures are too obvious to be substituted by any other known human endeavour, be it Yoga or spirituality. However, Yoga and spirituality are higher pursuits. Higher knowledge and spiritual growth are not possible without them because they are integral to the cause of spiritual evolution. Individual peace, social harmony, universal love and soul knowledge, all flow from the founts of Yoga and spirituality. They are the permanent sources of individual's inner fulfilment and of universal love and peace on the global level.

The promotion of ethical and spiritual values, which form the essence of finer human life and the substance of higher human endeavours, can be promoted by scientific Yoga methods of education. This neglect may cost humanity heavily and may even jeopardize the aspirations to lay the foundation for a new world order. Due to this deficiency, human conduct is degenerating and greed and venality have become home to our role models, be it our political leaders, industrial captains or bureaucrats. The vacuum caused by the banishment of basic values in human conduct is being filled by greed and lust, which are causing mayhem across the world, yet many believe that the world is progressing. Let us not dither to ponder that the challenges confronting humanity are immediate and grave. We are mistaken to believe that man's mind and intellect alone will bailout us. Great challenges are always solved by spiritual power. The methods to tap the infinite spiritual source are taught by Yoga and its grace flows through God's mercy.

THE UPANISHADS

Upanishads reveal the holy science, rather the supreme spiritual science that enables a seeker to realize the self within. The self cannot be known by mundane arts, sciences or the technologies. It is a unique knowledge beyond the ken of human mind and intellect. The rishis of ancient India discovered this mystic knowledge about 5000 years ago. These rishis must have been genius par excellence like Newton and Einstein of the modern world of science. Their discovery was the great science of Yoga which was unique in many ways. It opened their minds to know the unknown, transform their hearts to love all and empowered them to humble the mighty death. No doubt they could not have achieved this rare knowledge without many trials and travails. It must have been through long and relentless pursuit of intuitive meditation that they discovered the self, the very base and essence of consciousness. It is the source of highest knowledge and the secret of the existence of everything and being. What we know through the senses, mind and intellect is incomplete and at times incorrect, which is why we feel insecure, fall sick and die. We do not fully understand humane and non-humane environment, therefore we have rampant violence, wars, terrorism and pollution all over the world. We live unhappy lives despite being masters of knowledge, power czars and material tycoons. In this world the growth of knowledge, pace of material progress and increase in violence are moving as if in tandem. The singled out victims of this entire bizarre bonanza are the peace and happiness of humanity.

If the purpose of life is attainment of happiness and the means to attain it is knowledge then obviously there is something wrong with our pursuit and the type of knowledge that we have been acquiring.

These rishis of ancient India, though few, came from a diverse social background. Some were princes, estate owners, scholars and even poor; but all of them were afire with the quest for knowledge to find one power or one source, which will answer all questions and resolve all problems. They wanted to know about such a supreme knowledge. Their concerns were basic issues like, what is life, what is death and whether life ends at death? Despite power, possessions and position why are people unhappy? Having failed to find answers to such questions in books, deliberations, debates and in the study of various peoples' lives; they must have studied the methods of meditation. Finding no answers in the vast outer world which the senses reveal, they must have stopped the contact of their senses with the outer world by disconnecting the mind from their senses and simultaneously turned their mind inwards by fixing their mind on the point in between the eyebrows or the lotus of the heart. The secret of this exercise was concentration. Sitting in isolation, they continued their meditation for hours. As they pursued this proactive method for days, months and years with longer and deeper concentration on one fixed point, they must have started experiencing peace. By fully turning the mind and attention inwards with laser like power of concentration, they started experiencing unexpected results. They saw that the mind which they thought was the only source of knowledge was not so. They saw in deep meditation on consciousness that senses, mind and intellect are mere objects like other bodily parts and not the source of ultimate divine knowledge. A few of them must have derived strength in their consciousness from scriptures and the relevant verses of *The Bhagawad Gita* where Lord Krishna categorically declared that intellect and mind are matter like ether, air, fire, water and earth. Consciousness of the self is the source of supreme knowledge and in deep meditation; these rishis themselves experienced and confirmed this great truth, which is enshrined in these great scriptures. These rishis therefore made the greatest discovery through self-realization that super consciousness is both supreme knowledge and the knower of all. With deeper concentrated and intuitive meditation, they discovered the fourth state of consciousness, *the turiya* that is the state of spirit realization or the realization of Brahmn. It was the discovery of Brahma vidya that teaches about both God and the world-spirit and matter. This was a masterstroke, opening the floodgates of bliss. They found the substratum, the one unifying principle underlying the cosmic diversities, the only source of all worlds, beings and angels.

THE ISHA UPANISHAD

Om. God is the whole, this universe is the whole. This whole (the universe) has emanated from that whole (God). The whole coming out of the whole, the whole ever remains the whole.

This opening Mantra reveals the inexhaustible, ever-existent glorious essence of the supreme God (Param *Brahmn*). It explains that this world, which emanates from the perfect *Brahmn*, is also complete because it is born out of Him who is the nimit (sentient) and upadana (material) cause of its birth and existence. However, the perfection of the supreme *Brahmn* is never affected or diminished by the emanation of the vast universe from *Brahmn* because Param *Brahmn* is the ever-existent inexhaustible whole. The emergence of various universes from Param *Brahmn* and their dissolution back into Him neither reduces nor adds to His unaffected and eternal existence.

Mantra-1: Whatever exists in this world, the animate or inanimate, God permeates the whole of it. Thus, remembering God enjoy it (the world) with a sense of renunciation; be not attached with anyone.

Explanation: The whole phenomenon world of senses, including the diversity of its goods and services, is permeated by its source; God. These things should be consumed and used carefully and creatively to attain fitness to perform one's duty in this life towards God, people and all other species. We must remember that man cannot create matter. This world is God's creation, which He has created to be enjoyed by all, keeping greed and covetousness at bay. One can enjoy it best by cultivating the spirit of giver rather than that of a grabber. We must remember that its creator is present in its every atom. It is also mentioned it *The Bhagawad Gita*, Chapter 10, verse 39-41. He has made it so abundant and beautiful for us all, the animate and inanimate, because He exists in both the seed and deed as mentioned in Kathopanishad. Therefore, we must not covet His things nor deprive others but enjoy this world with creative devotion, sense of service and sacrifice. It is this spirit that adds to joy. The idea is that while using and consuming the goods and services of this world to improve heath and acquire knowledge, we must take pain to beautify and conserve it. Only such an approach can endear us to God who loves us all.

Mantra-2: Performing righteous actions one should desire to live for hundred years. Performing actions with devotion for God does not bind a person (to this world); otherwise there is no escape from being tainted by work.

Explanation: There are only two powers in this world: spirit (God) and Maya (matter). Matter means human body, mind and all possessions and God means the soul within. There is no salvation unless man manifests or realizes his soul.

Esoteric techniques, as explained in Yoga and other scriptures, are difficult and cannot be used gainfully without the guidance of an enlightened guru. This Mantra of the Upanishad offers a great alternative. It says that you only have to perform your duty with devotion and dedication to God and it will earn you not only health and contended life up to hundred years but also salvation at the end. Otherwise, there is no escape because nobody can ever remain without action, not even for a moment, and every action that we perform is binding because we perform it with motive. It must be remembered that action also includes thoughts and speech. Every action related to matter (world), being non-spiritual, binds us to the world. Worldly progress, possessions and positions do not enable us to attain God or even gain proximate to Him. This theme is also well explained in *The Bhagawad Gita* (3-9), "All actions except yagya lead to bondage." Yajna means an action performed with a sense of sacrifice for God or for others with devotion. In fact, when action is performed with purity of heart it imparts a sense of freedom and contentment.

Mantra-3: The slayers of soul, after death,go to the godless dark and gloomy worlds of hell which are the centers of pain, trauma and delusion.

Explanation: According to scriptures, there are various worlds (Lokas) like our world. Some are better and some worse. All worlds fall in the realm of Prakriti (Maya), whether hell or heaven. Trauma, pain and ignorance afflict all worlds, including ours. In fact all worlds, including heaven, in comparison with the Divine Bliss are hell. The slayers of soul are only those who deny the existence of soul and perform negative, selfish, anti-social and irreligious acts. They take birth in such worlds where irrespective of their worldly positions and possessions reel as discontented lot, wasting their lives in hypocrisy, vindictiveness and greed. Slayers of soul (the bad doers and non-believers) may cunningly attain material gains and social status but the inner fire of discontent and restlessness burns them with ever-increasing fury, as is mentioned in *The Bhagawad Gita* (16/12,16,19, 20). That is why *The Bhagawad Gita* says in 6/5, that man is himself his own friend and his own foe; by sublimating his lower self, man can earn spiritual reprieve because the love of Lord is there for all to attract them to His abode to live in all bliss.

Mantra-4: God is still and yet faster than the mind, swifter than the senses. He is the primeval power and knows all; even gods do not know Him. Being still, He outpaces all. Nature and gods alike having faith in Him operates with His grace.

Explanation: This Mantra describes God's inscrutable and infinite powers. God as the absolute supreme power (Param *Brahmn*) is ever still in His quiet beatitude. But due to His uniqueness, omnipresence and omniscience, he is faster than the mind. He oversees and activates various actions of all gods like Indra, air, fire, god, etc. The omniscient God knows everything and everybody; therefore, all other gods despite their knowledge quest feel ignorant before God because God is omniscient. The ever still and motionless God can never be outpaced, outrun literally or metaphorically by any lesser gods and beings, because He is omnipresent and omnipotent.

Being the primeval omniscient power, He already knows all and nobody, not even Devas (gods), know Him as is also declared by God Himself in *The Bhagawad Gita* 10.2. All natural powers like air (the breath of life) and other gods operate due to the grace of God, who is both still and active.

Mantra-5: He moves and He does not move. He is the farthest and the nearest. He is within all and also without (all perfection).

Explanation: This Mantra may appear a contradiction or a paradox but it is the truth because who else can exhibit such immaculate perfection in simultaneously operating the negatives and positives of an event so artfully always and everywhere. An absolute spirit (God) is always still but due to omnipresence He is always everywhere. He is farthest because there is no point and particle in farthest space where He does not exist and He is the nearest because He abides in every heart of a being. At the same time, He transcends all. This is also explained in *The Bhagawad Gita* 7.7 and 13.15. It can be explained in this way too that God for His devotee is the nearest, right inside their hearts and non-believers can never find Him.

Mantra-6: Hewho always sees all creatures in God and sees God in all creatures, knows no hatred.

Explanation: In the fifth Mantra the nature and qualities of God have been described. In this Mantra, the Upanishad explains the nature of a God-realized soul. Unless a person realizes the soul in his own heart, he cannot know God. Once the soul has been realized, such a person loves all because it is the same soul which abides in all hearts. Therefore, a soul-realized person loves all creatures like his own self and also knows God because soul is the presence of God in every creature. This concept may appear difficult to grasp but saints say that such indeed is the magic of the power of soul knowledge because it bestows the sixth sense, which can see the unseen and can know the unknown. It converts the human heart into an ocean of universal love. Therefore, such a yogi always sees God in all creatures and all creatures in God. This thought is well explained in *The Bhagawad Gita* VI-30.

Mantra-7: When for a God-realized person all creatures appear the same soul, in such a state of divine consciousness how can grief and attachment assail him?

Explanation: Such is the ever-existent glory of the divine essence that he who attains it, he attains a state of ever new bliss. Grief and delusion are characteristics of the mind (world life) and not of the spirit (soul realization), which is a state of super happiness in which such a person spontaneously loves all creatures from the core of his heart. The soul-realized person feels the soul of every being, which is the same in all due to the omnipresence of God. A glimpse of His omnipresence banishes grief and fills the heart with bliss.

Mantra-8: That great soul joins the Supreme who is all-pervading, all-effulgence, beyond astral form, body-less, invulnerable, pure and untouched by sin. He is all wise (Kavi), master of mind (Manishi), omnipotent (Prabhu), self-existent and eternal. He is the great creator of all objects too, since time immemorial.

Explanation: The Supreme God having the characteristics, explained in the 8th Mantra, can be realized by a sage who sees all creatures in God and God in all creatures. The various characteristics of God and His supreme nature, as described in this Mantra, reveal diverse facets of His unmanifest, indivisible being. God with his omnipotent, omnipresent, omniscient nature and as the fair distributor of all objects to all as per their Karmas can hardly be seen and realized by others, except by a sage who has attained the highest spiritual merit, as described in Mantras 6 and 7 above.

Mantra-9: Those who worship ignorance enter into blind darkness; into far worse darkness enters those who are intoxicated with knowledge (Vidya), the bragging lot.

Explanation: Worshippers of ignorance are those people who equip and educate themselves only with secular and mundane knowledge, which can fetch those worldly goods, services and status but are unaware of the spiritual science, which can uplift and enlighten them spiritually. Therefore, such people being materialistic and self-centered go on degrading themselves birth after birth in the direction of a descending downfall.

But still worse are those who perform neither good action nor possess the right knowledge of scriptures but with their unrealized shallow book knowledge brag like empty vessels misguiding others and misbehaving themselves. Such Pedants and social parasites fall into darkest and most gloomy hells.

Mantra-10: Different is the reward of knowledge (Vidya) and different is the reward of action (Avidya). This is how sages explain the essence of both.

Explanation: Vidya means spiritual realizations and Avidya means material knowledge. He who attains Vidya, the highest spiritual enlightenment, which enables a person to transcend the world of senses, which isa mixture of pain and pleasure and a storehouse of delusion, knows all and attains bliss.

Avidya here means performance of motivated worldly actions and acquiring the knowledge of worldly arts and sciences for self-projection. In this respect also, those who follow the worldly pursuits and perform their duty with full sense of duty, sacrifice and service, they also attain high rewards like heaven and other spiritual benefits. But selfish and greedy pedants cannot attain these rewards. They being hypocrites debase themselves. These are the views of the enlightened sages as is also mentioned in *The Bhagawad Gita* 2.16.

Mantra-11: Those who know the essence of both knowledge (Vidya) and action (yagya), they through action (yagya) overcome death and through knowledge (Vidya) attain immortality.

Explanation: As explained above, Vidya means spiritual knowledge or Brahmavidya. Avidya (action) here means akarma (the non-binding action). Akarma is Yajna detached action performed with sense of sacrifice and service.

Undoubtedly, the knower of Vidya (Brahmavidya) attains spiritual realization but even those people who perform worldly actions as yagya as Akarma (detached actions with sense of service and sacrifice) also overcome death, which means to attain salvation. This Mantra clarifies that not only meditation and spiritual knowledge enlighten a person but action (Karma) performed as (Akarma) with a sense of service and sacrifice unbothered by danger and difficultly uplifts a person to highest spiritual reward of salvation.

Mantra-12: Who worship the perishable, they enter the blinding darkness. The imperishable worshipping hypocrites and pendants enter the worse darkness.

Explanation: The *asambhuti* word used here means attachment to worldly relations and worldly possessions and positions. The action mentioned here is motivated action and as defined in Mantra-11 above, is detached action. Therefore, the plight of that worshipper due to attachment, rooted in the selfish concerns of their families and personal worldly gains, being spiritually ignorant, is pitiable. Yet far worse and more pitiable is the condition of those pseudo spiritualists who are intellectually conceited but spiritual blanks. The underlying idea is that the material worshipers are bad but pseudo spiritualists are far worse and go to hell.

Mantra-13: Distinct is the reward of the worship of the imperishable and different is the reward of worship of the perishable. Thus has been explained to us by the knower of truth.

Explanation: The imperishable is the Param *Brahmn*; 'The worshippers of the Param *Brahmn*; are the knower of Brahmavidya. Therefore, they may attain the highest reward of salvation depending on the merit and purity of their commitment.

On the other hand, the sincere worshippers of lesser gods, Devas, guru, good people and performer of good and great actions, also get the lesser rewards. Every good action performed with sincerity and devotion has a reward because in this world every action is both a cause and effect. It is to be noted that the worship of the perishable performed must be done sincerely unlike in Mantra-12, which is based on conceit and hypocrisy. In the 10th Mantra is described the difference between Vidya and Avidya and here the difference is explained between the rewards of the worship of the imperishable and the perishable performed honestly.

Mantra-14: He, who correctly knows the imperishable and the perishable together, through the worship of the perishable, overcomes death and with the worship of the imperishable attains the imperishable Supreme God.

Explanation: He who understands the supreme imperishable God and His infinite powers and worships Him as such and simultaneously realizing the lower positions and limited powers of the lesser gods and other mundane dignitaries, worships them also sincerely treating them as the creation of God. He therefore gets both the benefits to overcome death with sincere worship of the perishable (will not take rebirth) and also worshipping the imperishable Supreme God, finds Him.

Mantra-15: The face of Lord, the true provider of all, is covered with a dazzle of the golden disk; Lord uncovers it so that I who love the truth shall see it.

Explanation: Dazzle of the golden dusk means the divine auras and manifestation of the various glories of God (shrishti), behind which rests the still and eternal blissful God. A true God lover is always impatient to see this supreme and serene divinity. Nothing else can satisfy the divine quest of seeker for the divine truth. Such a true God lover prays to God to intercede to remove all deluding obstacles and bare His divine serenity to the seeker's devotional quest.

Mantra-16: O Lord! the protector of devotees, knower of the self, the controller, the sun, the loved of Prajapati, withdraw the dazzle of your blinding shine or absorb it in your radiance and radiate the soft glow of the serene self which I behold in mediation as the soul of the cosmos and I am also the same soul.

Explanation: A sincere devotee, who is 'Divine Lark', finds the dazzle of the golden disk a mere dissuading distraction. His only concern, rather passion, is the Lord of the cosmos who is the only source of supreme and secret knowledge (Brahmavidya) and is the protector and controller of the universe. The true God lover knows his God through the eye of intuition and insight of intelligence because as a soul, he is part of the supreme soul but to quench the desire of his human heart, the devotee prays to the Almighty God to reveal His glorious divine form even to his physical vision and therefore bless him on both counts.

Mantra-17: May my breath enter into cosmic breath and body into cosmic ashes. O Cosmic intelligence, remember my actions, O supreme power, remember my actions.

Explanations: This Mantra reproduces the theme propounded in *The Bhagawad Gita* 8.5, "Whoever at the time of death, goes forth remembering only Me, he attains Me, and this undoubtedly is the truth." These being the words of God

Himself, therefore, there can be no wiser council for a dying person to follow. But remembering God from the core of heart at the death bed and expecting Him to reckon his actions gracefully, presupposes that a person must have lived a pure and creative life; performing pure actions dedicated to serve good cause and God.

Mantra-18: O Fire God, being aware of our actions, lead us through pure and pious path, forgive us for our vices, we pray to you, we bow to you.

Explanation: The contents of these Mantras, 15 to 18, reveal that there is no substitute to the performance of good actions to uplift and purify life. No doubt, spiritual contemplation and meditation are very important but the real test of their effects is only reflected in the type of actions that we perform in life. Only our good actions can attract the love of fellow beings and the divine grace. Fire God being the purifying power, the devotee therefore begs for mercy for his unwontedly performed obstructive actions and to guide him to the abode of the supreme God as he (the god of Fire) is always aware of the qualities and purity of a devotee's action/mind.

MUNDAKA UPANISHAD

Mundaka Upanishad
Mundak-I
(The Origin of Brahma)

1. *Brahma,* the creator of the universe, the protector of the worlds and of all the gods, was the first to arise. He taught the knowledge of Brahma Vidya, the origin of all knowledge, to Atharwa, his eldest son.
   Explanation: The birth of Brahma is a mystical event. It is different from the happenings of ordinary mundane births. It is an event shrouded in spiritual mystery. The Supreme God created Brahma (the Prajapati) to create the universe. His first appearance is as Prajapati, the cosmic mind. Brahmavidya, which Brahma taught to his eldest son Atharwa, is the spiritual science and it is only through this supreme knowledge that the cosmic spirit and spiritual mysteries can be understood.

2. That Brahmavidya, which Brahma taught to Atharwa,

the same knowledge was taught by Atharwa to Agni rishi. Agni rishi told it to Satyavaha of Bhardwaja lineage, who in turn told this supreme knowledge, in its both forms, to Angira rishi.

Explanation: Agni and Angira are two great rishis of the yore who are among the Sapta Rishis. The two forms of Brahmavidya are called Para and apara. Para (higher) reveals the Divinity and spiritual mysteries and apara teaches about the phenomenon worlds.

3. *Shaunaka*, a known personality heading the great centre of learning, devotionally approached Angira rishi and humbly asked, "Sir what is that by knowing which everything becomes known?"

   Explanation: Shaunaka rishi's question shows his deep spiritual quest. He wanted to know the one basic cause, which explains the diversity of multiple effects. His craving for knowledge can be compared to the quest of noted scientists who are working overtime to find out one theory which will explain many questions staring at the mankind in the eye.

4. Famous rishi Angira told Shaunaka muni that the knower of *Brahmn* say that there is a two-fold knowledge which ought to be known – Para (the higher) and Apara (the lower).

5. Of these, the Rig Veda, the Yajur Veda, the Sama Veda, the Atharva Veda, rituals, phonetics, etymology, metrics and astrology are covered in Apara Vidya. The

Para (higher) knowledge is that which reveals the un-manifest or the Imperishable.

Explanation: Shaunaka muni must have felt ill at ease to hear from the great Angira rishi his enlightened views that rituals, grammar and the other disciplines which he had mastered, cannot lead to the highest knowledge which reveals everything including immortality and bliss. It is only the Para (higher knowledge) which has the power to lead to the Supreme. Shaunaka muni was the acknowledged authority on Vedas and Vedanga (which are ten in numbers) but not on Para knowledge because it cannot be learned through mind and human intelligence.

6. That which is invisible, in-cognizable, un-create and beyond attribute, has no eyes, ears, hands and feet, is eternal, and all pervading, infinitely subtle, that is the un-decaying which the wise perceive as the womb of creation.

   Explanation: This Mantra is an immaculate attempt at defining the imperishable *Brahmn* who is the source of the unmanifest and its all manifestations. This definition covers all aspects— the unmanifest, the manifest, animate and inanimate which emanate from the subtle source of the omniscient *Brahmn* to whom the Para (higher) knowledge leads. The other human senses, mind and intelligence, cannot know this Supreme Source. Only the Para (higher knowledge) can apprehend the Imperishable.

7. As the spider projects and draws in its web, as the herbs grow on the earth, as the hair grow on the head and body of a person, similarly this universe arises from the imperishable.

   Explanation: This Mantra shows that the creation (universe) spontaneously emerges from the cosmic spirit (Brahma) as hair, nails, etc grow on human body without human effort. The reason for creation is not indicated here, as it cannot but be the supreme will of the divine.

8. From deep meditation on *Brahmn* emerges the creative will of Brahma, which expands into creation from whom are born food, from food Pranaa, the mind, the Maha Bhutas (five elements), the world, the Karma and from Karma the varied world.

   Explanation: This Mantra reveals that the emergence of the universe is a cosmic design of the *Brahmn*. Food (anna) here means Avyakta (the un-manifest) from which rises Pranaa (life and the mind), the five unmanifest elements, Karma and the ensuing world of cause and effect nexus.

9. He who is all knowing, all wisdom, whose meditation is intuitive, from Him are born Brahma (Prajapati, the Cosmic Mind), name-form and foods.

   Explanation: This Mantra answers the questions of Shaunaka muni that what is by knowing which everything becomes known. Angira rishi briefly tells that it is the supreme Param *Brahmn*, who through His deep and intuitive meditation creates *Brahmn* (Prajapati, the cosmic mind) who creates this universe of name and form from life up to its diverse manifestations of being and becoming, including individuals, worlds and food.

Mundak-I
Section-2
(Religious Ceremonies)

1. This is the truth; the Karmas (good actions) which the great Rishis observed in the Mantras (hymns), are variously spelled out in the Tretayama. Practice them regularly with devotion. In this human body this is the path for you to harvest rewards of pure actions.

   Explanation: The word Tretayama used here means the three Vedas. The fourth, Atharwa Veda, is presumed to be included in these three Vedas. Various hymns prescribe the right methods to perform yagya (offerings made to gods). Only those devotees, who perform acts of yagya, according to the Vedic hymns, can attain the rewards of heavenly joys and successful life on earth.

2. When the flame blazes after kindling the fire, the oblations should be offered with faith in the centre, between the point of (two) first offerings.

   Explanation: Scriptures guide that the first two oblations in yagya are offered each to Agni and Soma, the second two oblations in yagya are offered with devotion to Indra and other gods. The remaining oblations must be offered in the centre of the blazing flames.

3. He whose yagya is not followed by the yagyas of the new moon, the full moon, by the fourth month yagya, by the harvest sacrifice, in which guests are not welcome, is without sacraments, is without oblations or is not, according to rules, regulating yagya that will destroy his seven worlds.

   Explanation: If the performer of regular yagyas does not complete the chain of subsequent sacrifices (yagya) of the new moon, the full moon, the four months' yagya, does not entertain guests in yagya and does not complete other activities, as mentioned above, then such a person will forfeit the spiritual rewards and joys of the seven heavens which he would have earned by performing yagyas according to the rules as laid down in the three Vedas. Fire yagya is important because it is the fire god who leads a person to heaven.

4. The black, the fierce, the restless the attractively red, the delightfully smoky, full of sparks, blazing and effulgent blessed goddess- these are the seven twitching tongues of the blazing fire.

   Explanation: It is only when the fire kindled on the yagya altar is blazing in its full forms and colours that the oblations should be poured with full faith and devotion. Seven tongues of fire flames means the seven fierce and bright colours of the yagya fire. To secure access to heavens, concentrated devotion while offering the oblations is the secret.

5. When the performer of yagya offers oblations into these shinning flames of fire at the right time, these oblations becoming the shining rays of the sun do take him along with them to the abode of Lord Indra.
   Explanation: To attain peace and glory of heaven, performance of yagya on regular daily basis is the sure means.

6. The radiant oblations welcome the performer of yagya and respectfully leading him with the rays of the sun to Brahmaloka (heaven) declare, "This, you have won through your holy Karma."
   Explanation: It is the reward of faithfully offering oblations in yagya due to which the performer of yagya is welcome and led respectfully through the sun-lighted path to the heaven. Here Brahmaloka does not mean the abode of God but the abode of Indra. The former is eternal and the latter has an end.

7. Inconclusive indeed are the boats of the eighteen kinds of sacrifices, which are not said to be the highest Karmas. Deluded are those who vainly delight and think it (these actions) to be the supreme path. They cannot escape old age and death.
   Explanation: There are said to be eighteen forms of sacrificial Karmas, which are performed with devotion for worldly or heavenly rewards. Such sacrificial yagyas

being sakam cannot lead the performer beyond heavens. The afflictions of old age and death (disease and fear of death) can only be escaped by the knower of the supreme virtue-Nishkama karma and divine love.

8. The ignorant, wise in their own esteem and thinking themselves to be learned, foolish people, victims of pains, move about like the blind led by a blind.

   Explanation: Those who ignore the scriptures and the words of the truly wise, due to arrogance and hypocrisy, become the victims of self-inflicted myopia. It is only the wise who can distinguish between the seeming and the real truth.

9. The deluded and self complementing lot, performing various sakam yagyas, for worldly benefits without devotion and detachment, know not the path of righteousness which is why after exhausting their Karmas they fall from the higher regions.

   Explanation: Only devoted and detached actions performed for God and not for worldly rewards can lead a person to salvation. The two categories of sacrificial acts and ceremonies performed are —Ishta (desire for gods) and Purak (done for others) sakam karmas. They being unaware of the higher righteous and holy acts, after exhausting the good effects of their good karmas return to earth to be born in low wombs.

   Ishta and Purak sakam actions can provide good worldly life and heavenly life after death. Both these sacrificial and meritorious acts are good but only earn heavenly peace and joys which have an end. At the end of their effect, the performer must return to earth as per his/her Sanchit karmas.

10. But those learned souls of austere and devotional nature, peacefully meditating in forest dwellings or living on alms, depart by the solar path to the abode of the imperishable.
    Explanation: It is the austere, pure and enlightened spiritual life afire with the divine quest which earns the highest reward of salvation. The worldly life despite performance of various sacrificial acts of yagya can only earn an entry to heaven, which must meet an end even if after a very long time.

11. Appreciating the limits of the motivated worldly sacrificial performances, the wise should take to non-attachment. The performed actions cannot lead to the un-create (God). Only a God-realized guru can reveal God to a committed ascetic who must therefore respectfully approach the former with samidha (a mark of devotion to light the fire) in hand; this is a traditional mark to honor the guru, who would not accept a valuable offering.

12. He who with pure and tranquil mind in a spirit of self-surrender has approached the guru, the guru is to teach him the truth, the Brahmavidya (the only knowledge which leads to the realization of the Supreme God) analytically and intuitively.

Explanation: When a devoted ascetic approaches the guru with samidha in hand, it is a spiritual tradition that the enlightened guru will reveal the Divine knowledge to that ascetic who is afire with the divine quest and who surrenders unconditionally.

MUNDAK-2
Section-I
(*Brahmn*-Atman-The Self)

1. O beloved one, this is the truth; just as from the blazing fire thousands of similar sparks rise, similarly from the imperishable Brahma various beings issue and return to Him.

   Explanation: The theme of the self is being explained by rishi Angira to Shaunaka rishi with an illustration, that at the time of creation (shrishti) countless beings (having form and formless) emerge from the *Brahmn* and at the time of dissolution (pralaya) they all dissolve back into Him.

2. Undoubtedly, the primeval divine personage (Purusha) is formless. He is within and without. He is unborn, has no breath, no mind and therefore is the purest, the highest and higher than the self.

   Explanation: In this verse is explained the imperishable *Brahmn* from whom the universe emerges. The unborn and formless, even without intelligence, mind and senses, is capable of knowing and doing everything because He is omnipotent and omniscient. He is immeasurably purer than the human soul because the soul though His reflection is in bondage within the body.

3. From Him are born Pranaa (life force), mind, senses, ether, air, fire and the earth, the supporter of all.
   Explanation: Here the Supreme God is shown as the prime power and prime source of the animate and the inanimate. The cosmos is not shown as His creation but as an emanation, evolving from Him.

4. His head is the fire, His eyes are the sun and the moon, space His ears, Vedas His speech, and air His Pranaa (subtle life energy). The world is His heart. The earth is His feet. The Param *Brahmn* permeates all beings.
   Explanation: In the second Mantra, the formless self of the Param *Brahmn* has been depicted and in this Mantra His form is projected. In brief, it is the similar cosmic form of God which is described in chapter eleven of *The Bhagawad Gita*.

5. From Him is born the Fire God whose fuel is the sun; from the fire is born the moon; from the moon clouds (rain) are born. Rain produces numerous herbs. Herbs produce seed (semen in males), which in females plants the creation.
   Explanation: In these Mantras (verses), the chain of evolution is described. *Brahmn* is the source. The sun and moon are born from Him. From the energy of sun and moon are born the rain and the herbs (food grains),

which produce procreative energy in the beings and thus the evolution progresses.

6. From Him are born Rig Veda verses, Sam Veda chants, Yajur Veda hymen, the initiation rites, all the sacrifices, sacraments, rituals, sacrificial gifts, time factor (the year), the performer of yagya and all the worlds, the moon and the sun which generate light.

   Explanation: From *Brahmn* are born the tri-Vedas, which reveal knowledge to perform acts of yagya and karatu. Karatu yagya is more elaborate in which various flags are hoisted. From Him are born the performers of sacrifices and gifts at the right time due to which the worlds prospers and are nourished and lighted by the solar and lunar forces.

7. Many different gods are also born from Him. Devas (celestials), enlightened men, people, cattle, birds, Pranaa-Apana currents, rice, barley, austerity, devotion, truth, celibacy and the spiritual codes are all born from Brahma. He is the source of all existence.

   Explanation: *Brahmn* is the source of the entire chain of creation—from the animate (breathing), inanimate (non-breathing) up to angels and gods and also the source of all knowledge forms and all foods.

8. From God are born seven Pranaas, seven flames of fire, seven senses, seven yagyas and seven worlds in which seven Pranaas pervade. These seven-fold groups, which during sleep relax in the cave of man's heart, are His creation.

Explanation: Seven Pranaas here signify seven senses because all senses are enlivened and activated by the Pranaa power. In fact, the senses are ten but here the rishi has mentioned the seven main senses (of the upper region of the body). Seven flames of fire are the seven powers of seven senses, which mean the seven respective sense objects of these seven senses. Seven homas (yagyas) mean the seven oblations offered in yagya respecting each of the seven senses. According to scriptures, these seven lokas (worlds) are enlivened and activated by the Pranaa energy. These seven fold groups, which operate the world and during sleep rest collectively in the heart of people, are the creation of God. Therefore, God is the source of all activities of the senses.

9. From Him are born all oceans and mountains, from which flow all the rivers. From them rise all herbs and their juices, which breed healthy bodies in which along with the individual souls abide the Supreme God.

   Explanation: God Himself is alone the creator and enjoyer of the entire world. Therefore, He is the immanent self of all objects of the world.

10. All austerities, yagyas and gods are nothing but the Supreme God Himself. Dear Shaunaka, he who can realize in this life, this Supreme God, hidden in the heart of man, by untying the knot of ignorance, undoubtedly realizes God here in this life itself.

    Explanation: The Supreme Purusha can be discovered

within the heart itself but only after untying the knot of ignorance through pure performance of yagyas.

Section-2
(Param *Brahmn*- Supreme God)

1. The effulgent, the closest (but) unmanifest, omnipotent, omniscient and accessible is the great God. In Him are centered all sentient, breathing and winking beings. You must know Him. He is cause and effect (sat-asat), the power to be desired, the highest beyond reach, beyond human intelligence.

   Explanation: The Supreme God who is the source of all power, knowledge, creatures, the immanent, in whom is centered the entirety of the animate and inanimate universe and who is both the cause and effect of the cosmos and who is beyond human intelligence, must be known. The question is that the God who is beyond mind and intelligence, how can He be known? The answer is by following whole-heartedly the spiritual briefs imparted by the God-realized guru as is mentioned in Mundaka 1-2 (12-13) Mantra, and in *The Bhagawad Gita* 4 (34).

2. That who is all effulgent, the most subtle, in whom are anchored all the worlds and all their beings, such is the imperishable *Brahmn*. He is Pranaa (life force), He is speech, He is the mind, and He is the truth. He is immortality. Dear one, that Supreme fathomable must be fathomed.He must be known..

Explanation: Angira rishi is telling Shaunaka rishi that the Supreme Param *Brahmn*, who is immanent, transcendent and absolute, must be known; in the following verses is suggested the way.

3. Using the great bow Aum as described in the Upanishads, put in it the arrow sharpened with meditation, draw it with the force of mind, target the Brahma and shoot.

   Explanation: The Param Brahma can only be realized through deep intuitive meditation on 'Om'. This special technique of meditation on Aum, its pronunciation and concentration on it can be learnt from a God-knowing guru.

4. Om syllable is the bow, the self (soul) is the arrow, and Param *Brahmn* is the target. The hit must not miss; as you hit the target, the arrow dissolves in it and you become the *Brahmn*.

   Explanation: Unless the ardent seeker is afire with the divine passion, *Brahmn* cannot be targeted. Purity, devotion and divine quest are the pre-requisites to target the *Brahmn*. Long and deep meditation on Om, as per the guru's imparted brief with concentrated mind is the requirement.

5. He in whom the heaven, earth, space and also the mind along with all forms of life force are interwoven, the indwelling supreme soul of all; He is the secret, the only link to immortality. Never bother about anything else.

Explanation: A spiritual seeker can only bind himself to God with deep love and meditation. To leave all the rest means not to remain attached to the world because mind can remain attached only to one thing at a time, i.e. either to the world or the divinity. Attachment to the divine has got to be totally undiluted otherwise the arrow will miss the targeted*Brahmn*,who is too subtle.

6. Like the spokes of a wheel joined to its centre are the arteries of the body joined to the heart. In this centre abides the multi-manifested (God). This immanent universal soul must be meditated upon through Om. This will successfully take you beyond the sea of darkness to the fold of the Divine.

   Explanation: The syllable Om is the indicator of God as is mentioned in Patanjali Yoga Sutra and also in Mandukya Upanishad. Om being the vibratory source of creation, therefore, accessing the un-manifest God becomes easier by meditation on God's vibratory power of Om, which vibrates all body nerves.

7. He who is omniscient, knows all in every respect and who is so acclaimed in this world – this supreme universal soul resides in the Divine *Brahmn* loka and permeates the life and hearts of all. The wise manifest this imperishable effulgence through the practice of spiritual science.

   Explanation: The omniscient and omnipresent *Brahmn* permeates the universe from every individual heart up to the *Brahmn* loka. He is not subjected to the limits of space and time. The wise through love and scientific meditation, realize *Brahmn* in their own heart.

8. By knowing God, the cause and effect creator, the knot of Jiva's heart opens. All his doubts dispel and all his Karmas, the binding effect of actions, end.

   Explanation: On knowing the Supreme God of the universe, through love and meditation as described above, a being (ego) becomes enlightened. All his doubts come to an end because he knows the secret of the cause-effect nexus of the world. All his Karmas end. This means that all effects of all actions performed by a being in the past dissolve. He becomes a free, enlightened soul. It is only actions and their effects which bind a person to the world; when the effects of actions come to an end, a person transcends the mind and ascends to spiritual consciousness, which is a state of true freedom and knowledge. Therefore, the final deliverance can be attained through the vision of the *Brahmn*.

9. That effulgent (shining) indivisible Param *Brahmn* lives in the superb luminous abode. He is the light of all lights and all luminous objects. Only the self-illumined wise, knows Him.

   Explanation: *Brahmn*, being the source of all lights and luminosity literally and metaphorically, can only be known by the knower of the self. This means that only a devotee who has experienced his soul spark can realize the *Brahmn*.

10. There neither the sun shines nor do the moon and the stars; the lightening and electricity of course not, then why talk of the shine of the fire; because all these (objects) shine due to the shining power. The whole universe is illumined due to His light.

    Explanation: The Supreme God literally and figuratively is the only source of all lights and light-emitting objects—the sun, the moon the stars or the lightening and fire. These objects emit their light in the world due to the cause of His light. But in the *Brahmn* loka, their light can never shine because it is beyond their luminosity.

11. Truly, this *Brahmn* is immortal. In the front is *Brahmn,* in the back is *Brahmn,* to the right and to the left is *Brahmn*. Below and above is *Brahmn*. The whole universe is *Brahmn*. *Brahmn* is the greatest.

    Explanation: The omnipresence of Brahma extends from a grain of sand to the farthest galaxies. In fact, this universe is the manifestation of His cosmic presence and cosmic power.

MUNDAK-3

Section-I

1. Two birds who are inseparable companions live together on the same tree. Of these two, one eats the

sweet and bitter fruits of the tree and the other non-eating one, is the witness.

Explanations: The tree is the human body and the two birds living together in it are the soul and Jiva (ego). The soul being pure, the inseparable part of God present in the body does not eat anything, because soul like God, never eats, never drinks or breathes, and is always blissful and watching as an objective witness. On the other hand, the Jiva being involved in the world due to ones Karmic effects, is always busy eating the sweet and sour (good and bad) things of the world and therefore, reacts accordingly and remains bound to the world due to the cause and effect nexus.

2. The Jiva (ego), sitting on the same tree is plunged into sorrows, grieves helplessly due to his delusion. When he sees the other different blissful bird (the Divine) worshipped (by devotes), he also becomes free from grief.

   Explanation: The reason for the sorrow and grief of the Jiva, who lives in the same body along with the free soul but unaware of him, is his attachment to the world. Due to God's grace, good actions and meditation when he acquires the ability to know the free companion bird, he also becomes free. Therefore, without seeing the soul Jiva cannot attain spiritual liberation.

3. When this Jiva is able to realize, God of Gods even the creator of *Brahmn*, the radiant Param Purusha (Supreme God) then rising above the duality of good

and bad, attaining the stainless, he attains supreme equanimity.

Explanation: It is only the experience of the soul through which a devotee can realize supreme god, the creator of even *Brahmn* and can attain supreme equanimity in which he is constantly in touch with God and is not born again.

4. This Pranaa (life force) shows in all and the knower of this does not brag. Performing devotionally in the world, attached to the indwelling soul, always remembering God, living in all hearts the knower of the *Brahmn*, such a devotee is the greatest.

   Explanation: All actions, which are performed, are with the power of Pranaa (the life force) which emanates from God. Most people due to ego think themselves to be the doers. But the wise, knowing this secret, uses this Pranaa power to discover God and remain devotedly absorbed in Him. Such a devotee is the dearest to God.

5. This (self) pure and luminous indweller of all hearts can be known by the sinless ascetics through truthful speech, austerity and pure knowledge acquired through chastity.

   Explanation: Banishing all impurities and attaining soul knowledge is the path to the secret of God-realization. When the impurities of the mind are banished, the God present inside the heart becomes visible.

6. Only truth triumphs and not untruth because the path leading to gods is the path only of truth by which the wise who have purified their desires ascend to the true supreme abode of God.

   Explanation: "Truth alone triumphs" is the motto inscribed on the emblem of the Indian nation. The power of truth is so great that it purifies and spiritualizes a person. The unfailing speaker of truth needs not perform any other acts of asceticism. Truth is the sure path to find God because truth is God.

7. The *Brahmn* is infinite and unimaginable is subtler than the most subtle and the most effulgent. He is farther than the farthest; being the indweller in the body is the nearest. For people to see, He is the cave of their hearts.

   Explanation: Despite the infinite size and form, the unthinkable subtle *Brahmn* is seated in all hearts and can only be seen by the pureness of the heart.

8. He can neither be seen by the eye nor cognized by the senses or speech, austerity or actions. He can be cognized only by His light and attained by detached pure mind transcended with meditation.

   Explanation: The mind is always attached to the world of senses. Unless purified with meditation, it can never cognize the subtle God. World is not to be abnegated nor performance of actions is to be relinquished; only attachment to the goods and services of the world is to be banished, which only the art of renunciation and deep meditation can teach.

9. In the same body which is full of power of the five Pranaas, this indwelling subtle soul can be known, but the mind being full of Pranaa power and externally preoccupied the soul can be known after the purification of the mind.

   Explanation: Five forms of Pranaa are Pranaa (crystallization), Viyan (circulation), Samana (assimilation), Udana (metabolism), and Apana (elimination)—always keep the mind activated and fully attached to the body and the world. Therefore, the mind must be freed from the grip of the five-fold Pranaas, which can only be done by pure actions and long, deep meditation. Banishing the hold of Pranaa from mind can liberate the mind; the mind then becomes still and can cognize the soul within.

10. A person of so called purified mind, whatever worlds or enjoyments internally seek, he attains them. Therefore, he who seeks the self must worship the source of the self.

    Explanation: The true knower of the self has the power to bestow that knowledge on genuine seekers. Therefore, an ardent seeker must bow to such a master.

Mundak-3
Section-2

1. That person cognizes the luminous supreme abode which appears supporting the whole universe. Any

desire-less devotee who meditates on the supreme power (*Brahmn*), that wise man crosses the reproductive world.

Explanation: The Guru or a devotee, who through meditation has become desire-less and has cognized the supreme luminous power of *Brahmn,* frees himself from this world which is based on the reproductive chain of rebirth. Such a wise knower of *Brahmn* attains salvation.

2. He who broods on desires and clings to them due to attachment, takes birth where they exist. But a person who has transcended desires and has attained perfection; his desires end here in this world.

   Explanation: Only such a devotee can be called desire-less who by purifying his mind has so banished the very seed of desires that he does not even dream of them. Such a pure person is perfect and attains salvation. But the desires of the desirer are born again in place where the object of his desires, animate or inanimate, exists.

3. This self cannot be cognized by deliberation or intellect, nor by hearing. Only he, whom He (soul) likes, can cognize because this soul (God) reveals his true self to a pure devotee.

   Explanation: The self (God) knows the true seeker and reveals Himself only to an ardent devotee whom He chooses and such a pure devotee is the one who cannot live without God. It is such deep intensity of God love which attracts a devotee to God.

4. This self cannot be attained by the weak or by indolent nor by performance of aimless austerity, but by that devotee who seeks God ardently with these means..
   Explanation: The term 'with these means' signifies shunning indolence and aimlessness and concentrating on God with full strength of spiritual ardor. Attaining God is a serious business and half-heartedness can never succeed in approaching Him.

5. Pure and detached God-realized souls, having perfected themselves with spiritual knowledge and saturated with divine peace on all sides; after attaining God they merge with the cosmic spirit.
   Explanation: After soul-realization, when a perfected spiritualist ascends to the Cosmic Spirit, he submerges with the spirit and attains supreme bliss.

6. With the knowledge of Vedanta science (Upanishad), who have fully realized God, who have purified their ante-karna (mind and intelligence) with the Yoga of renunciation and detachment, such perfected yogis at death enter Brahmaloka and attaining perfection realize eternal freedom.
   Explanation: The Yoga of renunciation and detachment means when the desire for the fruits of all actions and desire for worldly possessions and positions have been fully burnt and banished from the mind. Entering brahmaloka, such a person at the opportune time merges with the supreme.

7. When the fifteen body powers (kala) and all senses dissolve in their respective causal (deities), then all actions and the omniscient self dissolve, attaining unity in the imperishable *Brahmn*.

   Explanation: The fifteen parts are faith, Pranaa (life force), (shardha), space, air, light, water, earth, senses (indriya), mind, food, virility, austerity, intonation (Mantra), sacrifice, the worlds and name (individual). At the time of death of a spiritual master, these fifteen parts including senses and mind revert to their causal forms because there is no rebirth of a spiritually enlightened person. His enlightened soul merges with the Supreme Spirit.

8. Just as the flowing rivers disappear and merge with the sea losing their forms and names, similarly the knower of the Brahma freed from name and form merges with the supreme Divine Spirit.

   Explanation: The above-mentioned fifteen parts, including name and form, are the symbols of the mundane life which are subjected to rebirth and death. An enlightened person who becomes the soul does not need a body and frees himself from the perishable fifteen parts and merges at death with the Cosmic Spirit like the rivers of this world disappear, losing their forms and names into the ocean. This concept of sixteen parts (kala) is well explained in the sixth question of Prashna Upanishad.

9. Undoubtedly, he who knows the Supreme God himself

becomes God. In his family there is none who does not know the *Brahmn* (God). He rises above sorrow and sins. Freed from all knots of the ignorance of the heart, he becomes immortal.

Explanation: Nobody can know God without knowing the self and on knowing the self; the seeker becomes the Supreme Self (God). Mahatma Tulsi Das also says the same thing. *"Jo tumhein jaanat tum hi ho jat."* In his family nobody is born who does not know the *Brahmn*, because the knower of *Brahmn* attracts progenies with deep spiritual leanings. The knower of *Brahmn* cannot be affected by sorrows and sins. He is always blissful and beyond ignorance.

10. About this Brahmavidya it has been declared that "it should only be told to those who perform rites, know scriptures, are the devotees of *Brahmn*, have faith, who offer oblation in the sacred fire and who are devout and chaste."

    Explanation: Those who are not faithfully devoted to *Brahmn*, are not pure and chaste, do not study scriptures, Brahmavidya cannot be preached to them because such less-evolved people find it difficult to realize spiritual truths and start adverse commentary on them. Secondly, its requirement is devotion and is not meant only to be read with mind but with full faith and is to be lived in life.

11. This Brahmavidya (the sacred spiritual science) was first duly revealed by Angira rishi to Shaunaka rishi. He

who is not pure and chaste cannot grasp and learn it.

Explanation: Purity of body and mind (Brahmcharya), faith and devotion are the pre-requisites to learn and imbibe Brahmavidya.

KATHA UPANISHAD

Kathopanishad is a unique story revealing the spiritual truths in a dramatic way. It resolves the great mystery 'as to what happens to a man when he dies'? It is a dialogue between a precocious child and Yamraj (the god of death and knower of the ultimate). The young lad (Nachiketa) questions Yamraj on the eternal truths in this ephemeral world and succeeds to know what sacred fire is, what is the first cause and the last refuge and what is the self (atman). Yamraj, delighted by the spiritual curiosity of the young lad, lovingly explains to him the need to destroy ignorance and attain equanimity; explains the Aum power, the way to still the mind with Yoga, the role of Aditi (the cosmic mother), the reality of the self, the thumb-sized flame without smoke hiding in the cavity of the heart, and explains that the only way to access the self is to meditate with love. It is a wondrous dialogue dealing with basic human values in family and society such as intra-parent progeny relationship reflected in Nachiketa's concern for his father and father's anguish for his son due to his spasm of anger; man's weakness for recognition and aspiration for emancipation and yet falling short of doing the right to attain the best and the highest. The following pages will reveal the unfailing remedy to reach the spiritual summit, as revealed by Yamraj to Nachiketa.

It is said that Udalak rishi, the son of Vajshrava was famous for distributing food liberally in alms, and father of his precious son Nachiketa, to attain recognition and spiritual rewards, performed the Vishvajit yagya (in which the performer must give away in alms everything; especially the dearest possessions). Nachiketa seeing the old, dry and even sick cows being offered in charity became concerned about his father, who would be visited by nemesis for violating scriptural injunctions which required the dearest possessions to be offered in charity and not the old cows which would prove a burden to Brahmins. Knowing himself to be the dearest possession of his father, he said to his father, "To whom will you offer me in charity?" Asking it in good faith, for the third time, the irritated father said in anger, "To Yama (death) I give you." Being a loyal son Nachiketa seeing his father in anguish, tried to console him by saying that he should conduct himself like his worthy ancestors and like worthy contemporaries shall perform his duties, fear of death should not stop him (Nachiketa) from going to Yamraj. Seeing his determination, Vajashrava, regretting for the spasm of his anger, swallowed the bitter pills of patience. Nachiketa entered the abode of Yamraj but the text does not explain how and when Nachiketa, a mere boy, reached the abode of Yamraj (obviously he must have discarded his physical body). It must be borne in mind that around that time in ancient India, when this great event occurred, Yoga science was well advanced as is revealed by the study of the Puranas. In Yoga Sutra (chapter three, 'Vihuti *paad*'), Patanjali explains various

Yoga techniques to attain occult powers, including the power to attain the astral body. Even now perfected yogis attain the astral body at will and get back into physical body. Instances of such yogic feats are mentioned in a masterpiece on Yoga, 'The Autobiography of a Yogi' written by the world famous yogi Paramhansa Yogananda. Nachiketa was no ordinary boy. His karmic attainments in Yoga science must have been great. When a right Yoga technique is practiced by a pure person with intense desire and concentrated will power, focused on an objective or object, it materializes. Such is the power of esoteric science of Yoga. Nachiketa, who was afire with the passion to meet Yamraj to serve him, must have practiced the Yoga technique with full purity of heart and concentrated with intensity of mind. No doubt, it must have taken him time and exceptional will power to master the rare art which landed him in Yamraj's abode. At that time Yamraj was not present in his abode. For three nights, Nachiketa waited without food and water for Yamraj. On his return, Yamraj heard an intuitive voice say, "A pure Brahmin like a bright flame has entered your house; he is hungry for three nights, offer him water, wash his feet and extend warm hospitality to him." A pure Brahmin remaining hungry at a householder's place could be a curse, resulting in loss of courteous behavior, loss of cattle, sons and loss of acquired spiritual knowledge.

Respectfully bowing to the pure and bright Brahmin guest, Yamraj with warm humility extending his hospitality, regretfully told Nachiketa that to atone for the inconvenience that he suffered for passing three nights without food and water, "I offer you to choose three boons of your accord and I will grant them."

Nachiketa said, "Sir, Lord of Death, the first boon I ask is that my anguished father must feel peace and tranquility. He should get rid of his anger and be contended. When with your permission I go back home, my father should recognize me as his son and should receive me with affection." Yamraj granted this boon with assurance that his father finding him safely returned from the jaws of death will receive him with deep affection and he will be fully at peace with himself and will enjoy sound sleep.

Asking the second boon, Nachiketa spoke, "Swarga (heaven) is a great place. It is wonderful in many ways. There is no fear, not even of death, because you are not there. There is no anxiety and no affliction. Age, hunger and painful death don't bother there. Heaven is a place for all to rejoice. Nachiketa said, "Since heaven can only be reached by mastering the Agni Vidya, therefore, I must know it. I am pure and I am loyal to you. Therefore, Sir, teach the Agni vidya to me. This is my second boon." It is Agni which takes a devotee to heaven as is also explained in Mundaka Upanishad. Yamraj said, "Nachiketa, I know the Agni Vidya and will teach you this science therefore, listen to me carefully. This esoteric fire knowledge leads to heaven and sustains the world. It is a secret knowledge and lies concealed in the heart of the learned, which means that scholars do not know it really. It is the cosmic energy which emanates from Aum — the unmanifest vibratory structure of the cosmos. Its knowledge can be mastered with Yoga science." Yamraj revealed the secret along with the technique to erect the altar of the sacred fire for worshipping it and explained the skill to lay its bricks numerically according to a special secret design. After his briefing, Nachiketa, on being asked, correctly repeated the instructions with clarity. Seeing Nachiketa's intelligence and poise, Yamraj was so delighted that he gave an additional boon to him saying, "Nachiketa, this Agni Vidya, fire sacrifice, shall be called after your name." Yamraj also offered one multi-hued garland of gems to him, as a reward.

Yamraj declared, "He who thrice performs the worship of Agni vidya (as explained by Yamraj to Nachiketa), becomes the knower of three Vedas and by performing yagya, charity and austerity with purity and detachment would attain to this level of eternal peace. Nachiketa, this Agni vidya which leads to heaven will henceforth bear your name; now ask the third boon."

Nachiketa said, "When a person dies there is a doubt. Some say that after death this (soul) lives; yet others say it does not live. Sir, from you I want to know the truth, this is my third boon." Yamraj replied, "Nachiketa, earlier this doubt was raised even by Devas but being too subtle even they could not understand this. Therefore, do not persist and return this boon to me." Nachiketa said, "Sir, since you say that even Devas could not understand this secret, therefore, who else but you can explain this truth to me. Sir, I must know it from you."

Yamraj said, "Ask for sons, grand sons, who will have long lives. Ask for rare horses, cattle wealth, elephants, lands, and vast possessions, gold in bulk and ask for a very long life, as long as you desire to live and also ask for the capacity to enjoy the pleasure of the long life wholeheartedly. Nachiketa, be the emperor of a vast kingdom where all will bow to you. Ask for accomplished women of rare beauty never seen on earth before who will serve you and riding in chariots, skilled in music, full of learning they will dance to the tune of your wishes. But Nachiketa, do not press to know about the secret of death." Nachiketa respectfully replied, "Life on earth is ephemeral and so are its possessions and pleasures. The worse is that indulgence in them denudes the vital energies of life. Sir, therefore, keep your horses, elephants, chariots, music, dancing damsels for yourself. Wealth and possessions never are the means of happiness to mortals, particularly when they are aware of your presence (that death ultimately swallows all). After seeing the great immortal like you, how can I bind and enslave myself to the ephemeral pleasures of the ever-changing senses and to the rigors of old age and death. O Lord of Death, therefore, grant me the third boon of unraveling the mystery of soul. After testing Nachiketa's deep spiritual concerns and depth of spiritual commitment, Yamraj started to explain the spiritual (soul) essence. In this world there are two eternal paths: (1) Shreya (good and spiritually liberating) and (2) preya (pleasant but ultimately leading to bondage). Both these powers try to attract a person to their respective folds. The power of Shreya liberates its staunch follower from worldly pains and pleasures and leads him to the highest source of eternal bliss—the Param *Brahmn*. The follower of the path of preya being rooted in the denuding pleasures of wife, son, material possessions, worldly pleasures, heavenly desires and the like, ultimately succumbs to his weakness and fails to find the supreme. Brooding over these two alternatives, the wise opting for the spiritually liberating shreya path makes it to the Supreme Divine and the myopic follower of the preya path running after Yog-Ksham (protection of the attained and desire for the unattained) forfeits his spiritual prospects and may court self-destruction.

"Nachiketa, I have seen the spiritual merit in you and you exhibit the strength of a staunch renunciate who knows the worthlessness of the fleeting pleasures of this ephemeral world. You are different from the self-deluded so called intellectuals, who missing the grain rejoice in the chaff of self-esteem and thus tumble like the blinds following a blind man such people are at the mercy of Yamraj.

I am glad to see that you bear the merit to acquire the Vidya (spiritual science of Yoga). Vidya (spiritual science of Yoga) and Avidya (material knowledge) are antithetical because a person of materialistic disposition (fond of worldly goods) cannot discern the subtle essence of spirituality."

In 1-2-7, Yamraj reveals to Nachiketa that spiritual realization is a wonder of wonders. When a person succeeds in realizing the soul, it is the rarest of rare attainments. When a spiritually realized master finds an ardent seeker of the soul essence, it is even a bigger wonder because in this world such a rare union is a unique event. On earth there are very few who are interested in knowing the soul; most of them do not even get the opportunity, due to their worldly struggles, to listen about the soul and may find it too subtle to grasp with their materially engrossed senses. Indeed wonderful is the person who sincerely engages himself in this great pursuit and one who realizes it is the real hero of this divine mystery. Explaining the challenges of soulrealization, Yamraj says that in the vast astral universe of all the abstract and subtle things, soul is the most subtle. Unless a soul-realized master (guru) is found, it cannot be taught by anybody. Mind cannot comprehend it, intellect cannot analyze it and reason fails to visualize it because it cannot even be imagined (as is also mentioned in the Bhagwad *The Bhagawad Gita* 2.25). "Nachiketa, the awakening that you have acquired is not a reward of logic or intellectual scholarship; it is the reward of your deep spiritual quest and the effect of the association of the spiritually enlightened personalities. Pray, there are more ardent seekers like you." Now with the proof of personal example, Yamraj tells Nachiketa that the pursuit of the performance of action done with desire, however ideal the desire be, is a trap of bondage. "Therefore, all yagyas (including Agni yagya) I performed with a complete detached mind as a part of duty, never for rewards but as an oblation and therefore I could establish God contact" (this is also mentioned in The Bhawad *The Bhagawad Gita* 3.9). Nachiketa now humbly said, "Sir, I know that earthly treasures are mere tinsels; they are obstructions to reach the supreme; therefore, I have renounced all worldly desires and have determined to experience the eternal bliss through your spiritual revelations." Commending the renunciate in Nachiketa, Yamraj started praising him "Nachiketa you have emerged as pure, unaffected by all the allurements, I sprawled before you. Lure of wealth, rule over earth, charm of women and celestial glories. Promise of powers beyond space and time, they all failed to budge your poise. Nachiketa, I commend your will and wisdom to renounce the best of earth and heaven."

This world, like a deep and dark vast forest, is full of chaos and confusion but the omnipresent permeates this all (The Bhagwad *The Bhagawad Gita* 9-4) and is hidden in the cave of the hearts of all (*The Bhagawad Gita* 13.17, 15.15, 18.61). Despite His omnipresence and abiding in the hearts of all, there is none who sees Him because for that, the veil of Maya is to be pierced (The Bhagwat *The Bhagawad Gita* 7.25). No doubt, the glimpse of the omnipresent is very difficult. But one who can focus his will and mind with deep concentration on this hidden omnipresence, he succeeds to envision Him and bids adieu to the duality of pleasure and pain.

"This sacred spiritual secret must be learnt from a realized master and then is to be deeply meditated upon with deep concentration and will power. Once a seeker glimpses this truth and tastes its nectar, he gets lost in the magic of its bliss. Nachiketa, I see the gates of joy opening for you to lead to the abode of the supreme," Yama said to Nachiketa.

Inspired and boosted in morale, Nachiketa said, "Sir, reveal that to me which exists beyond (the duality) right and wrong, cause and effect, and past, present and future." (1-2-14).

"Yes Nachiketa," delightfully Yamraj beamed, "I will reveal to you the word which holy spiritual texts (Vedas) adore and spiritual masters extol. To experience its glory, ascetics perform extreme austerities and observe Brahmacharya because impure of the heart can't make to it. This holy word is the essence of the Supreme God and it is Aum. This (Aum) is Brahm, it is the Param *Brahmn*. Knowing this wonder word, the seeker gets all that he wants. The blessed seeker feels his heart filled with contentment.

Knowing Aum is the supreme attainment. It is the highest ideal of all the true seekers in whose heart longing to know Aum reverberates; knowing the mystery of the Divine finds Him within. After revealing Aum as the essence and indicator of both *Brahmn* and Param *Brahmn*, He now answers Nachiketa's question about the soul.

The omnipresent and omniscient soul (self) is neither born nor dies. It neither creates anybody nor is it created by anybody.

It is neither the cause nor the effect. It is always the same; not even the slightest change happens to it. With the bodily death it never dies. It can never be destroyed or damaged. Unless a seeker completely disengages oneself from identifying himself as a body (Jiva) which changes and dies, he cannot experience the ever existent pure soul. The soul and the body are not only two separate entities but are completely different from each other. Body is made of the ever-changing and perishable atoms, is born and dies. But soul has nothing of these things. The pure soul is always there; it is eternal, and so is in fact man, because he is not the perishable body but he must realize this; only then he becomes the soul, and man must banish his ignorance, that he is body (Jiva).

The soul, which is subtler than the most subtle and bigger than the biggest, lives in the cavity of the heart of every person but due to his delusion (body consciousness), he cannot see it. It is the same theme as described in Mundaka Upanishad; two birds sitting on the same tree, one is ruffled eating its sour and sweet fruits and the other eating nothing is the ever blissful witness. Only that rare person who through meditation emerges above body attachment and worries of the world can see God as soul in his own heart. The Supreme God is incomprehensibly unique; sitting at one place He reaches far and wide; even sleeping he walks everywhere. Similarly, when a true seeker finds the self (soul) who is formless, changeless, and omnipresent and supreme, he rises above sorrow and becomes contented.

Yamraj says that the self cannot be known through the study of scriptures. Even for the sharpest intellect, it is too subtle. Discourses and deliberations are of little help in its realization.

Only God knows who loves Him, therefore, He reveals himself only to such a devout lover of Him.

Yamraj also points out the type of people who cannot find God or see the self. A person who is not pure and righteous, whose senses are not under control and mind is not steady, he who does not meditate, cannot find God; such people fall to death, the cosmic destroyer. However pure Brahmins and duty-bound Kshatriyas can find Him through the purity of heart attained through deep meditation and deep love which attract God.

In the second part, Jiva-Atman (individualized soul) and God have been discussed and it has been concluded that God reveals Himself only to him who He likes because God alone knows the true seeker who is pure of the heart and loves God alone above everything else. Therefore, the ways and means to find the Supreme God are more clearly spelt out in this third part.

It is due to his good actions that a Jiva takes birth as human being. The supreme self (God) and Jiva (ego-tainted soul), both live in the secret cave of the heart of a being to savor the truth. But both are different form each other like the shadow and sun light. The former is dim (less evolved) and the latter is fully illumined.

Ego soul (Jiva) will always grope in the darkness despite sharing proximity of the illumined. Therefore, unless the light of inner illumination is lit, the tow will always remain mutually apart like the sunlight and the shadow.

Yamraj says that, therefore, it is necessary to pray to God so that He grants the capacity (purity) and will to the Jiva to perform pure actions and yagya (spiritual sacrifices) to attract

His grace, to attain equanimity with which he may know and find God.

The way to access God is explained with the illustration of a chariot and it's Lord. This body is a chariot. The intellect is the charioteer, the mind is reins, senses are the horses, and the desires for sense objects are the roads to travel on. The master of the chariot is the self. It is the self (soul) which imparts directions to the charioteer (intellect). In this world, who lacks discrimination and is at the mercy of his undisciplined mind, his senses like the wild horses of a dumb charioteer run amuck in all directions. But when a person makes the best use of his discrimination, keeping the mind disciplined, his senses remain fully under control like the horses under the command of an alert charioteer. But one, who lacks discrimination and control over his mind, falls prey to impure thoughts and fails to find God. He falls and suffers the pangs after death. On the other hand, he who equips himself with discriminating intellect by exercising effective control over his mind and senses, rises to attain the supreme and never reincarnates. He liberates himself from the cycles of birth and death.

The wise understanding this highest spiritual knowledge, imparted by Yamraj to Nachiketa, becomes entitled to enter *Brahmn* loka. The word wise means that a person will have to acquire intuitive capability, through meditation, to grasp the purport of this spiritual dialogue between Yamraj and Nachiketa. Mere listening to it in a discourse cannot entitle a person to enter *Brahmn* loka. Those full of devotion, who recites the mystery of this spiritual dialogue in the august gathering of learned and pure Brahmins and to the devout Brahmins during shradha at meal time, also attain eternity.

In this part, it is explained from Verses 3 to 15, that the unmanifest omnipresence of *Brahmn* is the power which confers on the pure seeker, the ability to pray and meditate when the Supreme knows the sincerity of devotion of the wise, then alone He, sitting inside the heart reveals Himself to the devotee. Even the wise without complete surrender and faith cannot cognize the Supreme. This means that the soul within is the best guide to the pure of the heart, to accomplish the pilgrimage to blissful salvation.

The Supreme God has created the doors and directions of all senses outwards. Therefore, the being (Jiva) looks outward not at the soul within and knows the external world. A rare wise man inspired by the will to find the supreme abode, turns the flow of his senses inwards and succeeds to behold the self (soul) and becomes enlightened. The ignorant and unwise, running after the lure of sense pleasures and seeking various sense objects, falls in the trap of death and cycles of reincarnations. But the wise, through discrimination knowing the indestructible self, shun the lure of the sense objects.

The wise know the mystery that in this world man enjoys all ephemeral sense objects (sound, touch, sight, taste and smell) and sex due to the hidden presence of the omnipresent power. This mysterious and perennial power outlasts all contacts of varied sense pleasure enjoyed by man. The wise, therefore, understand the existence of this eternal cause behind the perishable pleasures of all sense contacts. It is that inexhaustible *Brahmn*, which Nachiketa had asked about.

The wise man knows that his capability to know and enjoy the world in waking and dream states, lies in the hidden self within. Therefore, taking the world in its stride he ever worries.

The wise knows that the causing power is the supreme God, the source of life to all, the sovereign of the universe, past, present and future, the provider of the fruits of action to all, abides in his heart (and also in the hearts of all), never talks ill of anybody. The idea is that the wise get the equanimity due to His grace. It is that hidden power about which Nachiketa has asked.

Who first emerged as *Brahmn*, due to His own will, even before the Panchtatva, and who entering the cave of the hearts of all beings lives (hidden) with them, he who knows this mystery, is the perfect knower. Therefore, (the hidden omnipresence) is the *Brahmn* about whom Nachiketa has asked. Yamraj now describes the same Param *Brahmn* in the form of Aditi.

The supreme angelic mother, Aditi, who is the source of life force (Pranaa energy) in all beings, is born with every being and lives hidden with each in the cave of his heart, he who sees and knows this (unmanifest) reality sees correctly. The underlying idea is that it is *Brahmn* Himself who manifests as Aditi.

The supreme mother goddess Aditi is the cosmic Maya, the creative and manipulative power of God. Nobody can know this supreme and unmanifest Maya except the wise through the grace of *Brahmn*. It is this Supreme *Brahmn* which Nachiketa wanted to know.

The life hidden in the foetus protected in the mother's womb and the fire hidden inside logs, which the knower of Agni vidya knows, reveals the wonder of the *Brahmn* which Nachiketa wanted to know.

The Supreme God from whom rises the sun and in whom it sets, on whom all Devas (angels) depend and to whom they surrender and who can be transcended by none, He is the *Brahmn* that Nachiketa asked.

This Param *Brahmn* is one and the same everywhere. In this world, and in the various other worlds and lokas of this universe. He who does not know this (cosmic) unity and sees and believes in the multiplicity of the manifestations cannot rise above the cycle of deaths and births; because for Moksha (salvation), realization of *Brahmn* as the supreme unity and supreme substratum of this universe is necessary. All forms and names are mere delusions because they are transitory. To overcome this delusion of relativity, duality and multiplicity, the imperative is purity of the heart, only the pure of the heart can see the divine unity behind the diversity.

"This Divine and Supreme Purusha of the size of a thumb dwells in the centre of the body of a being. He is the sovereign of time ruling over past, present and future. He neither fears nor hates anybody. He is the pure, smokeless, ever-shining bright light, ever constant and permanent effulgence. Such is the *Brahmn*," Nachiketa asked.

"As the rain water falling on the hill-top goes down differently in different directions, assuming different forms and colours due to earth contours and its hues, and therefore, people seeing the same water differently in different forms (unmindful) are unaware of the sameness of the rain water. Similarly, a person who looks at different religions differently oblivious of the underlying divine unity of God, does not know the lord and keeps wandering in this deluding world.

This abode of the self, called human body has eleven gates (tow eyes, two ears, two nose apertures, one mouth, Brahma Andhra, navel, anus, reproductive organ). This abode, the human body, is the city which is ruled by the omnipotent, ever-existent, ever-effulgent Supreme God, who dwells in its heart. He who worships and meditates on this Supreme Self secures freedom from the cycle of birth and death and finds the supreme omnipresent God, about whom Nachiketa asked.

Describing the cosmic form of the Supreme Self (*Brahmn*), Yamraj says, "He is the sun shining in the heaven, self-effulgent purity; He is the air in the sky, is the chief of the eight vasus, He is the sage at the altar of sacrifice, He is the guest who blesses the house, He dwells in human heart, in gods, in firmament, He is river, He is the highest truth and the supreme being. Sitting as a king in human heart, He pulls the Pranaa up and pushes the Apana down (Pranaa and Apana autonomous currents cause the regular activity of inhalation and exhalation and automatic regulation of our cardio-vascular system through the silent supervision of our soul). All devas (sense gods) adore Him (the soul) with full devotion."

On death, when the soul, senses and Pranaa leave the body and enter a new one, what remains behind? To this question, Yamraj says that the Supreme God of whose stuff is made everything, animate and inanimate, in this universe remains present even in the dead even though our senses cannot see (because inanimate matter is also made of the God stuff)."

Yamraj tells Nachiketa, "All living beings one day are bound to die and neither Pranaa nor Apana can sustain them beyond death. The secret of life is the soul (who is obeyed by Pranaa and Apana). Nachiketa, now I will reiterate about *Brahmn*, tell you about the soul and about what happens after death. (This is explained in verses 2/6-8. This theme is also explained in the Bhagwat *The Bhagawad Gita* 15/7-8). Nachiketa, according to the quality of their actions and according to the quality of their thoughts as influenced by scriptures, guru's grace, association, education and profession and in accordance of their mental leanings, at the end many people (at death) take rebirth. Whose good and bad actions are balanced they are born as human beings. Whose bad Karmas outweigh their good Karmas are born in lower forms as birds, beasts, etc. and performers of many bad actions take the form of immobile bodies like plants, grass, water, hills, etc.

"The creator of countless goods and services for people befitting their Karmic pattern is awake when all sleep (at night or in parlay time when the awareness of all is at rest or non-existent). He is pure supreme *Brahmn*, He is the immortal eternity, He is the substratum of all, He never sleeps, never awakes, He is the omniscient. None can transcend Him, the one that you asked about. Like the fire which has no form of its own and takes the form of the object that it enters in the world, similarly, the formless soul (or omnipresent *Brahmn*) assumes the shape of what it enters, be it human or non-human. In addition, as air assumes the shape and form in this world of the object that it enters, unaffected in its essence, similarly, Param *Brahmn*, the soul of all, remaining always the same, looks indistinguishable from the being it enters. Such, Nachiketa, is the nameless, formless, omnipotent and omnipresent *Brahmn* you asked. Just as the one sun makes everything in the universe visible with its lights and remains unaffected by the defects of the objects, the *Brahmn* (soul) inside all remains unaffected by the deeds and trauma of the beings. The idea is that despite being inside the being, soul is separated from him. The same, one indivisible self manifesting itself through its unlimited powers in many forms, is the sovereign of all beings. He who sees the supreme self (soul) abiding within himself, attains eternal happiness but not who fail to see the soul as the substratum of all."

Yamraj declares in verse 2-3-13, that a true seeker must have the faith at irrevocable conviction that God exists eternally among the transitory and non-eternal things of this world and that He certainly reveals Himself to the ardent seeker. In everyone who is conscious, He is the sole source and secret of consciousness. He alone has the generosity to fulfill the countless desires of all. Only those who fail to perceive the presence of God within, deprive themselves of this divine gift of eternal peace.

Now Nachiketa asks Yamraj with humble curiosity vide verse II-2-14, "Sir, you say that the wise realize that the *Brahmn* within the supreme, indescribable and all effulgence, is the cause of their peace and bliss; is that *Brahmn* self effulgent or does it shine with the light of some other source?" Now Yamraj explains that Param *Brahmn*, or the Supreme Abode, is beyond the reach and effect of the sun, the moon, the stars and fire. They do not have the super effulgence by which the Supreme Abode of the *Brahmn* will shine. The supreme effulgence shines with the light of *Brahmn* which lights the sun, moon, stars and the fire.

The opening verse of this portion compares the world with massive ancient Ashvatha tree (massive papal tree), the roots (origin) of which (this world) are above (in heaven in the Param *Brahmn*) and branches are below on the earth. The origin of this massive worldly tree is the eternal *Brahmn* Himself. All the worlds and their beings rest in Him and no power can transcend Him. This massive tree (the world) is paradoxically both ancient and perishable. It is ancient because nobody knows its beginning or when it was born but it is perishable (changefully) because its living beings, plants and all other things are subjected to death and decay but the world endlessly survives in its progenies and successive generations. Such is the *Brahmn* that Nachiketa asked.

The entire cosmos animate-inanimate, imaginable, emanates from this *Brahmn*, moves in Him and is supported by Him. The resonance of His power resounds in this cosmos like thunder reverberating in the sky; only those who know Him have no fear of death. Yamraj says that all forces of the universe fear the *Brahmn*. The fire burns from his fear, the sun shines due to His fear, the clouds rain and the winds blow from His fear; even Death. God wipes out people due to His fear. Fear here signifies the universal causal power of *Brahmn* which causes and mobilizes all natural, physical and astral forces. If one is unable to realize this self (*Brahmn*) in this world before the call of death, he must under the chain of birth and death cycles. It is an indication to Nachiketa that therefore he should not miss any opportunity in this life to realize the soul. If one fails to realize the *Brahmn* in this life before death, then it is a great failure. Losing the golden opportunity to meet God in this human life is indeed a colossal failure because this human life with sound mind is a rare chance. After death the effects of the Karmic law cannot be escaped and one may undergo the long and varied cycle of births and deaths. By the self-realized person, *Brahmn* (soul) can be seen clearly like an object placed before a mirror is seen in it. But those who are not self-realized but are conventional devotees, the self looks to them unclear as in dream (as per his own leanings and mindset). In Gandharva loka (when a seeker is less devoted), he sees the self merely as reflection in water. But in Braham loka (when the devotee is well realized), he sees the self clear and near, like the sun and the shadow next to each other. This verse explains that the vividness of the appearance of the soul to the seeker is relative to the level of his degree in spiritual realization.

The wise, realizing that different senses perform different functions in different states of consciousness (in waking, sleeping and dream states) and knowing their fleeting nature (in different stages of age and health), knows that senses are separate from him who is the ever unchanging self. Therefore, seeing the mind and senses denuding, he does not grieve. This theme is further explained by elaborating that mind is superior to senses, intelligence is superior to mind, and the soul (ego) is superior to them all. But the causal body (the unmanifested Prakriti) is superior to the ego tainted soul (Jiva). The Jiva (ego-tainted soul) is part of the unmanifested Prakriti (the cosmic Maya). Maya or Prakriti is superior to all except the Supreme God. Therefore, avyakata (the un-manifest Prakriti) is superior to the ego-tainted soul (Jiva) but the formless omnipresent Param Purusha (*Brahmn*) is the supreme. Knowing Him, the Jiva attains blissful state and stands released from the cycle of birth and death.

But *Brahmn* is formless and subtle. He can never be seen with our two gross worldly eyes. He reveals himself to the faithful devotee in his heart purified with deep mediation after fully conquering the senses and mind. Realizing the *Brahmn*, the seeker attains bliss and eternity. But this ultimate spiritual state can only be attained; when through Yoga and deep meditation, the senses have been stilled (they do not see external objects), when the mind is stilled (its restlessness is banished and is fixed), the intelligence is stilled and ceases to work because in that state it sees the most subtle and the most attractive. Only such a state of complete stillness of the senses, mind and intelligence enables a yogi to enter the highest state of intuition, the state of being one with the *Brahmn*. It is the state of complete unity where the seeker becomes the sought and the sense of separate existence is banished. It is the genius stroke of the Upanishad rishis who divined that the bliss is in the whole, not in the part. The whole, the infinite, is our native state. Having fallen from that state through every activity, we strive to fill this vacuum. The feeling of being separate is the cause of our restlessness. But life cannot help us to fill it from outside. There is inner path to this union through intuitive meditation and intense love.

This state of the highest union (intuition) cannot be attained with words (Mantras), thoughts (mind), or eyes (senses). Only one who has full faith, only that *Brahmn* exists and not the body (ego), can find Him. Because there are two selves—the ego soul (Jiva) and the pure indivisible soul (Atman)—only when one rises above the ego-consciousness (that I am this body, senses, mind and intelligence), the feeling of I, me and mine, only then a devotee realizes his Atman, the pure indivisible soul. This realization only dawns when all the worldly and supra-worldly desires of the mortal heart cease to surge in it and the ascetic is gripped by the master desire to grip the cosmic spirit and the yogi spontaneously finds all the worldly knots of his heat untied; then he attains immortality.

There are one hundred and one important nerves in the heart radiating in various directions. One of them (Sushmna) leads to the brain and the yogi (at death), following Sushmna nerve reaches the supreme abode and finds the blissful eternal God. The other hundred nerves involve the being with the body and the world. Others who fail to master the Sushmna nerve, according to their Karmas, return to the world. The thumb-sized supreme divinity is always enshrined in the hearts of all. The devotional seeker must therefore know the difference between the weed and the seedling, should know the art to separate the sun from the moon and the spiritual skill to separate the ego from the soul. Knowing from Yamraj and mastering the supreme art of Yoga and meditation (Brahmavidya), Nachiketa, purified of the heart and released from death, embraced the Divine. Therefore, to be similarly blessed everyone should endeavor to become soul-realized in this birth itself.

GLIMPSES OF YOGA AND SCIENCE

Many thinkers have offered different views on the origin and evolution of the universe. But the views advanced by Yoga masters and scientists are considered authentic because they are both based on reliable evidence. Yoga views are based on intuition based knowledge and experiences. Intuition being the higher and direct knowledge of the facts perceived, is said to be flawless by Yogis. The views of science being based on demonstratable evidence are therefore irrefutable.

The Views of Yoga: The science of Yoga has the oldest theory to explain, 'the origin and evolution of the universe along with the course of descension of man from God and the adventure of his ascension back to the spirit. The science of Yoga reveals that the evolution of phenomenon universe and man, including all forms of life, is a long drawn-out cosmic process of descension emanating from God, the cosmic spirit, and an equally long process of man's ascension back to God from where he descended. According to Yoga and other Hindu scriptures, this universe evolves from the Divine Spirit who is the sentient and material cause of creation. God wills the creation and produces it along with natural laws from His own Self (*ekoaham bahushyam* – I am one, I am becoming many) using His vibratory power of *Aum* and executes the process through *Prakriti*. Therefore, this process begins as descension, following the descending order of life and twenty-four evolutes: chita, intelligence, ego, mind, ten senses, five tanmatras and five elements, i.e., ether, air, fire, water and earth called *para* and *apara Prakriti*. Then the evolution reversing its course follows the ascending order. Following this course a person must reverse the course of descension of 24 evolutes, which he adopted to descend from the spirit to become man. Every soul, after descending from the spirit to dawn this body, passing through the process of descension of 24 evolutes, now to go back home to God must reverse this descending process of 24 evolutes by following the course of ascension. Therefore, Yoga prescribes a course of action to follow for every person to enable him/her to ascend back home to God from where he/she has descended during the course of cosmic descension.

According to the theory of Yoga, this universe is a divine design. Its creation, preservation and dissolution, both at cosmic and individual levels, are the unique feats of God's creative will. As *Brahmn-Sutra* also reveals in its second aphorism of the first chapter, "The birth, existence and dissolution of the universe are from *Brahmn*." The supreme God is the Master Creator. The truth that God with His will produced this universe out of Himself is revealed by Holy Scriptures and visioned by the seers. According to *Chandogya Upanishad*, God willed: "I am one, I shall become many." None of the Upanishads that

I have read contradicts this view. In fact, all the Upanishads are votaries of the theory that the universe is a product of the creative will of God.

Master yogis of all times, including the living masters accept and support this theory of creation of the cosmos on the basis of their samadhi based intuitive experience. Voluminous writings of the world famous modern yogi *Paramhansa Yogananda* reveal his *Samadhi*-born intuitive experiences, proclaiming that God is the source of creation. All yogis and spiritual masters, whether of the past or present declare, based on their intuitive knowledge and experiences that God, through His *Prakriti* (*Aum*-creative power) has created this universe. Their intuitive knowledge is based on the infallible experience of *samadhi*. *Samadhi* is an advanced state of God-contact, a state of bliss and omniscience, in which everything is visioned directly.

Many formulaes are provided in the scriptures (*Sahintas*) to measure space and time from *parmanu* (the constituents of atom) up to galaxies and from kshan, *pal-kaal* (constituents of a second) up to years and *kalpa* (cosmic eons of time), which are based on the commonly accepted principles of evolution and involution. Hindus believe in the theory of four *yugas* which have their different spans: *Kaliyuga* (spanning over 4,32,000 years), *Dwapar yuga* (8,64,000), *Treta yuga* (17,28,000) and *Sat-yuga* (34,56,000).

The total life span of these four *yugas* forms one *chaturyugi*. One thousand *chaturyugis* make one day of *Brahma*. This one day of *Brahma* does not include the night of *Brahma*, which has the same duration as one day of *Brahma*. To convert one day of *Brahma* in worldly terms (a day of Brahma is 360 times bigger in duration) would mean one thousand *chaturyugis* multiplied by hundred and again multiplied by three hundred sixty and also one night of *Brahma* lasts the same duration.

During the day of *Brahma*, various parts of creation emerge and evolve from the spirit and during the night of *Brahma*, various portions of creation are dissolved (move back to their causal state) from where in due course new creation (*shrishti*) re-evolves. During these cycles (*yugas*), human beings who attain spiritual realization, ascend to God and the rest are reborn through countless cycles of births and deaths as per their karmas. At the end of one hundred years of *Brahma* (365 days of *Brahma* multiplied by 100 years of *Brahma*), God creates a new *Brahma*. This is called *Mahapralaya* (cosmic dissolution); the entire creation dissolves and merges in its causal state. This new creation, when the new *Brahma* is created, is called *Mahasarga* which lasts for one hundred years (the age of the new *Brahma*). This cosmic process of evolutions and involutions, involving trillions of years, is an unending and a continuous process which is why scriptures say that *Prakriti* (nature) is *anadi* (beginning less); it changes from its physical form to astral and then to causal and keeps on obversing and reversing its infinite phases of evolution and involution but it has no permanent end. Little wonder, it is called the *Leela* (sport) of the cosmic creator.

Here it is important to mention that in the 19th century (in AD 1894), a sage scientist and a God-realized yogi *Swami Sri Yukteshwara Giri*, the guru of great modern yogi *Paramhansa Yogananda*, in a masterpiece book 'The Holy Science', has propounded an astronomical theory based on mathematical calculations and intuition that the present age of our world is *Dwapara yuga*, which has started in AD 1700 at the transition of *Kaliyuga*. This theory explains that the age of four *yugas* (*Satyayug, Treta, Dwapara* and *Kaliyuga*) is based on the calculations of the time, our sun along with the solar system, takes to revolve around another big star in the galaxy and this circle of revolution is completed (in descending and ascending order) in 24,000 years. The descending order takes 12,000 years and the ascending order also takes 12,000 years to complete the circle of one revolution. The time taken in descending course of 12,000 years is divided into four segments, of which 4,800 years are taken by *Satyayuga*, 3,600 years by *Treta yuga*, 2,400 years by *Dwapara yuga* and 1,200 years by *Kaliyuga*. Similarly, during the ascending order commencing at *Kaliyuga* and culminating in *Satyayuga* the process of revolution is reversed but period of each of the *yugas* remains unaffected. Human intelligence in *Kaliyuga* is at its lowest due to the farthest distance of our earth from the seat of *Vishnunabhi* (the grand centre of intelligence). In *Dwapar yuga*, when the earth moves closer to the grand centre, human intelligence increases and man's knowledge expands to know the subtler secrets and laws of nature. This view is confirmed by the fact of various important inventions made by man in and around the 17th and 18th centuries, the time of commencement of the present *Dwapar yuga*. No wonder, in this age of *Dwapar yuga,* man's creative and innovative adventures are progressing fast. In *Treta yuga*, human knowledge will grow faster and man will know a lot more. In *Satyayuga,* a person ascends intellectually, emotionally and spiritually to very high level and universal love reigns supreme in human heart. After the next descending course of the *yugas,* the order reverses again to restart its ascendance. The alternately descending and ascending orders of these four *yugas* are regularly followed by each other and the divine design goes on ad infinitum.

Swami *Sri Yukteshwara* has pointed out that the period of *Kaliyuga* (4,32,000 years as shown in almanacs), was calculated due to the error that 1200 years of *Kaliyuga*, were the *Deva* years and not the ordinary years of our earth. Each *Deva* year is 360 times bigger than our terrestrial year. If we multiply 1200 years by 360, the figure is 4,32,000 and the error is confirmed. The age of the other three *yugas – Dwapar, Treta and Satyayuga* – too, shown in Indian almanacs is based on this error. This miscalculation occurred because at the time of the transition of *Dwapar yuga*, and advent of *Kaliyuga*, the social scene in the country was in total disarray and 'there was none in the court of *Raja Parikshit* (the time when this mistake crept into almanacs about BC 700)' who could understand correctly the principle of calculating the ages of the several *yugas.* The present age of *Dwapar yuga*, according to this calendar, is 310 years in AD 2010. This theory is worked out strictly adhering to the occurrence and timings, of vernal and autumnal equinoxes. Due to its mathematical and intuitive basis, I believe in the correctness of this theory to measure the age of four *yugas* of the Hindu almanacs.

According to Yoga, life emanates from God who is the source of creation. God, the cosmic spirit, is the *nimit* (sentient) and *upadan* (material) cause of the universe, which means that except the cosmic spirit (the supreme God), nothing else exists permanently or is real (eternal)(Gita 7/4 to 7/7). The cosmic spirit plans and out of its own self creates the universe. God Himself becomes the mind and matter (the raw material of the universe). Just as a spider weaves its web out of its own body material (taking nothing from outside), similarly, God also creates the prime forces of *Akasha* and *Pranaa* out of His vibratory Aum power. Aum, the creative vibratory power of God is the source of life force and other twenty four evolutes of *prakriti* (the unmanifest nature). This *prakriti* is the creative powerful cosmic power of God and it has three gunas (qualities). *Satvik* (positive), *Rajsik* (dynamic) and *Tamsik* (negative). These three gunas are the basic structural material of the universe. From *Satvik* quality evolves the five knowledge senses. From *Rajsik* quality evolves five action senses and from *Tamsik* attribute evolves the five tanmatras (causal forms of the five elements). These five tanmatras following the panjikaran process evolves into five gross elements, the objects of five senses. These elements are *akash* (ether), *vaya* (air), *agni* (fire), *apa* (water) and *bhumi* (earth). These 20 elements and chita, intelligence, ego and mind, complete the 24 evolutes of *prakriti*. Prana, the cosmic energy also emanates from the Om power of God. *Akasha* is the basic element and prana is the basic energy.

Through the interaction of *Akasha* and *Pranaa* evolves this universe. *Akasha* is the primal matter and *Pranaa* is the primal energy. This *Akasha* is a unique phenomenon. It becomes infinitely fine and finer and infinitely gross, grosser and solid. Everything physical that exists in this universe, from an atom up to the galaxies and from an amoeba up to the angels, all forms, all colours, sounds and textures, are made of *Akasha*. *Akasha* is the material and *Pranaa* is the power that form and forge with their interactive and interpenetrative action in this myriad cosmos. The *tanmatras* (causal forms) of other four elements (air, fire, water and earth) also emanate from *Akasha tanmatra* (causal state) and evolve into their gross forms, following the process of panjikaran through the power which *Pranaa* exerts on a*kasha*.

The 24 evolutes mentioned above, constitute the body and mind of a person. Human body has three forms: causal, astral and physical. God first creates the causal body, then astral and then the physical body. The causal body is made of ideas from which evolve the astral and gross objects. As already mentioned, this process of creation is started by God from His creative power of '*Aum*' (the un-manifest *Prakriti*).

In *Bhagwad Gita,* in verses 3 to 7 of the seventh chapter, verses 5 and 6 of the thirteenth chapter and verses 4 to 6 of the fourteenth chapter, Lord Krishna describes the origin, creation and evolution of the universe. God declares that His two prakrities; para (higher – the life element) apara (the lower – energy or matter element) emanate from Him (His Om attribute) and are the source of creation. This is how the animate and inanimate worlds are produced by prakriti in accordance with God's supreme will (Gita 9/10). Every being and object of the universe is born of these two prakrities due to God's will who puts His seed (consciousness) in the Mahatbraham (mool prakriti) from which the worlds are born.

Yoga and *vedanta* holds a unanimous view that universe is the creation of God. All schools of Yoga; *Karma Yoga, Bhakti Yoga, Kriya Yoga, Raja Yoga, Upnishadas, Bhagwad The Bhagawad Gita* and *Brahmn Sutras* are votaries of this conclusion and conviction. In *The Bhagawad Gita,* which is a unique source of both *Vedanta* and Yoga and is the speech of God Himself, Lord Krishna repeatedly declares that He is the source – creator, preserver and dissolver of the universe in its manifest and unmanifest forms. All knowledge, power, love, creativity and intuition and also energy and matter emanate from Him. "I am one, I will become many" is the refrain of the Upanishads. The Upanishads are called *shrutti* because they contain the highest intuitive knowledge gained in *Samadhi* through direct communion with the spirit.

Now let us elaborate on the basic theme of origin and evolution of the universe, as explained by Hindu scriptures. Hinduism holds that nobody knows correctly about how and why of the universe; and the one who knows does not share because the audience does not understand his medium, he knows that human intellect and the mind are mute instruments which cannot cognize subtle intuitive knowledge of Yoga regarding the universe. However, according to Hindu scriptures, broadly speaking there are two theories, which explain the origin and evolution of the universe. One is an evolutionary theory and the other is based on *Maya*. Both these theories conclude that God is the source of origin and evolution of the universe. Even the evolutionary view of Hinduism holds that the universe has no beginning in time. Its cycles of beginning, continuity and dissolution appear and disappear at regular mathematical intervals. These cycles have vast time spans and keep on repeating in regular succession of ascension and decension. Creation, preservation and dissolution are the three components of each cycle of the evolution. According to this view, *Ishwara* is the prime power who controls and creates the universe. *Ishwara* creates *Brahama* – *Hiranyagarbha* – the first born who creates the universe. In fact *Hiranyagarbha* himself is the astral universe or the cosmic mind and individual minds are the parts of this cosmic mind like the countless cells in human body. Creation, preservation and dissolution (*srishti – sthiti* and *pralaya*) correspond to *Brahama's* one day and one night. Creation and preservation make the day of *Brahama* and dissolution (*pralaya*) is the night of *Brahama*. During the night when *Brahama* sleeps, it is *pralaya* (dissolution) and during the day when *Brahama* wakes up, it is the phase of creation and preservation. But when *Brahama* wakes up he does not create a new universe and its beings. It is like when we go to sleep, practically for us in sleep there is no world and when we wake up the world appears in our consciousness. *Brahama* being the cosmic mind, its sleep is called dissolution (*pralaya*) for us all and when *Brahmn* wakes up it is our creation and the phase of preservation. As already said, the day of *Brahama* lasts a thousand *Chaturyugis* (four billion years) and the night of *Brahama* also lasts a thousand *Chaturyugis* (four billion years). These are the smaller phases of *srishti – sthiti* and *pralaya* (creation, preservation and dissolution) which affect only small parts of the universe. As already said, after every one hundred years of *Brahama* (trillions of years) God appoints a new *Brahama*. At the completion of one hundred years of *Brahama's* age there is cosmic dissolution which lasts for one hundred years of *Brahama* then the whole universe dissolves and reverts to its causal state along with all animate and inanimate objects, who as per their karmic pattern, reemerge at the dawn of the new creation at the installation of the new *Brahama*. This is a recurrent cosmic rhythm of creation, preservation and dissolution coinciding with the appointment of every new *Brahama* at every new creation.

As explained below, scientists say that the evolution

starting from the big-bang takes billions of years to become earth and what we see around. It is a long evolutionary course of burning gases, radiations, supernovas, nebulae and then evolving hydrogen, helium and ultimately evolving life affable atoms and oxygen. The view of Hindu scriptures is somewhat similar. It is an evolution from extremely minute *suksham bhutas* – much too subtle to be caught by a microscope. The evolution takes billions of years involving the days and nights of *Brahama* to reach the stage fit to support human life. But the basic difference between these two disciplines is that universe for scientists begins at big-bang and nothing is known of pre big-bang era. Hindu view is that universe evolves from God and it follows a regular rhythm of appearance and disappearance. It is eternal appearing-disappearing and re-appearing cycle of trillion years. The aspect of some similarity between these two views is stated by the great modern scientist Carl Sagan in his famous book, "Cosmos, the story of cosmic evolution, science and civilization".

A summary of the *Vedantic* view of Hindu scriptures is that God is the material and efficient cause of the universe. It is He from whom or under whose supreme will the *suksham bhutas*, which evolve into twenty four evolutes and three *gunas* emerge from the *avyakta – Prakriti*. It is His *leela* that He appears as *Brahama* the creater, *Vishnu* as preserver and *Shiva* as destroyer of the universe. The process of creation, preservation and dissolution of the universe is an eternal divine sport, changing its forms in cosmic rhythm from causal to astral, astral to gross and vice-versa. Carl Sagan in his great book "Cosmos, The story of cosmic evolution, science and civilization" complements Hindu mythology about its views on the origin of universe. A serious student may read about it in its 10th Chapter (The Edge of Forever).

Now let us briefly talk of *Advaita,* which is the achievement offer genious par excellence and therefore, not easy to comprehend. *Advaita* view or experience is that that only *Brahmn* is the absolute reality, the only truth and the universe, in fact, is non-existent because it is only a relative reality. To *Advaita,* spirituality is the absolute reality that never changes, is above time, space and causation, is un-create beyond beginning and end, imperishable and everlasting. Such is the *Brahmn* of the *Advaita*. The universe is an appearance (*vivarata);* an illusionary or a seeming reality. The universe including its names, forms appearing as distinct objects is a mere illusion which has no absolute existence the acid test of which is *Samadhi* because in *Samadhi* no relative object exists but only the absolute truth – *Brahmn* is there. Our incomplete and illusionary worldly vision least affects the reality of *Brahmn*, like the reality of a rope when misconceived for a snake is never affected. The apparent cosmic reality is the handy work of *Maya*. *Maya* is the mysterious and powerful power of God which is why it is said in scriptures that God is both *sat* and *asat,* real and unreal, absolute and relative. In spirit, God is absolute and in nature, relative. It is *Maya*, which creates the illusionary worlds of names and forms. This mysterious power of God is known by various names; *Avyakta, Prakriti* and *Maya*. In scriptures, it is called nescience (*Avidya)*. In Hindu scriptures, *Maya* is made of two letters: *Ma* and *ya*. *Ma* means 'no' and *ya* means 'yes'. Therefore *Maya* always reverses the reality so deftly that no human intellect can know it. *Maya* does it with its two power components: *avarni shakti* (the power to hide) and *Vikshepshakti* (the power to project). This *Maya* is said to be invincible and infinite like God. No cosmic power can defeat *Maya* because man's intellect and mind are the seats of *Maya*! As long as one is under the spell of nescience, (non-spiritual knowledge) *Maya* is supreme. God reveals that the only way to defeat *Maya* is to know the supreme self— the soul within. This truth is confirmed by the spiritual seers and yogis with personal experience as is also laid down in *The Bhagawad Gita* 2/16. *Advaitis* say that the illusory and relative nature of the world can be compared with the dream experience. In dreams, whatever we see appears real. Our foods, places, travel, working, socialization, planning, fighting, all appear undeniably real as long as the dream lasts. Only when we wake up the unreality of the dream is known. Similarly, when a yogi enters *nirvikalpa samadhi* the unreality of the world is revealed to him.

It is a positive sign that in India and in other countries like U.S.A., a number of science students are showing interest in Yoga and Yoga practitioners are showing interest in science. Keen followers of these two disciplines are becoming convinced that Yoga too is a science like other physical sciences but with a degree of difference. There are different ways, methods and experiments to know the physical sciences. These sciences are taught and learnt in class rooms and experimented in labs. Their results are demonstrated in fields. In Yoga, it is only the minor theoretical part which can be taught in small classes. For experiments, its lab is the human mind and body. Esoteric concentration and intuitive meditation along with observance or vairagya (nonattachment) are its methods of learning which are to be pursued in isolation and occasionally in silent group meditations. Physical sciences are learnt through the mind but Yoga uses mind to ultimately transcend it. The results of Yoga may not be easily demonstrated but are observable and are experienced by its practitioners. A Yoga practitioner can observe the change in his blood pressure, pulse rate, feeling of peace, feeling of liking and love towards others and increase in his/her sense of service to others. These developments in Yoga practitioners are observed even by others who are in contact with them. These are elementary experiences and benefits of the science of Yoga. The higher experiences and spiritual benefits of Yoga are attainable by committed and dedicated practitioners of Yoga occult science. It takes time but the results attained are said to be unmatched and unique. As the yogi advances in the endeavor of concentration and meditation he/she begins to watch and feel ambrosial and ecstatic scenes, sounds and experiences. These are said to be astral in nature. With advancement in meditation, the astral and causal dimensions of animate and inanimate objects start unfolding before the intuitive vision of a yogi. This process for a few lucky and blessed ones culminates in *Samadhi* and slowly into higher *Samadhi*— even beyond *nirvikalpa Samadhi*. More details in this regard have been discussed in Chapters, 'Why Yoga and What is Yoga'. The *Samadhi* realized yogi is the real Yoga scientist who can demonstrate the wonders of Yoga science if and when he/she thinks it necessary because ordinarily a yogi does not interfere with the divine scheme of creation. Great modern yogi Sri Sri *Paramhansa Yogananda* demonstrated among many others, two feats of Yoga science to two Americans, Dr. Lewis (a devoted catholic) and Mr. James J. Lynn, a rich successful businessman. *Swami ji* seeing with his intuitive vision the karmic background of these two men, on their request, lifted their consciousness to the super-conscious and made them experience the divine! What an ecstatic wonder they experienced and both dedicated their lives to the pursuit of Yoga. These events and many other similar instances are mentioned in two books, 'Autobiography of a Yogi' and 'Treasures Against Time'. There is another book for students interested in Yoga, 'Man's Natural Quest' by Yogananda. Yogis on the basis of personal experience have been saying that Yoga undoubtedly is a higher science, people even scientists, not knowing Yoga cannot understand the pure nature of the higher science of Yoga which can correctly know and explain the hidden secrets of mundane and higher regions. Yogis who have mastered the science of Yoga have always said that physical sciences and the science of Yoga are both sciences; one higher and the other lower, the higher science deals with both the world of senses and the worlds beyond the senses. Both are two fruits of the same tree, one is raw and the other is sweet and ripe. Therefore, they are not opposed to each other but represent two levels of the same discipline.

These two branches of knowledge are moving to the same destination by two different routes. Their common goal is to serve and uplift mankind to make living easier and better and to raise it to higher planes. Physical sciences cater to physical and intellectual planes by improving social, economical, academic, cultural, political and physical environments. Yoga science opens up vast spiritual and ethical dimensions of life which reveal the secrets to build character and attain the finer and higher aspects of life. Yoga teaches the art of love, peace, fellow feeling and inculcates a sense of sacrifice. These relationships in life promote harmony and peaceful healthy social life. Most importantly, as has been repeatedly said, Yoga teaches the unique art of creatively changing the mind set and thereby, making its practitioner realize the Self within and the bliss effect. Therefore, in the wake of the increasing complexity of life and increasing challenges confronting the world, there is now a greater need to benefit from both these great sources of knowledge so that prosperity, security and peace are evenly promoted.

According to God-realized Yoga masters, the conclusion of the science of Yoga, about the origin and evolution of the universe, are authentic because they are based on the direct flawless spiritual knowledge attained in *Samadhi*, the condition when yogi is in contact with God/Cosmic spirit, the creator and preserver of the universe.

The Views of Science: Modern age is the age of science. Therefore, it is important to spell out briefly the views of science, about the origin and evolution of the universe. At the outset, it maybe said that at the present juncture, eminent scientists and physicists of the world are wholeheartedly engaged in unearthing the cause of the origin and evolution of the universe. The ongoing 'Large Hadron Collider Project' is a landmark adventure undertaken by the scientists to discover that after the Big Bang, in a split second what must have happened instantaneously, which caused the evolution and existence of the universe? This is the world's largest experiment to resolve this concern of the scientists. From this experiment scientists are hoping to get many important answers about Black holes, anti-matter, Higgs Boson or the God particle. No doubt the scientists are now hopeful that their endeavour will lead them to discover scientific evidence about the origin, age and evolution of the universe. However up till now, the scientists approximately know that the universe came into being as a consequence of the Big Bang about 14 billion years back.

According to some scientists, cosmologists and physicists, humanity remained oppressed for thousands of years by the views that the universe was a creation of God. Even Aristotle, an acknowledged scientist of the ancient Greek world, believed that the laws governing the universe being pure thoughts were above questioning and needed no experiment and scrutiny. Aristotle, like Ptolemy, believed that earth was the centre and all other heavenly bodies orbited around it.

Another Greek philosopher, Democritus, believed that atom was the smallest unit of matter and everything in the universe was made of atoms. Ancient Hindu yogis already knew that even atoms, the building blocks of the universe, had constituents (*parmanu*) yet more abstract which evolved from the basic source of the cosmic energy called *Pranaa* (the life force).

In the Western world, it was Copernicus, who declared in 1514 that earth orbited round the sun and the sun was stationary. In 1609, Galileo, among other things, demonstrated with his telescope that moons of the Jupiter orbited around it. Later, Kepler proved that planets moved in elliptical orbits and not in circles as held by Aristotle and Ptolemy. These were major strides in the field of science which these pioneers had proved despite the rage and opposition in the general climate of Papal orthodoxy. However, the major landmark in the field of science was the singular contribution made by Newton's theory of gravitation. In 1687, with the publication of 'Principle Mathematica', his theory not only explained with convincing reason to show how various bodies move in space and time but also developed mathematical formulas to analyze movements of heavenly bodies.

Newton with his laws of gravity showed that moon orbited planets in elliptic paths and planets, in turn, orbited the sun in elliptical motions. Newton's three laws of motion became the force to push the progress of physical sciences in many directions. Now, during the last one hundred years, the progress of physical sciences has changed the surface of our plant. It may be concluded that there have been three master achievements that have revolutionized modern science: Einstein's theory of General Relativity, Hubble's discovery of the expanding universe and the theory of Quantum Mechanics.

For modern astronomers and scientists, age of the universe is about ten to fifteen billion years. They trace the origin of the universe to the unique event called Big-Bang. Scientists have offered various theories and models to explain big-bang and the course of evolution that the universe followed through billion of years encountering many astronomical cycles, glacial ages and biological phases. Astronomers and scientists do not tell anything about the universe preceding the big-bang. For them big-bang is the epoch when the universe began. Therefore, it could be said that for want of evidence for scientists before big-bang, there existed no worlds, no galaxies, no planets and of course, no living species. But scientists say that on the basis of scientific models and theories they are convinced that the universe began at big-bang and in the absence of conclusive evidence for them universe did not exist before big-bang.

These theories as briefly discussed in some of the books, that I have read, make an interesting and useful study: one by Carl Sagan (Cosmos — the story of cosmic evolution, science and civilization), the other is by Stephen Hawking (A brief history of Time) and the third is by Simon Singh (Big-Bang). I must acknowledge that studying these books inspired me to write this chapter. I have also found some similarity between the Hindu views on the origin and evolution of the universe and the views of these scientists, at least in respect of the astronomical vastness of time, ascribed to the origin and evolution of the universe. Hindu scriptures and yogis declare God as the creator and preserver of the origin and evolution of the universe, but as far as I know scientists by enlarge appear silent on this basic issue except Wallace, the contemporary of Darwin, who in his theory of biological evolution sees the hand of God behind evolution unlike Darwin for whom evolution is randomness.

Einstein in his general theory of relativity predicted that the universe (space-time) had a beginning at the big bang. Later Einstein's prediction to some extent got contradicted in the wake of the theory of Quantum Mechanics – a great theory which has revolutionized the modern economy and technology, even though originally the theory of quantum mechanics was the brain child of Einstein. It was the theme of the theory of uncertainty principle of quantum mechanics, the theory of microcosm unlike Einstein's general theory (which was the theory of the macrocosm), which perhaps did not quite explain the scope and extent of the cosmic microcosm. Reacting to the theory of uncertainty principle, Einstein, somewhat irritated, is said to have commented that God does not play dice – which meant that God is always certain. There are various other important theories discussed in these books i.e. the steady state theory, Friedman model, Heisenberg's uncertainty principle etc.

Now I may attempt to explain in layman terms that what is the big-bang theory, which is assumed to have happened ten to fifteen billion years back. Let us be clear that there is no positive or tested proof of the occurrence of this 'spectacular' event. But it is also not a hypothetical conjecture and is based on tested scientific predictions. Despite some disagreements, many scientists say that it did happen. But strangely enough as already said, the authors and supporters of this theory say that for them there existed no universe before this event or more precisely that for science, the universe began only with the big-bang. Could it have happened in a cosmic vacuum? Yet scientists say that they are not concerned with whether there existed or not anything before the big-bang and they do not have any answer as to why it happened ? But this epochal event is no speculation because it is assumed and predicted on the basis of reasonable scientific theories and models. But all these theories by eminent scientists are the product of twentieth century and the big-bang happened ten to fifteen billion years back. This distinctly explains the ingenious endeavor of the scientists, who devised the scientific methods to measure such stellar times and distances. In fact, the age and distance of stars and galaxies which are so vast, are measured and verified on the scientific basis of red shift and the doppler effect, which measure the time and distance of light and sound waves.

Astronomers describe big-bang as a cosmic explosion not because it created a massive thunderous or deafening resound, as the term would suggest, but because from this exploded, the unending gaseous source of the expanding universe which is still continuing. Therefore, the term big-bang may be called a misnomer as it was neither 'big nor a bang'. It is said to be an explosion of an infinitesimally small substance from which emerged and evolved this infinite universe. At the point of big-bang, the universe is said to be of zero size having infinite heat, infinite density and infinite pressure under which it exploded. Carl Sagan so beautifully explains this beginning phase of the universe in the 10th chapter (The Edge Forever) of his above mentioned book. The same theme with more scientific details is wonderfully presented by Stephen Hawking in his book "A brief History of Time" in its chapter – 'The Origin and Fate of the Universe'.

There are several theories and models advanced by scientists to explain the origin and evolution of the universe. More important of these are the General Theory of Relativity of Einstein, the Theory of Quantum Mechanics, the theory of Entropic Principle and the great revelation made by American astronomer, Edwin Hubble. In the 1920s, Hubble with his big telescope pleasantly surprised the community of scientists that the universe is not static. It is an expanding vastness of some hundred thousand million galaxies, which were running away from us (earth). This landmark discovery revolutionized the science of astronomy and was followed by more scientific discoveries and models explaining the universe. Till this discovery, Newton's theory of gravity was the basic theory holding the fort in the realm of astronomy. After Newton the major theory which revolutionized the knowledge of universe was the theory of relativity of Einstein, its fundamental postulate being that the laws of science should be the same for all freely moving observers irrespective of their speed. Connected to this, another landmark contribution of Einstein was his equation 'E=MC2' which led to the splitting of atom and proved that all matter is made of energy and vice versa. Einstein also proved that space and time are not absolute but are dynamic. Space-time is a single unit not divided into parts and space is an active agent among forces at work in the evolution of this universe because these forces are the part of a larger whole – the space time continuum. His research resolved that gravity was not a force like other forces but a consequence of the truth that time space is not flat; it is curved. Later, Einstein modified his theory of relativity which was based on the premise that the universe is static. In his general theory of relativity, Einstein predicted that space-time began at the Big-Bang singularity about ten to fifteen billion years back. Singularity is a point in space at which the matter is compressed to an infinite density. The curvature of space-time at this point becomes infinite, which means that at this juncture, no laws of mathematics and physics apply to the universe. Therefore, at that point the situation is beyond the comprehension of science and it can be called a point of knowledge vacuum, which means that nothing is known to the scientists prior to the event of Big-Bang.

In fact, the Big-Bang theory is not about what Big-Bang is and how it happened. It explains what followed the Big Bang. Therefore, for science, the time (universe) begins from the event of the Big Bang. Scientists therefore conclude that time (read universe) had a beginning at this epoch-making cosmic event. At this point of time the universe is predicted to be infinitely contracted as already said, under the intense pressure of gravity and density causing its explosion. At the outset of Big-Bang, the universe is supposed to have zero size and is supposed to be immensely hot. The explosion thus resulted in infinite heat and enormous expansion. At Big-Bang, the intensity of heat was predicted to be trillions of time more than what it is at the centre of our burning sun. With extremely fast expansion the enormity of heat dropped and slowly during the course of evolution, first gases like hydrogen and helium were formed. As temperatures cooled and radiations appeared, more gases like oxygen were formed. With passage of millions of years, microwaves and radiations of neutrons, photons, etc. and other particles were formed. The cosmic drama for millions of years was a melodrama of supernovas (explosion of a big star releasing light and energy equal to trillion suns) breaking, reforming, some vanishing into massive black holes, new sources of planets and galaxies emerging and moving apart. With the passage of more eons of time, particles were formed and then atoms led to the formation and motion of matter, which at last evolved into the universe as the physicists find it now. This model of the universe is called the hot Big-Bang model. Its basic postulate is that, as the universe expands, all matter and radiations in it become cool. With drop in temperatures; energy, particles, atoms, matter, planet and galaxies are formed.

Lately some scientists concluded that since all laws of science break down according to the general theory of relativity at the Big Bang singularity, therefore, one cannot predict how the universe began. On the other hand, this theory explains the macrocosm and does not apply to microcosm. In fact, it applies to the large-scale structure of the universe and does not apply to the uncertainty principle of quantum mechanics, which governs the microcosm of the universe. There are many other theories i.e. Inflationary theory, Steady state theory, Entropic principle theory and Theory of Quantum Mechanics.

The theory of Quantum Mechanics is more comprehensive and perhaps the latest to describe the universe. It is said to be based on a totally different type of mathematics and it is said that it does not describe the world in terms of particles and waves but recognizes the duality between particles and waves. Somewhere it is useful to think of particles as waves and somewhere it is useful to think of waves as particles. This may also indicate the intrinsicness of the will of a person to the process called the 'observer induced change effect'. It is a theory said to be developed from Plank's Quantum Principle and Heisenberg's Uncertainty Principle. Plank's Quantum Principle states that light cannot be emitted at an arbitrary rate but only in certain pockets called quanta. Hinesburg's Uncertainty Principal relates to the position and velocity of a particle and states that the position and velocity of a particle cannot simultaneously be known accurately. If the position of a particle is known correctly, its velocity cannot be known as correctly; Quantum Mechanics, therefore, heralds the factor of uncertainty and unpredictability in science but it works with precise adjustability. Thus, its results after experiments have yielded laudable effects which have been commended by a large section of the community of scientists who claim that but for the Quantum Mechanics, the modern world could not have benefited from the invention of computers, Internet, television, etc. Quantum Mechanics is the basis of modern technology on which is based the working of transistors and integrated circuits, which are the basic pillars of the electronic revolution. Similarly, wonders achieved in the fields of modern chemistry and biology are no less due to the contribution of Quantum Mechanics. Apart from major industries, the areas of agriculture (due to genomics and MAS-Marker Assisted Selection Technology), medicines, plant, protection, etc. are benefiting in a big way.

This theory is being used by physicists to describe the elementary states of universe. It rectifies shortcomings of the general theory of relativity due to its singularity factor. The quantum theory of gravity declares that the laws of science hold good in all situations and everywhere, even at the Big Bang (the beginning of time). The singularity factor, therefore, ceases to operate because there is no scope for singularity in the quantum theory.

Simultaneously, the quantum theory of gravity postulates that space-time has no boundary either at the beginning or at the end and therefore the common laws of science will explain various situations and events moving hand in hand with the uncertainty principle of theory of Quantum Mechanics, which through its uncertainty reveals the wonder of evolution as unfolded by science.

Now scientists having made rapid and land mark advances in the field of Astronomy sound hopeful that they may stumble on a great theory, which among other things, may explain the origin and evolution of the universe some thing like the unified theory of science. This may hopefully explains the universe as a whole from microcosm to macrocosm. Such a theory, when discovered, will indeed be a master achievement which will discover and explain many hidden truths and serve as a means for many useful inventions. Such a theory will not only be an ideal mix of general theory of relativity and the Quantum Mechanics but may have to even borrow and benefit from philosophy and mysticism because Yoga has the power to fathom the field of mysticism. No wonder, Lord Krishna long time back declared, "Man is not only mind but the all-knowing soul. Therefore, man must endeavor to discover his soul, the true self, all-knowing and all-loving like God." This achievement is possible not only through reason but also by developing intuition. Eminent scientists and psychologists are already veering round the wonder of spirituality, not only to draw inspirations but also to probe the claims and convictions of yogis that life emanating from God is the source and cause of matter and not the consequence. The cycle of evolution involves both descension and ascension and culminates in enlightenment. Eminent scientists like Von Neumann, Eugene Wigner, David Bohm, Roger Penrose, Erwin Schrödinger, etc. are of the view that consciousness is the field deserving respect and scientific enquiry. Commenting on Heisenberg's uncertainty principle (duality of behavior between particle and wave), Einstein could not have remarked without his spiritual belief that 'God does not play dice'. But nobody can deny the scientific element of precision behind this uncertainty principle, which has revolutionized the field of microscopic science. In fact, this uncertainty principle is also reminiscent of the unexceptionable demeanor of Lord Krishna whose only certainty was in his unpredictability and which was invariably correct and befitting to each situation. Despite His disarming smiles, He destroyed demons; despite His overpowering love, He overawed the mighty. He decimated the titans, played with *gopies,* fought the mighty and embraced the humble.

He surprised all, loved all and hated none, not even enemies. He never was wrong but never straight either. In His pictures, Krishna is rarely seen standing straight; either His legs are bent, waist is twisted or arms and neck are tilted indicating that this world is not straight. It is too subtle for the human eye to discern its microcosms. Only Yoga reveals its true inside behind a ceaseless series of the ever-changing dynamics of *Prakriti*. Lord Krishna also repeatedly reveals in *The Bhagawad Gita* that this vast universe is His creation. He permeates its every atom and it emanates from His thought and will, "I am the origin of the universe." However, with the creation of supercomputers, scientists appear hopeful to change the world beyond human dreams. Media has started reporting that biotechnology is going to defeat death and make us immortal. The claims of scientists about the creation of artificial intelligence no longer seem to be the stuff of science fiction. But these claims of scientists must delight and not surprise us. Yogis always have been saying that if a person, through Samadhi (trance) can become divine and create what he wants to, then why not should a scientist, with his creative flair create wonderous things. In fact, the joint endeavour of wonderment of science and spirituality based on Yoga education can produce even greater wonders.

Natural Selection: Evolution is the basis of natural selection. This discovery was made by Charles Darwin and Alfred Russell Wallace. At the outset, it must be mentioned that the conclusions arrived by these two men of genius were based on the use of two different means and methods employed by them in their research. Darwin's method was scientifically based on observation and experiments, involving inductive and deductive methods. It is said to be a revealing example of thoughtful plodding and careful experimenting. On the other hand, Wallace arrived at similar conclusions through faith and the flash of spiritual insight. His approach was based more on intuition than reasoning. Surprisingly enough, the conclusion of both are reported to be similar to the point of identity. The element of surprise fans curiosity to see that during the relevant time, there existed no physical contact between them because then Wallace was living on a distant continent in the east. However, later on Wallace is said to have taken to spiritualism more seriously as is mentioned in an interesting and useful book "A Short History of Nearly Everything" by Bill Bryson. It may be pointed out that Darwin does not explain the origin of life but deals with its evolution. Therefore, the origin of life and universe is a mystery at least so far, to the physicists and biologists and this may be a reason that the theory of evolution and not of origin is ascribed to Darwin. According to this theory of Darwin, nature produces all kinds of life including plants and animals in abundance. All of these plants and animals do not survive for various reasons of inability to live. Of the abundance of plants and animals, environment selects only those which due to their intrinsic qualities are more suited for survival. The intrinsic qualities of these adjusting and adapting plants and living beings are by accident and not by design. According to this theory, sudden changes in heredity called mutations, which 'breed true', are responsible for this selection of the surviving plants and beings. This process takes place randomly but at the same time environment selects only those few mutations (changes in heredity) which enhance the chances of survival. Due to this process of mutations, gradual changes occur slowly over long durations of time, which cause gradual transformation of one form of life into another form. Thus new species are created. This gradual growth and transformation of species based on the fact of natural selection has been the cause of evolution. Its main features are: nature is prolific, environment is selective. Mutations introduce changes in heredity; this has no design and happens over a long period of time by accident in a random manner. This factor of variability (mutations) improves the quality of life through the process of struggle for survival by adaptation. The improved life reproduces itself and the continuous process of mutations brings about transformations and species of these transformed organisms gradually cause new species and the evolution continues.

The keynote of the theory of natural selection is survival of the fittest through adaptation to environment, helped by factor of mutations and selection. In support of the theory of natural selection, its supporters say that artificial selection (man made) is an open evidence to illustrate that how efficiently human efforts have changed and radically improved the varieties of plants, flowers, animals. If human efforts, through artificial selection, have been able to revolutionize the animal kingdom and the realm of plants, how and why could not nature had done so during the last four billion years, when the earth had assumed a state of fitness to support some sort of rudimentary life bacteria? Now with rapid progress in bio-sciences and bio-technology, despite the discovery and mapping of the human genome, cloning engineering, neural unlading and the knowledge of nano-technology, there appears to be a change in the scene. On the basis of evidence, opinion is building among scientists that consciousness is the source of man and matter both. Some of the eminent bio-scientists have convincing reasons to believe and conclude that life is neither an accident nor a random development and not only a consequence of mutations or clash and cohesion in matter. They believe that life element or consciousness outlasts the bodily death because life is a continuity of consciousness preceding and following the body-death factor. Life being the universal unmanifest force, it vibrates and enlivens each individual living being carrying forward the life experiences of each birth to the successive ones. Mind creates and changes the brain and it is believed to have evolved much before the body. Some views of scientists like Bells indicate belief in the existence of cosmic mind guiding the cosmic events. These views read like the contents from the pages of Yoga and *Vedanta* volumes aired long time back by the *rishis* on the basis of their intuitive knowledge, which is the highest branch of knowledge. Scientists like Roger Sperry, John Eccles, etc. are the well known authorities supporting the power and precedence of mind and consciousness over matter and body.

In the wake of change noticed in the attitude of some leading scientists to recognize spirituality and metaphysics as the forces to be probed, and particularly in view of the thesis of the 20th century, sage, savant and scientist *Swami Yukteshwara Giri*, a very concise gist of a part of which has been narrated above to illustrate that it is the *Dwapar yuga* in progress, which signifies marked advancement in human intellectual capabilities and spiritual stance, it is obvious that people will take to more creative pursuits and innovative adventures. This should happen because these realities are inbuilt in the ascending order of these four *yugas*. In current ascending order of *Dwapara yuga,* which has set in since 1700 AD, the world will experience and enjoy the gifts of its creative forces and innovative powers. But individual and group creative initiatives can always accelerate and maximize the results of their efforts to benefit themselves and to inspire others. It is therefore the right time for all creative people of science and spiritual backgrounds to accelerate their efforts to organize their activities in order to motivate intelligent people who will endeavor to mobilize right people to follow them, to create a new order of enlightenment based on selfless service for creating a peaceful global society. The greatest achievement of this 'New Age' will depend on its ability to forge the syncretism between science and spirituality. It is this union of these two forces, which can usher in prosperity and enlightenment, which is the aim of Yoga-based education.

GLOSSARY

A

ABHAYA	Fearlessness which dawns at spiritual realization
ABHYAS YOGA	God-realization through practice as per scriptures/guru's guidance
ACHAL	Stationary (always there)
ADHIBOOTA	All perishable beings and objects
ADHIDEVA	Spiritually realized souls (all astral beings)
ADHIYAGYA	God (the supreme sacrificer)
ADHYATAM	Spiritualism (presence of soul in beings)
ADIPURUSHA	God
ADITI-DITI	Aditi gave birth to Devas and Diti gave birth to demons
ADITYA	The Sun, astral forces; scriptures mention of 12 Adityas-they are among the 33 gods or devtas
ADVAIT	Monism

AHANKARA	Egoism
AJAPA YAJNA	Speechless devotion such as watching the breath or inner sensations
AKARMA	Actions which do not bind (detached action) or liberating actions
AKASHA	Ether
ANAADI	That which has no beginning
ANANTNAAG	King of non-poisonous snakes (also signifies awakened Kundalini)
ANTE-KARNA	Centre of consciousness, feeling, intellect and mind
ARANYKAS	Spiritual texts on Vedas concerning the knowledge aspects
ARJUNA	Also named as Dhananjaya, Gudakesha, Konteya, Partha, Bharatashreshtha, Parantapa, Mahabaho, Bharata
ARTHA	Aterial means (money)
AASANA	Seat for meditation and meditation posture
ASAT-SAT	Signifies imperishable (God) and the perishable (relative world)
ASHTANGA YOGA	Eight-fold path of Yoga
ATHRVA-VEDA	One of the four Vedas
AUM	Denotes God and His un-manifest power which creates all beings/objects
AVIDYA	Material or mundane knowledge
AVYAKATA	Unmanifest

B

BHAKTI	Devotion to God

BHAKTI YOGA	God-realization through pure and deep devotion
BHAYA	Fear instinct
BHOOTA	Signifies phenomenon world including Common people
BHU-LOKA	Earth
BHUVAR-LOKA	One of the seven lokas above earth (astral region)
BRAHMA LOKA	The highest among seven lokas
BRAHMA RANDHRA	Spiritual space inside Sahasrara (brain)
BRAHAMA	Signifies God the creator
BRAHAMAVASTHA	State of God-realization
BRAHAMASTRA	Enormously destructive weapon which Arjuna could wield
BRAHAMN	God as infinite vastness inclusive of sentient and insentient universe
BRAHMAVIDYA	The highest spiritual knowledge which leads to God
BRAHMANAS	Commentary on Vedic Mantras regarding Yajna, they yield desired results
BRAHMACHARI	A celibate; pure person
BUDDHI YOGA	Equanimity attained through spiritual realization

C

CHATURYUGI	Also called MAHAYUGI is the sum total of the age of four yugas: Kali-yuga, Dwapara-yuga, Treta-yuga and Sat-yuga

CHITTA SHUDHI	Purification of the heart/mind
CHITTA VRITTI	Modifications of the mind
CHITTA-VRITTI-NIRODH	To stop the modifications of the mind through Yoga

D

DEVAS (great ones)	God-realized, spiritually advanced souls (astral beings)
DHAARNA	Very long spiritual concentration without break
DHARMKSHETRA	The field of righteousness
DHARMA	Righteousness (which is good for body, mind and soul)
DHRUVA	Always fixed, means spiritually realized
DIKHSHA	Spiritual brief gifted by a Guru to disciple
DRASHTA-DRISHYA	The seer and the scene
DURMATI	Unwise
DWANDWA	Pair of opposites, duality

E

EKO AHAMBAHU SHYAM	The primeval will of God before creation of the universe (let there be many)

G

GANESH	God; Son of Shiva and Parvati
GAYATRI	Source of Vedas (spiritual incantation)
GOPIS	Lord Krishana's devotee maids of Vrindavan
GUNA	Qualities

GUNA-KARAM-VIBHAG	It means that all desires, actions and qualities are in the mind (nature), not in soul, which being pure does not act
GUNATEET	One who has risen above the three gunas.
GURU-SHISHYA	Teacher and disciple.
GYAN YOGA	God realization through the path of knowledge

H

HIRANYAGARBHA	Cosmic, mind, the image of the first person created by God (Brahama)

I

IDA-PINGLA-SUSHMNA	Three astral nerves in spine which control breathing.

J

JAGAT	The phenomenon world
JAGATMITHYA PRABHUSATHYA	God is absolute truth, world is false
JAPA YAGYA	Religious sacrifice performed with chants.
JIVA	Ego-pseudo soul.

K

KAAMDHENU	Mythological cow with head of a women, which grants all correct wishes.
KAARAN SHAREER	Causal body.
KALIYUGA	One of the four yugas.

KALPA	Means aeons
KAMA-KRODH, MOHA, LOBH, AHANKAAR, BHAYA	Lust, anger, attachment, greed, ego and fear, respectively.
KARAMA	Means spiritual action
KRIYAMAN KARMAS	Means our current action
KARMA YOGA	To realize God through pure actions.
KARMA NISTH	Karma yogi
KARATHU	Highest form of religious sacrifice
KARMIC	Law regulating results of actions
KAVI	Poet
KOSHAS	Five astral covers of the soul
KSHATRIYA	The warrior class
KRISHNA	Lord Krishana.
KRISHNA PAKSHA-SHUKLA PAKSHA	Dark half and bright half of the moon respectively
KRIYA YOGA	A spiritual rite based on special Pranayama teachnique to realize God.
KUBER	The chief of collectors and protectors of wealth
KUMBHAK-PUIRAK-RECHAK	Kumbhak means breathless state; Purak means inhaling; Rechak means exhaling, respectively.
KUNDALINI	Astral (spiritual) power lying coiled up at the base of the spine (Mooladhara).
KUTHASTHA	Spiritual consciousness

M

MAHA PRALAYA	Cosmic dissolution
MAHABALI	Highly powerful
MAHAT	Comic intelligence
MAHAT BRAHAMAN	The womb of creation (Prakriti)
MAHESH	The name of God Shiva
MANAN	Concentrated mental repetition of a religious image, thought or aphorism
MANN SHUDDHI	Purity of heart.
MANTRA	Incantation
MAYA	Cosmic delusion
MARUT	Denotes power, there are 49 Maruts (astral forces)
MAYA YUKTA	In-bondage of maya
MAYAMUKTA	One who has conquered maya
MOOL PRAKRITI	Causal form of Prakriti
MRITYULOKA	This world
MUNI	Silent spiritual seer.

N

NAAD (BRAHMAN NAAD)	Astral sounds (melodies) heard in Samadhi.
NAAD BINDU	Astral sound and luminous point seen and heard in Samadhi.
NARA NARAIN	Krishana and Arjuna
NARAK	Hell
NETI NETI NETI	No this-not this-not this; beyond the mind.

NIRGUN	Formless, above and beyond gunas of Prakriti
NIRVIKALPA SAMADHI	The highest state of Samadhi or God realization
NIRVANA	Salvation.
NISHKAM KARMA	Selfless actions performed as service without desire/attachment
NIKDHI DHYASAN	Method of meditation observed in Dhayan Yoga
NISHPRIYA	To be above material desires
NIYAMA-YAMA	Ten religious dos and don'ts.
NIYATI	Destiny
NYAYA	One of the six schools of philosophy based on reason.

O

OM/AUM	Denotes God in all beings and objects. The unmanifest vibratory creative power of God.
OM TAT SAT	Immanent, transcendental and absolute God.

P

PAAP-PUNYA	Vice and virtue
PANCHBHOOTA	Five gross elements
PARA-APARA (PRAKRITI)	Higher and lower forms of natures created by God.
PARAM BRAHAMN	The Supreme God-pure consciousness
PRANAAYAMA	Special breathing technique
PITRA-PITRALOKA	The dead and their abode

PRAJAPATI	Brahma
PRAKRITI	The unmanifest (hidden) cosmic power which is made of three gunas.
PRAJNA	Soul
PRALAYA	Cosmic dissolution or involution
PRANAA-APANA	Life force
PRANAAVA	Om
PRATYAHARA	Turning mind and all senses inwards in meditation
PRAVRITI-NIVRITI	Worldly orientation and Spiritual orientation
PURUSHA	Soul

R

RAJRISHI	Prince Rishis like Arjuna and Janaka
RAJOGUNA (RAJAS)	Which generate desires and activities
RAJ-VIDYA-GUHYA-VIDYA	The sovereign knowledge and the supreme secret.
RAJ-YOGA	One of the Yogas to control the mind for God realization
RAKSHAS-YAKSHAS	The producers and protectors of wealth.
RAM-RASAYAN	The chemistry of divine love.
RIG VED	the oldest of four Vedas
RUDRA	Having powers of Lord Shiva; there are 11 Rudras

S

SAGUN	Form and manifestation
SAGUN BRAHMAN	God with form/manifestation

SAHASRARA	The thousand petaled astral part of brain
SAKAAM KARMA	Desire based actions
SAKSHI	Silent spectator
SAMADHI	An advanced spiritual state of God contact in meditation
SANATAN DHARMA	The oldest Hindu religion
SANKHYA	One of the six schools of philosophy; also means spiritual knowledge
SANKHYA YOGA	Realizing God through the path of knowledge.
SANSKARAS	Mental dispositions as a result of past actions
SANYAS	Renunciation
SAPT LOKA	The seven spheres
SAPTRISHI	The seven great Rishis: Bhrigu, Marichi, Atri, Angira, Pulaka, Palstaya and Kratu).
SARGA	Evolution
SAT GURU	God-realized masters
SAT-CHIT-ANAND	Existence-consciousness-bliss
SATOGUNA	Sattva-which generate happiness and knowledge
SAVIKALPA SAMADHI	A state of meditation in which a seeker sees God in some form
SAVYSACHIN	One who fights with both hands
SHAMBHWIYOGA (MUDRA)	An advanced state of spiritual enlightenment in which eyes get transfixed.

SHESHNAAG	The Kundalini power which when awakened becomes Anant Naag (the limitless power).
SHRADDHA	Devotion to God.
SHRAVANA	Astral sounds
SRI CHAKRA	Tantra method of worship.
SRISHTI	Creation of God.
STHOOL SHAREER	Gross body
SUKSHAMA SHAREER	Astral body
SUSHPTI	Deep sleep
SWADHA	Offerings made to the dead (Pitras)
SWADHARMA	Soul realization

T

TAIJAS	Soul's spiritual power to guide individuals
TANMATRAS	The five astral forms of gross elements.
TANTRA	Form of worship for God realization
TAPA	Austerity and devotion
TAPASWI	An ascetic
TAT TVAM ASI	Thou-that-are; denotes God
TATVA GYAN	Spiritual knowledge/experience
TRIGUN	The three gunas of Prakriti
TRIVID	Three Vedas
TURIYA	A state of spiritual realization
TYAGA	Renunciation

U

UDHAVA	One of the devotees of Lord Krishna

UPANISHADAS	Spiritual books teaching God realization
UPASANA	Devotion
UTTAM YOGI-VIMURH YOGI	Successful Yogi-unsuccessful Yogi
UTTRAYANAN	The Northern path

V

VAIRAGYA	Renunciation
VAISHESHIK	One of the six schools of philosophy
VASU	The eight astrals powers
VASUKI	The king of poisonous snakes
VEDANTA	Culmination of Vedanta philosophy
VEDAS	Holy scripture-four in number
VIDEHA	Body-less (when a yogi manifests the astral body)
VIDYA	Spiritual knowledge attainment through spiritual enlightenment
VIKARAM	Forbidden action
VISHAYA BHOGA	Consumerism
VISHISHTH DWAIT	One of the three branches of Vedanta.
VIRATA	God's unmanifest divine power
VISHNU	God
VISHVA	Un-manifest divine power
VISHWA ROOPA	Cosmic form revealed by Lord Krishana in chapter 11 of the *The Bhagawad Gita.*
VRITI	Modification
VYAKT-AWAKT	Manifest-un-manifest

Y

YAJNA	Performing all duties with the spirit of sacrifice
YAMA- RAJA	The god of death.
YOGA	The science of God realization
YOGA-KSHEM	Materialistic approach
YOGA-MAYA	God's infinite power as creator of this universe
YOGA-RURH	Firmly established in Yoga
YUGA	Mythological period of cosmic cycles.